The Mormon Church and Blacks

The Mormon Church and Blacks

A Documentary History

Edited by
Matthew L. Harris and Newell G. Bringhurst

UNIVERSITY OF ILLINOIS PRESS
Urbana, Chicago, and Springfield

© 2015 by the Board of Trustees
of the University of Illinois
All rights reserved
∞ This book is printed on acid-free paper.

Library of Congress Cataloging-in-Publication Data
The Mormon Church and Blacks : a documentary history / edited by
Matthew L. Harris and Newell G. Bringhurst.
pages   cm
Includes bibliographical references and index.
ISBN 978-0-252-03974-4 (cloth : alk. paper)
ISBN 978-0-252-08121-7 (pbk. : alk. paper)
ISBN 978-0-252-09784-3 (e-book)
1. African American Mormons—History—Sources. 2. Race relations—
Religious aspects—Mormon Church—History—Sources. 3. Race
relations—Religious aspects—Church of Jesus Christ of Latter-day
Saints—History—Sources. 4. Priesthood—Mormon Church—
History—Sources. 5. Priesthood—Church of Jesus Christ of Latter-day
Saints—History—Sources.
I. Harris, Matthew L. II. Bringhurst, Newell G.
BX8643.A35M66   2015
289.3089'96—dc23   2015014681

To our wives, Courtney Harris and Mary Ann Bringhurst, who have patiently endured our long telephone talks and frequent conference excursions. This book is dedicated to them with gratitude and love.

Contents

Acknowledgments   ix

Introduction   1

1. Three Mormon Scriptural Works: Providing a Canonical Framework for Race, Slavery, and the Status of Black People   6
2. Joseph Smith and Evolving Mormon Attitudes and Practices on Slavery and Race, 1830–1844   18
3. Brigham Young, the Beginning of Black Priesthood Denial, and Legalization of Slavery in Utah, 1844–1877   30
4. Justifying and Perpetuating Black Priesthood Denial, 1877–1949   44
5. Church Growth, Confronting Civil Rights, and Official Affirmations of Black Priesthood Denial, 1945–1970   63
6. The 1978 Revelation and Its Implications   92
7. Confronting the Church's Problematic Racial Past after 1978   118

Notes   145

Bibliography   205

Index   213

Acknowledgments

This book would not have been possible without the help and encouragement of a number of individuals and institutions.

Particularly helpful were Armand Mauss and Lester Bush, whose own path-breaking studies on blacks and Mormonism provided a high standard to aspire to. Both scholars, moreover, provided essential materials, and each also read and critiqued preliminary drafts of this study, providing valuable suggestions. Also furnishing critical information was Gregory Prince, whose invaluable materials in the David O. McKay collection at the Marriott Library at the University of Utah provided both crucial insights and context to the all-important post–World War II period. Edward Kimball—son of late LDS church president Spencer W. Kimball—likewise provided equally important information concerning the religious milieu and the role his father played and other LDS general authorities in the issuance of the 1978 revelation lifting the black priesthood ban.

Two scholars, Paul Reeve and Laurie Maffly-Kipp, also carefully read and critiqued our preliminary manuscript, imparting important insights, thereby greatly improving it.

Other scholars providing useful information include Michael Quinn, Craig Foster, Michael Marquardt, John Hammond, Darron Smith, Gary Bergera, and John Seidel. The volume further benefited from materials provided by David Jackson, Darius Gray, Cory Bangerter, Dennis Gladwell, Eugene Orr, and Keith Hamilton.

The LDS Church History Library staff was most helpful in providing essential materials, specifically Richard Turley and William Slaughter, along with Brittany Chapman, Ardis Smith, Jay Burrup, and Brandon Metcalf.

In addition, a number of universities, through their libraries and faculty, proved most helpful. At Brigham Young University these include John Murphy, Mark

Grover, Gordon Daines, Russell Taylor, Cindy Brightenburg, Margaret Young, and Galen Fletcher. Assisting at the University of Utah were Walter Jones, Elizabeth Rogers, Betsey Welland, Julie Huddleston, and Paul Mogren. Clint Pumphrey, librarian at Utah State University, provided access to information, as did the staff of the Utah State Historical Society. Also answering the authors' frequent requests for materials were librarians at Colorado State University–Pueblo, in particular Kenneth McKenzie and Karen Pardue.

The Department of History and Provost's Office at Colorado State University–Pueblo provided financial support for the completion of this work. This project also benefited from a Charles Redd Fellowship at Brigham Young University awarded to Matt Harris.

Family members deserve honorable mention too, particularly for their research assistance and willingness to share materials: Katrina Hammond, Jason Harris, Linda Leighton, Lawrence Harris, Joyce Harris, and especially Michael Harris.

Finally, the staff of the University of Illinois Press provided continuing aid and encouragement through the various stages of this project, specifically Larin McLaughlin, Willis Regier, Amanda Wicks, and especially Dawn Durante.

The Mormon Church and Blacks

Introduction

In June 1978, leaders of the Church of Jesus Christ of Latter-day Saints announced the end of its long-standing ban on the ordination of black males to the Mormon priesthood—a lay organization open to all worthy males over the age of twelve. The lifting of this ban, representing a drastic departure from past practice, raised two important questions: How did the ban originate? Why did it remain intact for some 126 years? These are crucial questions, given that blacks had been allowed ordination in the early church under the leadership of Mormon founder Joseph Smith. Following Smith's death in 1844, Brigham Young, as leader of the largest group of Mormons, prohibited the ordination of blacks.[1] The ban remained in force from 1852 to 1978.[2]

Mormon attitudes and practices toward blacks evolved in a complex, contradictory manner. On the vexing issue of slavery, Joseph Smith went through a threefold change of position: (1) initial opposition during the early 1830s; (2) support for slavery by the mid-1830s, evident in a strong anti-abolitionist position; and (3) by the mid-1840s, a return to an antislavery position, most dramatized in his 1844 presidential platform.[3] Smith, moreover, allowed the ordination of black males to offices in the Mormon priesthood. The status of blacks deteriorated following Smith's death in 1844 and the emergence of Brigham Young as Mormonism's primary leader. After the Mormon migration to the Great Basin, Young promoted both the legalization of slavery and implementation of the black priesthood ban.[4]

While Mormon racial attitudes and related practices reflected similarly negative trends in American society at large, they were as much, if not more, the product of five characteristics unique to Mormonism itself. The first was Mormonism's emergence as a so-called "new" American religion during the Second Great

Awakening—a time when Americans were particularly sensitive to the issues of slavery and race.[5] A second characteristic was Joseph Smith's role as a "prophet, seer, and revelator," resulting in a set of unique Mormon scriptures, specifically the *Book of Mormon*, *Book of Commandments* (later canonized as the *Doctrine and Covenants*), and *Pearl of Great Price*, canonized on a par with the Old and New Testaments.[6]

A third characteristic is the hierarchical structure of Mormonism, based on divinely endowed priesthood authority. This authority became paramount as church leaders implemented an increasingly esoteric set of doctrines and practices. The important role assigned to the Mormon priesthood is akin to the hierarchical structure within Catholicism. Mormonism's leadership structure functions like a pyramid, with the First Presidency constituting the highest governing body of the church, and below it the Council (or Quorum) of the Twelve Apostles. On a third level are the First and Second Quorums of Seventy. The all-male members of these top three levels, cumulatively known as general authorities, oversee a range of local lay leaders—specifically stake presidents and bishops—who in turn oversee local entities known as *stakes*, akin to Catholic dioceses, and *wards*, akin to parishes.[7]

The importance of priesthood authority notwithstanding, Mormonism manifested a fourth, albeit seemingly contradictory characteristic—its development of a lay priesthood organization, composed of virtually all worthy adult male members ordained into its ranks, including a handful black Mormon males ordained during Joseph Smith's lifetime.[8]

A fifth characteristic of Mormonism was its evolving sense of ethnic self-identity, particularly manifest following the death of Joseph Smith. In particular, Latter-day Saints viewed themselves as literal descendants of "chosen" Old Testament peoples, specifically the tribes of Joseph and Ephraim. In assuming a quasi-ethnic identity, Mormons were akin to Jewish people, who likewise viewed themselves as both a religious and ethnic group. Conversely, Mormons viewed other ethnic groups as less favored, particularly black people, whom they considered as literal descendants of Cain, Ham, and other biblical counterfigures.[9]

Mormonism's lineage theology harkened back to ancient Israel when Jews, Christians, and Muslims appealed to the Bible, positing that God had cursed dark-skinned Africans with eternal slavery and bondage.[10] After the emergence of the African slave trade in the sixteenth century, European Christians taught lineage as a way to justify slavery. Christians had interpreted these passages, rooted in the fourth and ninth chapters of Genesis, to mean that God had placed a divine curse on Cain for murdering his brother Abel. God continued the curse through Ham's posterity by punishing him for ridiculing his father's nakedness and for dishonoring his father's prophetic authority. The Bible makes no distinction of the skin color of either Cain or Ham, but European Christians had long identified this mark as a curse God had put on Africans to justify their enslavement.[11]

Mormon leaders, akin to some Protestant ministers of the nineteenth century, accepted the divine curse uncritically. Brigham Young and his successors appealed to the curse to justify priesthood denial.[12] In determining lineage, Mormons followed the "one-drop" rule codified into legal doctrine in the late nineteenth century.[13] Federal and state courts both asserted that anyone with "one drop of Negro blood" was considered black and therefore subject to racially exclusive practices then emerging in the United States. These practices constituted an effort by white southerners to separate the races both with Jim Crow legislation and antimiscegenation laws. Moreover, the one-drop rule became associated with the eugenics movement of the early twentieth century—the latter supported and sponsored by proponents of racial purity who vowed to keep the races apart.[14]

In the late nineteenth century and early twentieth century, Mormons advanced a second rationale for priesthood denial: church leaders drew a correlation between skin color and spiritual worthiness. In this interpretation, most prominently promoted by Mormon church leader Joseph Fielding Smith, blacks came to earth under a divine curse because they lacked spiritual valor in a pre-earth life.[15] This pre-earth existence culminated in a cosmic struggle—a "war in heaven"—pitting the followers of Jesus against the followers of Satan. Smith and other leaders taught that there were no neutrals in the "war in heaven," but some were "less valiant" in their support for God. These spirits, born into the African race, became the cursed lineage foretold in both biblical and Mormon scripture.[16]

This rationale became the standard explanation for priesthood denial for much of the twentieth century. It presupposed a racial hierarchy in which God favored whites over blacks.[17] But that interpretation came under increasing attack during the civil rights era in the 1960s, when critics began pressuring the church to lift the priesthood ban. Critics, both within and without the church, pressured the Mormon church to officially support civil rights and to renounce all racially offensive rhetoric demeaning black people. While the church would not renounce its theological rationale for priesthood exclusion, official spokesmen largely abandoned previous explanations calling blacks cursed or less valiant. By 1969, the new church position evolved to one of carefully nuanced ambiguity: "We don't know why God denied blacks the priesthood" became the standard reply.[18]

This new interpretation provided a third explanation for priesthood denial. However, remnants of LDS racist teachings manifest themselves on occasion.[19] The church lifted the ban in 1978, in what some LDS leaders called the "long awaited day." In doing so, the church was responding at least in part to tremendous legal and social pressure during the 1960s and 1970s. Accordingly, LDS president Spencer W. Kimball proclaimed through revelation that all "worthy male members" were eligible for the priesthood. The 1978 statement made *no* mention of previous rationales for the ban. But some general authorities and church educators implied that the new racial doctrine had mitigated past teachings.[20]

Concurrent with the priesthood revelation of 1978 there emerged a fourth explanation for the priesthood ban, overlapping the previous one. During Mitt Romney's two presidential campaigns, in 2008 and 2012, LDS leaders labeled as folklore previous explanations for the ban.[21] Such folklore, church leaders posited, had permeated earlier explanations for the ban, specifically those penned by earlier church leaders, including Joseph Fielding Smith, Bruce R. McConkie, and others. Thus relegated to folklore, the church's erstwhile teachings on the divine curse and the spiritual impiety of blacks were clearly passé in Mormonism as a growing worldwide religion. Simultaneous to this development, church leaders explicitly denounced residual racism in the church, spawned by such earlier teachings. This occurred at the turn of the twenty-first century when then president Gordon B. Hinckley, along with other leaders, labeled such elements of racism among rank-and-file church members as displeasing to God.[22]

In 2013, the LDS church provided yet a fifth explanation for the priesthood ban, most evident in its official "Race and Priesthood" document. The church asserted that the ban was based on the pervasive racism in the larger American society of the nineteenth century, when "many people of African descent lived in slavery, and racial distinctions and prejudice were not just common but customary among white Americans," influencing "all aspects of people's lives, including their religion." Accordingly, by the early 1850s, Brigham Young, largely influenced by "a highly contentious racial culture," imposed the priesthood ban. In essence, the ban resulted from "racial discrimination" rather than divine revelation.[23]

At present, the LDS church continues to struggle with racism despite its best efforts to teach that "all are alike unto God." Underscoring this problem is the stark fact that black Latter-day Saints constitute less than one percent of the church body.[24] It is further manifest in the absence of black people and black traditions in church-sanctioned art, literature, music, and temple rituals. Likewise, just three black Mormons have been called to the position of general authority since 1978.[25] And yet, since the lifting of the priesthood ban, the church has made progress, bringing the Mormon gospel to countries with a significant black population. Mormon missionaries now serve in many countries in black Africa, and many live in large metropolitan areas in the United States and elsewhere with large black populations.[26]

So, too, black celebrities like musician Gladys Knight, NBA basketball player Thurl Bailey, and others count Mormonism as their spiritual home. Less notable people of color have also embraced the Mormon message, despite the challenge of remaining active in a predominantly white church.[27] But most encouraging for church leadership is what the future holds. Mormons today generally embrace a racially inclusive church while simultaneously rejecting Mormonism's racially exclusive past. According to a public opinion poll in 2012, conducted during Mitt Romney's presidential run, over 90 percent of Mormons polled had either never heard of the church's racial doctrine or rejected it completely.[28] This is an encouraging sign for the Mormon faithful. It is proof that LDS racial attitudes are evolving, and that Mormons are more accepting of a people they had once shunned.

* * *

This volume offers an important new perspective of LDS racial history through the lens of authoritative documents.[29] The seven chapters contain official and/or authoritative statements tracing the changing status of black people during the period 1830 (the date of the founding of the Mormon church) down to the present. The documents include statements from relevant LDS scriptural works produced by Mormon founder Joseph Smith and canonized as scripture on par with the Old and New Testaments—in particular, the *Book of Mormon*, *Doctrine and Covenants*, and *Pearl of Great Price*. But the majority of documents are noncanonical statements given by Mormon leaders and/or church spokesmen, most of which were publically stated and/or circulated through official church publications and/or through the media.[30]

Each of the seven chapters begins with a brief introduction outlining the historical context and unifying theme. Also included are extended contextual essays for each document, carefully explaining its meaning, importance, and influence. While no claim is made that one general authority speaks for the church on doctrinal matters, it is clear that certain general authorities exerted a stronger authoritative voice than others. The only documents bearing the imprimatur of the church are a handful of First Presidency statements on race made in the latter half of the twentieth century, along with two official statements in 2012 affirming the equality of all races, and one in 2013, where the church disavowed its earlier teachings undergirding the priesthood ban.[31] Nevertheless, a sampling of the documents reveals certain patterns and themes in Mormon racial history, particularly the divine curse and other theological rationales for the ban.

One final note: To avoid repetition, we use the terms *priesthood ban*, *priesthood exclusion*, and *priesthood denial* interchangeably. All denote the restriction of black men from the LDS priesthood. Finally, we do not call LDS leaders by their preferred names of "elder" or "president" so as to avoid unnecessary confusion for readers not familiar with LDS nomenclature. We have opted for the more transparent title of "apostle" when describing members of the Quorum of the Twelve, "church president" when referring to the church prophet, or "First Presidency counselor" when referring to a member of the First Presidency.

1

Three Mormon Scriptural Works

Providing a Canonical Framework for Race, Slavery, and the Status of Black People

General Introduction

Three different Mormon scriptural works provided a canonical framework for Latter-day Saint doctrines and related practices involving race, slavery, and black people as they evolved, specifically the *Book of Mormon*, the *Doctrine and Covenants*, and the *Pearl of Great Price*. The Church of Jesus Christ of Latter-day Saints recognizes all three as canonized, divinely inspired scripture on a par with the Old and New Testaments of the Bible. Through these three works Joseph Smith strengthened his role and authority as Mormonism's primary leader.

I. *Book of Mormon*

Of paramount importance is the *Book of Mormon*—the foundational scripture of the Latter-day Saint movement.[1] According to Latter-day Saint teachings, Joseph Smith translated this work through divine inspiration from a set of gold plates.[2] The *Book of Mormon* published in 1830, just prior to the formal organization of the church, does not specifically address race and/or slavery involving blacks. Rather, it details the rise and fall of an ancient American civilization descended from a group of Israelites who migrated from the Holy Land to the New World about 600 BCE. Initially led by a man named Nephi, the "Nephites," as they were known, built up a complex, urban-based civilization, lasting until AD 400. At the beginning Nephi's two brothers, Laman and Lemuel, challenged his authority. The two rebellious brothers led a group of dissidents into the wilderness, where they declined from their civilized state, becoming a barbaric, nomadic people known as Lamanites. God marked or "cursed" these Lamanites with a dark skin.

Subsequently, the light-skinned Nephites and dark-skinned Lamanites fought each other in a series of protracted wars until the Nephites were ultimately wiped out, with only the Lamanites remaining. Joseph Smith and his Latter-day Saint followers viewed contemporary Indians or Native Americans as descendants of these Lamanites.[3]

The *Book of Mormon*, while not directly addressing race involving blacks or people of African descent, alluded to them through its use of the term *black* interchangeably with *red* in describing various dark-skinned peoples and the curse inflicted on them.[4] This scriptural work, moreover, contains an extensive discussion of the unrighteous behavior of Cain—a Biblical counter-figure considered by nineteenth-century Latter-day Saints to be a direct ancestor of contemporary black people.[5] Also, the *Book of Mormon* suggested possible black African origins for another ancient American civilization, the Jaredites, whose activities predated those of the Nephites and Lamanites.[6] While *Book of Mormon* references to the Jaredites' precise ethnic background are somewhat vague, it states that this people originated in a region near the Tower of Babel before moving to the Valley of Nimrod—areas identified with the descendants of Ham. In turn, Joseph Smith and his nineteenth-century Mormon followers viewed Ham as the common ancestor of all contemporary blacks. At least one important Mormon leader, apostle Parley P. Pratt, asserted that the "genealogy of the Jaredites" could be traced "back to Ham."[7] The Jaredites migrated to the Western Hemisphere and built up a civilization, but, with the later Nephites, they perished because of their unrighteousness.[8]

The following verses contained in the *Book of Mormon* provide insight into initial Latter-day Saint beliefs relative to race and slavery.

1. THE *BOOK OF MORMON* REVEALS WHY GOD PUT A "CURSE" ON THE LAMANITES, 1830.

   DOCUMENT INTRODUCTION, 2 Nephi, 5:20–25

   The *Book of Mormon* warned of racial degeneration, i.e., "the curse" of a dark skin for those individuals and groups who misbehaved and fell from divine favor, in particular, the Lamanites, Amlicites, and Zoramites. Others who fought against God's chosen people, i.e., the Nephites, were also threatened with "a mark" or a "dark skin."[9] Such concepts of racial degeneration were not unique to the *Book of Mormon*. Racial environmentalism—a belief that a particular social situation and/or a certain geographic setting promoted the evolution of particular races and ethnic groups—was widely held by racial theorists during the early nineteenth century, many of whom believed that such racial changes could occur within a relatively short time span.[10] *Book of Mormon* suggestions of racial degeneration mirrored similar views in the larger society that all contemporary, primitive, dark-skinned peoples had degenerated from a more "advanced culture."[11]

DOCUMENT

From 2 Nephi, 5:20–25, in Joseph Smith Jr., *Book of Mormon* (Kansas City, MO: Burd and Fletcher Printing Co., 1902), 72.

20. Wherefore, the word of the Lord was fulfilled which he spake unto me, saying That inasmuch as they will not hearken unto thy words, they shall be cut off from the presence of the Lord. And behold, they were cut off from his presence.

21. And he had caused the cursing to come upon them, yea, even a sore cursing, because of their iniquity. For behold, they had hardened their hearts against him, that they had become like unto a flint; wherefore, as they were white, and exceeding fair and delightsome, that they might not be enticing unto my people, the Lord God did cause a skin of blackness to come upon them.

22. And thus saith the Lord God, I will cause that they shall be loathsome unto thy people, save they shall repent of their iniquities.

23. And cursed shall be the seed of him that mixeth with their seed; for they shall be cursed even with the same cursing. And the Lord spake it, and it was done.

24. And because of their cursing which was upon them, they did become an idle people, full of mischief and subtlety, and did seek in the wilderness for beasts of prey.

25. And the Lord God said unto me, they shall be a scourge unto thy seed, to stir them up in remembrance of me; and inasmuch as they will not remember me, and hearken unto my words, they shall scourge them even unto destruction.

2. THE *BOOK OF MORMON* STATES THAT THE CURSE OF A DARK SKIN WILL BE LIFTED FROM THOSE LAMANITES WHO ACCEPT THE TRUE FAITH, 1830.

DOCUMENT INTRODUCTION, 2 Nephi, 30: 5–6; 3 Nephi, 2: 14–16

The *Book of Mormon* further states that the process of racial degeneration could be reversed, given the right conditions. Specifically, God removed the "curse" of a dark skin from those Lamanites who accepted the true faith and allowed themselves to be inspired by the righteous example of the fair-skinned Nephites.[12] This work also promised contemporary American Indians that if they became "civilized" and adopted the true faith they would lose "their scales of darkness" and become a "white and delightsome people."[13] The assertion that racial degeneration could be reversed echoed contemporary non-Mormon theorists who maintained that dark-skinned people had the capacity to regain the "original perfection" of a light skin and earlier "civilized state."[14]

DOCUMENTS

From 2 Nephi, 30: 5–6, in Joseph Smith Jr., *Book of Mormon* (Kansas City, MO: Burd and Fletcher Printing Co., 1902), 122.

5. And the gospel of Jesus Christ shall be declared among them [the Lamanites]; wherefore, they shall be restored unto the knowledge of their fathers, and also to the knowledge of Jesus Christ, which was had among their fathers.

6. And then shall they rejoice; for they shall know that is a blessing unto them from the hand of God; and their scales of darkness shall begin to fall from their eyes; and many generations shall not pass among them save they shall be a white and delightsome people.

From 3 Nephi, 2: 14–16, in Joseph Smith Jr., *Book of Mormon* (Kansas City, MO: Burd and Fletcher Printing Co., 1902), 480.

14. And it came to pass that those Lamanites who had united with the Nephites were numbered with the Nephites.

15. And their curse was taken from them, and their skin became white like unto the Nephites:

16. And their young men and their daughters became exceedingly fair, and were numbered among the Nephites, and were called Nephites. And thus ended the thirteenth year.

3. THE *BOOK OF MORMON* AVERS THAT GOD WILL NOT DENY ANYONE WHO "COME UNTO HIM," INCLUDING "BLACK AND WHITE, BOND AND FREE, MALE AND FEMALE," 1830.

DOCUMENT INTRODUCTION, 2 Nephi, 26: 32–33

The *Book of Mormon*, like the New Testament, promised universal Christian salvation for all humankind, without regard to race, color, or bondage. The atonement of Christ is "infinite for all mankind," with Christ manifesting himself "unto every nation, kindred, tongue and people."[15] The Nephites made a special effort to preach to all—"both old and young, both bond and free, both male and female."[16] Alma, a Nephite missionary and one of the book's principal heroes, strived to carry the true gospel "unto every soul." Other Nephite missionaries preached among the dark-skinned Lamanites, explaining that "All men are privileged . . . and none are forbidden from receiving the True Gospel."[17]

DOCUMENT

From 2 Nephi, 26: 32–33, in Joseph Smith Jr., *Book of Mormon* (Kansas City, MO: Burd and Fletcher Printing Co., 1902), 113.

32. And again, the Lord God hath commanded that men should not murder; that they should not lie; that they should not steal; that they should not take the name of the Lord their God in vain; that they should not envy; that they should not have malice; that they should not contend one with another; that they should not commit whoredoms; and that they should do none of these things; for whoso doeth them, shall perish;

33. For none of these iniquities come of the Lord; for he doeth that which is good among the children of men; and he doeth nothing save it be plain unto the children of men; and he inviteth them all to come unto him, and partake of his goodness; and he denieth none that come unto him, black and white, bond and free, male and female; and he remembereth the heathen, and all are alike unto God, both Jew and Gentile.

4. THE *BOOK OF MORMON* ASSERTS THAT IT IS "AGAINST THE LAW" OF THE NEPHITES TO HOLD "SLAVES," 1830.

DOCUMENT INTRODUCTION, Mosiah 2:13

In addition to race, the *Book of Mormon* addressed slavery within the context of its pre-Columbian American setting, stating it was "against [Nephite] law" to hold slaves.[18] The Nephites refused to enslave those less favored than themselves, namely, the dark-skinned Lamanites. They proclaimed: "Neither do we desire to bring anyone to the yoke of bondage."[19] Rather the idolatrous Lamanites practiced slavery and made repeated efforts to enslave the "civilized" Nephites.[20] Lamanite slaveholding was cited as proof of that people's unrighteousness.[21] Nephite resistance to these dark-skinned slaveholders was described as a struggle for freedom from "bondage" and "slavery."[22] There are, however, a number of *Book of Mormon* passages that could be construed as recognizing a master-servant relationship. These described bondage as a punishment for wicked behavior.[23]

DOCUMENT

From Mosiah 2:13, in Joseph Smith Jr., *Book of Mormon* (Kansas City, MO: Burd and Fletcher Printing Co., 1902), 164.

13. Neither have I suffered that ye should be confined in dungeons, nor that ye should make slaves one of another, nor that ye should murder, or plunder, or steal, or commit adultery; nor even have I suffered that ye should commit any manner of wickedness, and have taught you that ye should keep the commandments of the Lord, in all things which he hath commanded you—

5. THE *BOOK OF MORMON* DESCRIBES A "GOLDEN AGE" DURING WHICH ALL PEOPLES WOULD LIVE IN HARMONY, AND WHERE THERE WOULD BE NO SLAVERY NOR DISTINCTIONS BASED ON RACE, 1830.

DOCUMENT INTRODUCTION, 4 Nephi 1:3, 10, 17

The *Book of Mormon* foresaw a "golden age" when all peoples would be "exceedingly fair and delightsome" with no "Lamanites nor any manner of -ites." This concept reflected a general belief held by nineteenth-century Americans and Western Europeans that all humankind, given identical, "optimum" cultural-geographic conditions, might overcome all distinctions of race and become one universal white race.[24] Such ideas dovetailed with a general American millennialistic belief, rooted in Enlightenment optimism, that all humankind had the capacity to "return" to a pristine, pure white racial state akin to that enjoyed by Adam and Eve in the Garden of Eden.[25]

DOCUMENT

From 4 Nephi 1:3, 10, 17, in Joseph Smith Jr., *Book of Mormon* (Kansas City, MO: Burd and Fletcher Printing Co., 1902), 544–45.

3. And they had all things common among them: therefore there were not rich and poor, bond and free, but they were all made free, and partakers of the heavenly gift.

10. And now, behold it came to pass that the people of Nephi did wax strong, and did multiply exceedingly fast, and became exceedingly fair and delightsome people.

17. There were no robbers, nor murderers, neither were there Lamanites, nor any manner of -ites; but they were in one, the Children of Christ, and heirs to the Kingdom of God.

II. *Pearl of Great Price*

GENERAL INTRODUCTION

A second Mormon scriptural work, the *Pearl of Great Price*, also produced by Joseph Smith, more directly discusses race affecting African Americans.[26] This work focuses on certain Old Testament peoples considered ancestors of contemporary black people described in the *Book of Moses* and *Book of Abraham*.[27]

Joseph Smith produced the first of these sections of the *Book of Moses* as part of a larger effort to revise or "correct" both the Old and New Testaments, with portions of this work initially published in the *Evening and Morning Star*—the official Mormon church newspaper in 1832–33.[28]

1. ### THE *BOOK OF MOSES* REVEALS WHY GOD GAVE CAIN A "CURSE," 1832–33.

    DOCUMENT INTRODUCTION, Book of Moses, 5:23–26

    The *Book of Moses* details the deeds, or rather misdeeds, of Cain, the son of Adam, and brother of Abel, whom he purportedly slew. It discounts Cain's murderous act as a spontaneous outburst of anger, declaring that it was a carefully planned conspiracy between Cain and Satan. For his act, God punished Cain. In the words of the *Book of Moses*, Cain "was cursed from the earth," destined to be "a fugitive and a vagabond." In addition, "the Lord set a mark upon Cain," who was in turn "shut out from the Presence of the Lord."[29]

    DOCUMENT

    From *Book of Moses*, 5:23–26, in Joseph Smith Jr., *Pearl of Great Price* (Salt Lake City: Deseret News, 1907), 22.

    23. If thou doest well, thou shalt be accepted. And if thou doest not well, sin lieth at the door, and Satan desireth to have thee; and except thou shalt hearken unto my commandments, I will deliver thee up, and it shall be unto thee according to his desire. And thou shalt rule over him;

    24. For from this time forth thou shalt be the father of his lies; thou shalt be called Perdition; "for thou wast also before the world."

25. And it shall be said in time to come—That these abominations were had from Cain; for he rejected the greater counsel which was had from God; and this is a cursing, which I will put upon thee, except thou repent.

26. And Cain was wroth, and listened not any more to the voice of the Lord, neither to Abel, his brother, who walked in holiness before the Lord.

2. THE *BOOK OF MOSES* STATES THAT THE DESCENDANTS OF CAIN HAD A DARK SKIN AND WERE SEGREGATED FROM THE REST OF THE "SEED OF ADAM," 1832–33.

DOCUMENT INTRODUCTION, Moses 7:22

The *Book of Moses* also presented Cain's descendants in an unfavorable light. Lamech, one such descendant, entered into a "covenant with Satan" and killed one of his relatives.[30] For this deed, Lamech was "cursed" along with "his house," by the Lord, and further "despised and cast out" from "among the [righteous] sons of man."[31] It also described other descendants of Cain as a segregated, dark-skinned people.

DOCUMENT

From *Book of Moses*, 7:22, in Joseph Smith Jr., *Pearl of Great Price* (Salt Lake City: Deseret News, 1907), 39.

22. And Enoch also beheld the residue of the people which were the sons of Adam; and they were a mixture of all the seed of Adam save it was the seed of Cain, for the seed of Cain were black, and had not place among them.

3. THE *BOOK OF ABRAHAM* DESCRIBES PHARAOH, THE KING OF EGYPT, A DESCENDANT OF HAM AND PROCLAIMS HIM "CURSED . . . PERTAINING TO THE PRIESTHOOD."

DOCUMENT INTRODUCTION, *Book of Abraham*, 1: 21–27

The *Book of Abraham* reflects Joseph Smith's evolving ideas relative to race. Smith transcribed a set of Egyptian papyrus rolls acquired from Michael H. Chandler, a salesman of Egyptian artifacts.[32] The entire text was first published in 1842 in the official LDS church newspaper, the *Times and Seasons*, followed by its inclusion in the *Pearl of Great Price* some nine years later.[33] The *Book of Abraham* relates the experiences of the prophet Abraham during his sojourn in Egypt.[34] More important, it outlines a number of essential Mormon tenets ultimately embraced as fundamental beliefs. One is the concept of a premortal existence—the idea that the human spirit existed in an earlier state prior to being born in this world; and the second a belief in a plurality of Gods. The *Book of Abraham*, moreover, casts two particular groups in an unfavorable racial light—the Chaldeans and Egyptians. Of particular relevance are those verses asserting that these peoples were "cursed as pertaining to the priesthood." LDS leaders ultimately used this scripture as a "proof text" to justify black priesthood denial. But there is *no* contemporary evidence that

Joseph Smith did likewise. At least one historian suggests that these verses instead exhibited an "idiosyncratic type of racial thinking. Neither [racial] inferiority nor servitude was the issue only priesthood." This scholar further states that its concern "was with civilizations and lineage more than race. Pharaoh, Ham, and Egyptus figure in one lineage and Abraham in another. The implications for modern race relations interested Joseph [Smith] less than the configuration of family lines and the descent of authority."[35]

DOCUMENT

From *Book of Abraham*, 1: 21–27, in Joseph Smith Jr., *Pearl of Great Price* (Salt Lake City: Deseret News, 1907), 55.

21. Now this king of Egypt was a descendant from the loins of Ham, and was a partaker of the blood of the Canaanites by birth.

22. From this descent sprang all the Egyptians, and thus the blood of the Canaanites was preserved in the land.

23. The land of Egypt being first discovered by a woman, who was the daughter of Ham, and the daughter of Egyptus, which in the Chaldean signifies Egypt, which signifies that which is forbidden.

24. When this woman discovered the land it was under water, who afterward settled her sons in it; and thus, from Ham, sprang that race which preserved the curse in the land.

25. Now the first government of Egypt was established by Pharaoh, the eldest son of Egyptus, the daughter of Ham, and it was after the manner of the government of Ham, which was patriarchal.

26. Pharaoh, being a righteous man, established his kingdom and judged his people wisely and justly all his days, seeking earnestly to imitate that order established by the fathers in the first generations, in the days of the first patriarchal reign, even in the reign of Adam, and also of Noah, his father, who blessed him with the blessings of the earth, and with the blessings of wisdom, but cursed him as pertaining to the Priesthood.

27. Now, Pharaoh being of that lineage by which he could not have the right of Priesthood, notwithstanding the Pharaohs would fain claim it from Noah, through Ham, therefore my father was led away by their idolatry.

4. THE *BOOK OF ABRAHAM* DISCUSSES THE PREEXISTENCE, DESCRIBING DIFFERENCES AMONG PREMORTAL BEINGS THAT DETERMINED THEIR EARTHLY STATUS FOR PRIESTHOOD ORDINATION.

DOCUMENT INTRODUCTION, *Book of Abraham*, 3: 22–28

The *Book of Abraham* discusses the preexistence—a premortal existence for all humankind—and indicates a different status for such premortal beings, or "intelligences," as they were called. This in turn determined their status on earth, where

God "organized" the status of such beings before the creation of the earth with "the noble and great ones" destined to be Earthly "rulers." Abraham was among those so chosen. This work also describes a premortal conflict between two of the most important beings, neither of whom is specifically identified in the text itself. The first is referred to "one" who was "like unto God" or "like unto the son of Man," and a second described as simply "another." The two presented God with differing plans for human salvation, with the Lord accepting the plan of the first, causing the second to became "angry," provoking "many" premortal beings to follow "after him." This conflict came to be viewed as the "war in Heaven" between Jesus and Lucifer and their respective followers, with Satan's followers denied mortal or earthly bodies due to their errant behavior.[36]

While these verses did not specifically address race or the status of black people per se, certain Mormon spokesmen, beginning with apostle Orson Hyde in 1845, suggested that black people had failed to take either side in the conflict, hence their status as an accursed race.[37] Subsequent Mormon spokesmen through the late nineteenth and into the twentieth centuries suggested that black people's inferior status could be attributed to their behavior during their premortal existence.[38]

DOCUMENT

From *Book of Abraham*, 3: 22–28, in Joseph Smith Jr., *Pearl of Great Price* (Salt Lake City: Deseret News, 1907), 65–66.

22. Now the Lord had shown unto me, Abraham, the intelligences that were organized before the world was; and among all these there were many of the noble and great ones;

23. And God saw these souls that they were good, and he stood in the midst of them, and he said: These I will make my rulers; for he stood among those that were spirits and he saw that they were good; and he said unto me: Abraham, thou art one of them; thou wast chosen before thou wast born.

24. And there stood one among them that was like unto God, and he said unto those who were with him: We will go down, for there is space there, and we will take of these materials, and we will make an earth whereon these may dwell;

25. And we will prove them herewith, to see if they will do all things, whatsoever the Lord their God shall command them;

26. And they who keep their first estate shall be added upon; and they who keep not their first estate shall not have glory in the same kingdom with those who keep their first estate; and they who keep their second estate shall have glory added upon their heads forever and ever.

27. And the Lord said: Whom shall I send? And one answered like unto the Son of Man: Here am I, send me. And another answered and said: Here am I, send me. And the Lord said: I will send the first.

28. And the second was angry, and kept not his first estate; and, at that day, many followed after him.

III *Doctrine and Covenants*[39]

GENERAL INTRODUCTION

The Mormon church's third scriptural work, the *Doctrine and Covenants*, first published in 1835, "was meant to summarize the church's major beliefs and provide a handbook of its policies." Essentially a gathering of "items of . . . doctrine" for the "government of the church," it was canonized that same year, proclaiming "a law unto the church, a rule of faith and practice."[40] The bulk of this work consists of Joseph Smith's numerous revelations, along with a series of his official pronouncements, plus a handful of revelations issued by Smith's Mormon successors. These are arranged in "sections."

In three sections of the *Doctrine and Covenants* the Mormon church, through Joseph Smith, directly addressed slavery as it existed in antebellum America.

1. JOSEPH SMITH'S "REVELATION AND PROPHECY ON WAR," 1832.

DOCUMENT INTRODUCTION, *Doctrine and Covenants*, 87: 1–8

In December 1832 Joseph Smith issued his "Revelation and Prophecy on War," destined to be among the most famous of all of his revelations, ultimately included as Section 87. But it was not included in the work's first edition, published in 1835.[41] It is noteworthy for three major reasons. First, it reflected Mormon anxiety at the growing national controversy over slavery, as reflected in two unsettling events: (1) Nat Turner's rebellion, occurring in August 1831 in Southampton County, Virginia, staged by some sixty slaves, with fifty-seven whites and all of the slaves involved killed before being suppressed;[42] (2) the Nullification Crisis of 1832–33, pitting federal officials, led by President Andrew Jackson, against the rebellious state of South Carolina, whose state officials nullified an objectionable tariff enacted by the national government.[43]

Second, this revelation manifested a strong sense of apocalyptic millenarianism pervasive within early Mormonism—that is, a widespread belief that the End Times were imminent.[44] This was dramatized in 1834 in a change of the church's official designation from the "Church of Christ" to the "Church of the Latter-day Saints."[45] In promoting premillennialism, Smith's millenarian teachings were akin to those of contemporary rival religious leader William Miller.[46]

And finally, Smith's revelation, given its limited initial exposure, reflected a Mormon desire to remain aloof from the entire slavery controversy. Such a desire to remain aloof was prompted, at least in part, by the location of Mormonism's so-called Zion, or central gathering place, in Missouri, a slave state.[47] Accordingly, the church's official newspaper, the *Evening and Morning Star*, based in Independence, Missouri, avoided the slave issue altogether, ignoring Nat Turner's rebellion and the burgeoning abolitionist movement.[48]

DOCUMENT

From Joseph Smith Jr., *Doctrine and Covenants* (Salt Lake City: Deseret News Office, 1876), section 87, verses 1–8.

1. Verily, thus saith the Lord, concerning the wars that will shortly come to pass, beginning at the rebellion of South Carolina, which will eventually terminate in the death and misery of many souls.

2. The days will come that war will be poured out upon all nations, beginning at that place;

3. For behold, the Southern States shall be divided against the Northern States, and the Southern States will call on other nations, even the nation of Great Britain, as it is called, and they shall also call upon other nations, in order to defend themselves against other nations; and thus war shall be poured out upon all nations.

4. And it shall come to pass, after many days, slaves shall rise up against their masters, who shall be marshalled and disciplined for war:

5. And it shall come to pass also, that the remnants who are left of the land will marshal themselves, and shall become exceeding angry, and shall vex the Gentiles with a sore vexation;

6. And thus, with the sword, and by bloodshed, the inhabitants of the earth shall mourn; and with famine, and plague, and earthquakes, and the thunder of Heaven, and the fierce and vivid lightning also, shall the inhabitants of the earth be made to feel the wrath, and indignation and chastening hand of an Almighty God, until the consumption decreed, hath made a full end of all nations;

7. That the cry of the Saints, and of the blood of the Saints, shall cease to come up into the ears of the Lord of Sabaoth, from the earth, to be avenged of their enemies.

8. Wherefore, stand ye in holy places, and be not moved, until the day of the Lord come; for behold it cometh quickly, saith the Lord. Amen.

2. JOSEPH SMITH EXPLAINS THROUGH REVELATION WHY NO MAN SHOULD "BE IN BONDAGE ONE TO ANOTHER," 1833.

DOCUMENT INTRODUCTION, *Doctrine and Covenants*, 101:77–80

In December 1833 Joseph Smith through revelation proclaimed that "it is not right that any man should be in bondage one to another." Upon initial examination, it would appear that this statement, immediately following the Mormon expulsion from Jackson County, Missouri, the previous July, represents the Mormon leader's earliest direct condemnation of slavery. But according to one noted scholar of the Mormon-black issue, this statement "does not appear to have been used in early [Mormon church] discourses on either side of the slavery question,"[49] further noting that the "statement is traditionally interpreted as meaning economic bondage."[50]

DOCUMENT

From Joseph Smith Jr., *Doctrine and Covenants* (Salt Lake City: Deseret News Office, 1876), section 101, verses 77–80.

77. According to the laws and constitution of the people which I have suffered to be established, and should be maintained for the rights and protection of all flesh, according to just and holy principles,

78. That every man may act in doctrine and principle pertaining to futurity, according to the moral agency which I have given unto them, that every man may be accountable for his own sins in the day of judgment.

79. Therefore, it is not right that any man should be in bondage one to another.

80. And for this purpose have I established the constitution of this land, by the hands of wise men whom I raised up unto this very purpose, and redeemed the land by the shedding of blood.

3. AN OFFICIAL DECLARATION THAT CHURCH MISSIONARIES NOT BAPTIZE "BOND SERVANTS" AGAINST "THE WILL AND WISH OF THEIR MASTERS," 1835.

DOCUMENT INTRODUCTION, *Doctrine and Covenants*, 134: 12

Joseph Smith and other church spokesmen more directly addressed the issue of slavery in an August 1835 official declaration, stating that it was not "right to interfere with bond servants, nor baptize them contrary to the will and wish of their masters," nor "cause them to be dissatisfied with their situations in this life." LDS officials ultimately placed this statement in the *Doctrine and Covenants* as Section 134:12 under the title "A Declaration of Belief Regarding Governments and Laws in General."[51] Prompting Smith to issue this seeming pro-slavery statement was his desire to avoid identification with the fledgling abolitionist movement rather than a desire to embrace the South's peculiar institution. Kirtland, Ohio, the church's headquarters, was on the Western Reserve,[52] a hotbed of abolitionism during the 1830s.[53] Such abolitionist activity made Ohio the focal point of more anti-abolitionist violence than any other state in the Union.[54]

DOCUMENT

From Joseph Smith Jr., *Doctrine and Covenants* (Salt Lake City: Deseret News Office, 1876), section 134, verse 12.

12. We believe it just to preach the gospel to the nations of the earth, and warn the righteous to save themselves from the corruption of the world; but we do not believe it right to interfere with bond servants, neither preach the gospel to, nor baptize them, contrary to the will and wish of their masters, nor to meddle with or influence them in the least, to cause them to be dissatisfied with their situations in this life, thereby jeopardizing the lives of men; such interference we believe to be unlawful and unjust, and dangerous to the peace of every government allowing human beings to be held in servitude.

2

Joseph Smith and Evolving Mormon Attitudes and Practices on Slavery and Race, 1830–1844

General Introduction

The fourteen-year period commencing in 1830 with the birth of Mormonism and concluding in 1844 with the assassination of Joseph Smith Jr. was a critical time for emerging Mormon attitudes and practices affecting African Americans. Mormon attitudes relative to slavery went through three distinct phases. Initially, Joseph Smith and other church spokesmen remained aloof from slavery. The church's official newspaper, the *Evening and Morning Star*, which commenced publication in June 1832, avoided all such topics.[1] No mention was made of those *Book of Mormon* verses condemning slavery and/or human bondage.[2]

By the mid-1830s, however, Joseph Smith shifted his position, affirming support for slavery, doing so in an official 1835 church statement (discussed in the previous chapter).[3] Three major factors compelled Smith's changing stance. First was a growing Mormon presence in Missouri—a slave state whose population came primarily from the slaveholding South and neighboring border states. Throughout the 1830s Smith looked to Missouri, in particular Jackson County, as Mormonism's Zion, or primary gathering place.[4] Smith's desire to carry the Mormon message to potential converts in the slaveholding South also prompted him to support slavery. And finally, the Latter-day Saints were anxious to avoid identifying with the fledgling abolitionist movement.[5]

By the early 1840s, Joseph Smith shifted his position once more, condemning slavery, promoting this view until his death in June 1844. Other Mormon spokesmen followed suit along with the *Times and Seasons*—the church's official newspaper. Several factors motivated Latter-day Saint dislike for slavery. First was the Mormons' forced expulsion from Missouri, a slaveholding state, to Illinois, where slavery was prohibited. From the Latter-day Saints' new gathering place of Nauvoo, church spokesmen felt free to attack slavery. Secondly, Mormon antislavery convictions resulted from a shift in Mormon millennialistic expectations during the 1840s wherein church spokesmen moved away from their previous sense of immediate apocalyptic doom to a belief that the End Times were several decades away.[6] A third factor prompting Mormon disdain for slavery was that the vast majority of church members hailed from non-slaveholding regions, including New York, New England, the Ohio Valley, and Great Britain—regions that by this time had outlawed slavery. By contrast, Mormonism drew a limited number of new converts from the slaveholding South.[7]

Concurrent with Mormonism's shifting position on slavery was the church's acceptance of black members in full fellowship—albeit few in number. Church leaders ordained a handful of African American males to the priesthood during Joseph Smith's ministry—namely Elijah Abel, Joseph T. Ball, and Quock Walker Lewis.[8] Two other African Americans—Enoch Lovejoy Lewis and Black Pete—apparently also received the priesthood during this early period, though records are not clear regarding their ordination.[9] Still less clear is the total number of African Americans in the early church. According to apostle Parley P. Pratt, fewer than "one dozen free negroes or mulattoes" affiliated with the church as of 1839.[10] And during the early 1840s, following the Mormon settlement of Nauvoo, the number of blacks remained "relatively small," with only about twenty out of a total estimated population of twelve thousand. Some of these black members were closely associated with Joseph Smith; others were unknown to him, though he approved of their baptism when queried by missionaries who taught them.[11] In sum, a handful of blacks were ordained to the priesthood during Joseph Smith's ministry.

1. ESSAY TITLED "FREE PEOPLE OF COLOR" PUBLISHED IN THE CHURCH'S OFFICIAL NEWSPAPER, *EVENING AND MORNING STAR*, JULY 1833.

DOCUMENT INTRODUCTION

Among the earliest Mormon articles discussing the place of African Americans within the fledgling Mormon movement was "Free people of Color." A dramatic fourfold increase in the number of Mormons settling in Jackson County, Missouri, between May 1832 and July 1833 prompted editor William Phelps to publish "Free People of Color" in the *Evening and Morning Star*.[12]

Phelps stated that his article was intended "to prevent any misunderstanding among the churches abroad, respecting free people of color, who may think of coming to the western boundaries of Missouri as members of the Church." The bulk of the article consisted of a reprint of two clauses of the state laws of Missouri governing such migration. On slavery, Phelps affirmed that "Slaves are real estate in this and other states, and wisdom would dictate great care among the branches of the Church of Christ on this subject." He then concluded: "So long as we have no special rule in the Church, as to people of color, let prudence guide, and while they, as well as we, are in the hands of a merciful God, we say: Shun every appearance of evil." Phelps also penned a companion article published in the July 1833 issue of the *Star* wherein he revealed his own position on slavery, embracing colonization of blacks in Africa.[13]

Phelps's two articles generated anger among Jackson County non-Mormons already upset over the increasing number of Mormons in their midst. Accordingly, non-Mormon Missourians circulated a "Secret Constitution" in which they accused the Mormons of "tampering with our slaves, and endeavoring to sew dissentions and raise seditions among them," as well as "inviting free negroes and mulattoes" into the region. Most significantly, they called upon all Mormons to leave the county immediately.[14]

In response to the uproar caused by "Free People of Color," Phelps quickly penned a follow-up article contained in a *Star* "Extra" wherein he claimed that he had been "misunderstood," asserting that he intended to "not only stop free people of color from emigrating to this state but to prevent them from being admitted as members of the Church," adding that "none will be admitted into the Church."[15]

The *Star* "Extra" failed to reverse the deteriorating Mormon situation in Jackson County. Phelps's provocative statements coupled with other non-Mormon grievances, provoked mob violence wherein angry Missourians destroyed the office of the *Star*. Thus Phelps and his follow Mormons fled Jackson County, finding temporary asylum in Clay County.[16] Such violence reached its peak in the so-called Missouri Mormon War of 1838–39, forcing Joseph Smith and his Latter-day Saint followers to abandon the state completely.[17]

Portions of "Free People of Color" are included below.

DOCUMENT

From W. W. Phelps, "Free People of Color," *Evening and Morning Star* (July 16, 1833), 218–219 (excerpts).

To prevent any misunderstanding among the churches abroad, respecting free people of color, who may think of coming to the western boundaries of Missouri, as members of the Church, we quote the following clauses from the laws of Missouri:

> "Section 4.—Be it further enacted, that hereafter no free negro or mulatto, other than a citizen of someone of the United States, shall come into or settle in this state under any pretext whatever; and upon complaint made to any justice of the peace, that such person is in his county, contrary to the provisions of this section, if it shall appear that such person is a free negro or mulatto, and that he hath come into this state after the passage of this act,

and such person shall not produce a certificate, attested by the seal of some court of record in someone of the United States, evidencing that he is a citizen of such state, the justice shall command him forthwith to depart from this state; and in case such negro or mulatto shall not depart from the state within thirty days after being commanded so to do as aforesaid, any justice of the peace, upon complaint thereof to him made may cause such person to be brought before him and may commit him to the common gaol of the county in which he may be found, until the next term of the circuit court to be held in such county. And the said court shall cause such person to be brought before them and examine into the cause of commitment; and if it shall appear that such person came into the state contrary to the provisions of this act, and continued therein after being commanded to depart as aforesaid, such court may sentence such person to receive ten lashes on his or her bare back, and order him to depart the state; and if he or she shall not depart, the same proceedings shall be had and punishment inflicted, as often as may be necessary, until such person shall depart the state.

"Sec. 5.—Be it further enacted, that if any person shall, after the taking effect of this act, bring into this state any free negro or mulatto, not having in his possession a certificate of citizenship as required by this act, (he or she) shall forfeit any pay, for every person so brought, the sum of five hundred dollars, to be recovered by action of debt in the name of the state, to the use of the university, in any court having competent jurisdiction; in which action the defendant may be held to bail, of right and without affidavit; and it shall be the duty of the attorney-general or circuit attorney of the district in which any person so offending may be found, immediately upon information given of such offenses to commence and prosecute an action as aforesaid."

Slaves are real estate in this and other states, and wisdom would dictate great care among the branches of the Church of Christ on this subject. So long as we have no special rule in the Church, as to people of color, let prudence guide, and while they, as well as we, are in the hands of a merciful God, we say: Shun every appearance of evil. . . .

2. JOSEPH SMITH'S DISCOURSE ON ABOLITIONISM AND SLAVERY AS PUBLISHED IN THE *LATTER DAY SAINTS' MESSENGER AND ADVOCATE,* APRIL 1836.

DOCUMENT INTRODUCTION

Three years later in April 1836, Joseph Smith discussed slavery while forcefully condemning the growing abolitionist movement, doing so in an important discourse published in the *Latter Day Saints' Messenger and Advocate*—the church's new official church newspaper based in Kirtland, Ohio. A visit to that community by an abolitionist activist, James W. Alvord, culminated in the establishment in

Kirtland of a chapter of the American Anti-Slavery Society consisting of eighty-six members. *The Philanthropist*—a Cincinnati-based abolitionist publication—stated that Kirtland citizens received both Alvord and "his doctrines of liberty . . . kindly."[18]

Smith, while conceding that "'an abolitionist' had held forth several times to this community," was "happy to say that no violence or breach of public peace was attempted," claiming that "very few" responded to his "avocations."[19] In essence, he expressed five major objections to the abolitionist cause.[20] First, he raised the specter of racial miscegenation and possible race war, specifically that the abolitionist cause was "calculated to . . . set loose, upon the world a community of people who might peradventure, overrun our country and violate the most sacred principles of human society, chastity and virtue." Second, Smith asserted that any evil attending slavery should have been apparent to the "men of piety" of the South, who had raised no objections to the institution.[21]

Third, Smith stated that he "did not believe that the people of the North have any more right to say that the South shall not hold slaves, than the South have to say the North shall," adding that the circulation of antislavery petitions represented "a declaration of hostilities against the people of the South." Fourth, Smith felt that the abolitionists opposed the "decree of Jehovah," wherein the Old Testament declared that blacks were cursed with servitude.[22]

In a fifth and final objection, the Mormon leader pointed to several other biblical precedents for slavery, particularly in the histories of Abraham, Leviticus, Ephesians, and Timothy; and then, quoting Paul in the New Testament, Smith declared: "Servants be obedient to them that are your masters according to the flesh, with fear and trembling, the singleness of your heart." Finally, Smith stated that "It would be much better and more prudent not to preach at all to the slaves, until after their masters are converted."[23]

Smith's arguments were echoed in companion articles by other Latter-day Saint spokesmen, in particular Warren Parrish and Oliver Cowdery, with the latter condemning the "corrupting" and "dangerous" activities of the abolitionists, holding up the specter of slave rebellion, black pauperism, and miscegenation.[24]

Excerpts of Smith's letter to Cowdery are included below.

DOCUMENT

From Joseph Smith to Oliver Cowdery, April 1836, in *Latter Day Saints' Messenger and Advocate* (Kirtland, Ohio), 2: 289–301 (excerpts).

Brother Oliver Cowdery:

Dear Sir—This place having recently been visited by a gentleman who advocated the principles or doctrines of those who are called abolitionists; if you deem the following reflections of any service, or think they will have a tendency to correct the opinions of the southern public, relative to the views and sentiments I believe, as an individual, and am able to say, from personal knowledge, are the feelings of others, you are at liberty to give them publicity in the columns of the Advocate. I am prompted to this course in consequence, in one respect, of many elders having gone into the Southern States, besides, there now being many in that country who have already embraced the fulness of the gospel, as revealed through the book of Mormon,—having learned, by experience, that the enemy of truth does not slumber, nor cease his exertions to bias the minds of communities against the servants of the Lord, by stiring up the indignation of men upon all matters of importance or interest.

Thinking, perhaps, that the sound might go out, that "an abolitionist" had held forth several times to this community, and that the public feeling was not aroused to create mobs or disturbances, leaving the impression that all he said was concurred in, and received as gospel and the word of salvation. I am happy to say, that no violence or breach of the public peace was attempted, so far from this, that all except a very few, attended to their own avocations and left the gentleman to hold forth his own arguments to nearly naked walls.

I am aware, that many who profess to preach the gospel, complain against their brethren of the same faith, who reside in the south, and are ready to withdraw the hand of fellowship because they will not renounce the principle of slavery and raise their voice against every thing of the kind. This must be a tender point, and one which should call forth the candid reflection of all men, and especially before they advance in an opposition calculated to lay waste the fair States of the South, and set loose, upon the world a community of people who might peradventure, overrun our country and violate the most sacred principles of human society,—chastity and virtue.

No one will pretend to say, that the people of the free states are as capable of knowing the evils of slavery as those who hold them. If slavery is an evil, who, could we expect, would first learn it? Would the people of the free states, or would the slave states? All must readily admit, that the latter would first learn this fact. If the fact was learned first by those immediately concerned, who would be more capable than they of prescribing a remedy?

And besides, are not those who hold slaves, persons of ability, discernment and candor? Do they not expect to give an account at the bar of God for their conduct in this life? It may, no doubt, with propriety be said, that many who hold slaves live without the fear of God before their eyes, and, the same may be said of many in the free states. Then who is to be the judge in this matter?

I do not believe that the people of the North have any more right to say that the South shall not hold slaves, than the South have to say the North shall . . .

After having expressed myself so freely upon this subject, I do not doubt, but those who have been forward in raising their voices against the South, will cry out against me as being uncharitable, unfeeling, unkind, and wholly unacquainted with the Gospel of Christ. It is my privilege then to name certain passages from the Bible, and examine the teachings of the ancients upon the matter as the fact is uncontrovertible that the first mention we have of slavery is found in the Holy Bible, pronounced by a man who was perfect in his generation, and walked with God. And so far from that prediction being averse to the mind of God, it remains as a lasting monument of the decree of Jehovah, to the shame and confusion of all who have cried out against the South, in consequence of their holding the sons of Ham in servitude!

"And he said, Cursed be Canaan; a servant of servants shall he be unto his brethren." "Blessed be the Lord God of Shem; and Canaan shall be his servant"—Gen. 8: 25, 26, 27.

Trace the history of the world from this notable event down to this day, and you will find the fulfillment of this singular prophecy. What could have been the design of the Almighty in this singular occurrence is not for me to say; but I can say, the curse is not yet taken off from the sons of Canaan, neither will be until it is affected by as great a power as caused it to come; and the people who interfere the least with the purposes of God in this matter, will come under the least condemnation before Him; and those who are determined to pursue a course, which shows an opposition, and a feverish restlessness against the decrees of the Lord, will learn, when perhaps it is too late for their own good, that God can do His own work, without the aid of those who are not dictated by His counsel . . .

Some may urge that the names man servant and maid-servant, only mean hired persons, who were at liberty to leave their masters or employers at any time. But we can easily settle this point, by turning to the history of Abraham's descendants, when governed by a law from the mouth of Jehovah Himself. I know that when an Israelite had been brought into servitude, in consequence of debt, or otherwise, at the seventh year he went from the task of his former master, or employer; but to no other people or nation was this granted in the law of Israel. And if after a man had served six years, he did not wish to be free, then the master was to bring him unto the judges—bore his ear with an awl, and that man was "to serve him forever." The conclusion I draw from this, is, that this people were led and governed by revelation, and if such a law was wrong, God only is to be blamed, and abolitionists are not responsible . . . if we look at a few items in the New Testament. Paul says:

"Servants be obedient to them that are your masters according to the flesh, with fear and trembling, in singleness of your heart, as unto Christ; not with eye service as men-pleasers; but as the servants of Christ, doing the will of God from the heart; with good will doing service, as to the Lord, and not to men knowing that whatsoever good thing any man doeth, the same shall be received of the Lord, whether he be bound or free. And, ye masters, do the same things unto them, forbearing threatening: knowing that your Master also is in heaven: neither is there respect of persons with him" Eph. 6: 5, 6, 7, 8, 9.

Here is a lesson which might be profitable for all to learn; and the principle upon which the Church was anciently governed, is so plainly set forth, that an eye of truth might see and understand. Here certainly, are represented the master, and servant; and so far from instructions to the servant to leave his master, he is commanded to be in obedience, as unto the Lord; the master in turn, is required to treat him with kindness before God; understanding, at the same time, that he is to give an account. The hand of fellowship is not withdrawn from him in consequence of his having servants.

The same writer, in his first epistle to Timothy, the sixth chapter, and the first five verses, says:

"Let as many servants as are under the yoke count their own masters worthy of all honor, that the name of God and His doctrine be not blasphemed. And they that have believing masters, let them not despise them, because they are brethren: but rather do them service, because they are faithful and beloved, partakers of the benefit. These things teach and exhort. If any man teach otherwise, and consent not to wholesome words, even the words of our Lord Jesus Christ, and to the doctrine which is according to godliness; he is proud, knowing nothing, but doting about questions and strifes of words, whereof cometh envy, strife, railings, evil surmisings, Perverse disputing of men of corrupt minds, and destitute of the truth, supposing that gain is godliness' from such withdraw thyself."

This is so perfectly plain, that I see no need of comment. The Scripture stands for itself; and I believe that these men were better qualified to teach the will of God, than all the abolitionists in the world.

Before closing this communication, I beg leave to drop a word to the traveling Elders. You know, brethren, that great responsibility rests upon you; and that you are accountable to God, for all you teach the world. In my opinion, you will do well to search the Book of Covenants, in which you will see the belief of the Church, concerning masters and servants . . . Having spoken frankly and freely, I leave all in the hands of God, who will direct all things for His glory, and the accomplishment of His work.

Praying that God may spare you to do much good in this life, I subscribe myself your brother in the Lord.

JOSEPH SMITH, jr.

3. PATRIARCHAL BLESSING GIVEN TO ELIJAH ABEL, A BLACK LATTER-DAY SAINT, 1836.

DOCUMENT INTRODUCTION

All anti-abolitionist, pro-slavery statements by Joseph Smith and other church spokesmen notwithstanding, blacks continued to be accepted in full fellowship. Elijah Abel, the most famous early black Latter-day Saint, was baptized in 1832 after moving to Kirtland from his birthplace in Maryland.[25] Abel was subsequently ordained to the priesthood office of elder in March 1836, and later in December of that same year elevated to the higher office of Seventy. Also in 1836 Abel became a "duly licensed minister of the Gospel," serving as a missionary in Ohio. Abel was subsequently called on a second mission to Upstate New York and Canada. Contemporaries described him as "a powerful preacher [and] servant of the most high God."[26]

Abel's missionary activities generated controversy. Non-Mormon residents of St. Lawrence County, New York, accused him of murdering a woman and five children. According to one account, "Handbills were pasted up in every direction . . . and a great reward was offered for him." Abel successfully refuted such charges and left the community unmolested, but he ran into further difficulties, this time from his fellow missionaries. While top church leaders scrutinized Abel's controversial behavior, they took no disciplinary action against him. Abel, in fact, retained his status as a member in good standing, including his priesthood. After moving to Nauvoo, he maintained a close personal relationship with Joseph Smith.[27]

Enhancing his status as a faithful Latter-day Saint, Abel received his patriarchal blessing from Church Patriarch Joseph Smith Sr., the Mormon prophet's father. Typically through this blessing, according to Abel's biographer, "the recipient's lineage is declared . . . along with future blessings, responsibilities, and predictions, all attached to faithfulness. Information regarding the recipient's premortal state, as well as general advice for righteous living, may also be revealed. But the emphasis is on lineage—and the blessings connected with it." However, in the case of Abel's lineage, Patriarch Smith "pronounced nothing conclusively substantive . . . the closest thing to a declaration of lineage" was Smith's declaration to Abel: "I seal upon thee a father's blessing because thou art an orphan," giving as an ambiguous reason the fact "thy father hath never done his duty toward thee."

Abel's blessing also promised that he would "be made equal to thy brethren," declaring that his "soul shall be white in eternity and thy robes glittering." The blessing further promised that he would "receive these blessings because of the covenants of thy fathers." The language used here appeared to suggest "that Elijah Abel's skin color was considered something less than blessed, something that required changing," notes Abel biographer W. Kesler Jackson, who further suggests, "It was despite his blackness, then, that Abel was to achieve eventual glory." Particularly significant was the blessing's assertion that Abel would be "made equal to his brethren."[28]

In further examining Abel's patriarchal blessing, a second writer, Lester Bush, has suggested that Abel was promised that he was to be "the welding link between the black and white races, and that he should hold the initiative authority by which his race should be redeemed."[29] This latter statement was not a part of Abel's "blessing in any form whatsoever," according to biographer W. Kesler Jackson, suggesting that Abel "possibly understood himself to be a 'welding link' between the black and white races—and indeed . . . such a promise, in some form or another, had been made to him by" Joseph Smith.[30]

The full text of Abel's blessing is appended below.

DOCUMENT

From Patriarchal Blessing Book 1:49, LDS Church History Library.

Brother Able, in the name of Jesus I lay my hands upon thy head to bless thee and thou shalt be blessed even forever. I seal upon thee a father's blessing, because thou art an orphan, for thy father, hath never done his duty toward thee, but the Lord hast had his eye upon thee, and brought thee through straits and thou hast come to be rec[k]oned with the saints of the most High. Thou hast been ordained an Elder and anointed to secure thee against the power of the destroyer. Thou shalt see his power in laying waste the nations, & the wicked slaying the wicked, while blood shall run down the streets like water, and thy heart shall weep over their calamities. Angels shall visit thee and thou shalt receive comfort. They shall call thee blessed and deliver thee from thine enemies. They shall break thy bands and keep thee from afflictions. Thy name is written in the Lamb's book of life. Thou shalt travel in the East and visit foreign countries, speak in all the various tongues, and thou shalt be able to teach different languages. Thou shall see visions of this world and other worlds and comprehend the laws of all kingdoms, and confound the wisdom of this generation. Thy life shall be preserved to a good old age. Thou must seek first the kingdom of heaven and all blessings shall be added thereto. Thou shalt be made equal to thy brethren and thy soul be white in eternity and thy robes glittering: thou shalt receive these blessings because of the covenants of thy fathers. Thou shalt save thy thousands, do much good, and receive all the power that thou needest to accomplish thy mission. These and all the blessings which thou canst desire in righteousness, I seal upon thee, in the name of Jesus, Amen.

W. A. Cowdery Assist. Recorder
[March 3, 1836]

4. JOSEPH SMITH'S ANTISLAVERY VIEWS, AS CONTAINED IN HIS 1844 PRESIDENTIAL CAMPAIGN PLATFORM.

DOCUMENT INTRODUCTION

In 1844 Joseph Smith articulated explicit antislavery views within the context of his short-lived campaign for U.S. president. Smith's dissatisfaction with the two major political parties motivated him to run, specifically the Jacksonian Democrats and the Whigs, who ignored Mormon petitions for redress in the wake of their forced expulsion from Missouri. Smith ran on his own self-styled third party, promoting a broad, ambitious reform agenda articulated in a platform titled "Views of the Powers and Policy of the Government."[31]

Included within Smith's platform was his call for the abolition of slavery through gradual, compensated emancipation and colonization of freed blacks, which mirrored similar efforts by American politicians to relocate blacks to Africa.[32] Smith lamented that "Some two or three millions of people are held as slaves, because the spirit in them is covered with a darker skin than ours," demanding the "break down [of] slavery" and removal of "the shackles from the poor black man." He called on southerners themselves to petition their legislators to establish a program of compensated emancipation with the funds needed obtained through the sale of public lands. This program, he predicted, could bring about the complete elimination of slavery by 1850.[33]

Smith crafted his campaign proposals for compensated emancipation to appeal to Americans in general.[34] He sought to reconcile the differences between the proponents and opponents of Manifest Destiny—this the central issue in the 1844 presidential campaign. Manifest Destiny proponents favored the annexation of Texas and other western territories. Those in opposition sought to block the annexation of Texas and other potential slave territory in the Southwest. Both the Whigs and Democrats were deeply divided on this issue. So-called "Cotton Whigs" favored expansion, while "Conscience Whigs" were opposed, fearing the extension of slavery into new regions. The Democratic Party mirrored a similar split, as reflected in the campaigns of rival candidates for the party's nomination. John C. Calhoun, a former vice president and pro-slavery spokesman, favored expansion, whereas ex-president Martin Van Buren, seeking to return to the White House, assumed a free-soil position, opposing any and all westward expansion. And finally, James G. Birney, running as the Liberty Party candidate, assumed a strong antislavery, anti-annexation platform.[35]

Smith, through his antislavery, -pro-annexation platform, sought to reconcile such conflicting views. Expanding on his proposals, the Mormon leader announced that as president he would do away with slavery in Texas, then liberate "the slaves in two or three states, indemnifying the owners, and send[ing] the negroes to Texas, from Texas to Mexico where all colors are alike."[36]

Smith carefully differentiated his proposals from other abolitionists, specifically William Lloyd Garrison, Theodore Weld, and others calling for immediate uncompensated emancipation for liberated blacks in America. More instructively, Smith condemned what he termed "a hireling pseudo priesthood" for pushing "abolition doctrines and doings . . . into Congress and into every other place where conquest smells of fame, or where opposition swells to popularity."[37]

Portions of Smith's "Views of the Powers of the Government" are included below.

DOCUMENT

From Joseph Smith, "Views of the Powers and Policy of the Government," *Times and Seasons* (May 15, 1844), 5: 528–533 (excerpts).

BORN IN A LAND OF LIBERTY, and breathing an air uncorrupted with the sirocco of barbarous climes, I ever feel a double anxiety for the happiness of all men, both in time and eternity. My cogitations, like Daniel's, have for a long time troubled me, when I viewed the condition of men throughout the world, and more especially in this boasted realm, where the Declaration of Independence "holds these truths to be self-evident, that all men are created equal; that they are endowed by their Creator with unalienable rights; that among these are life, liberty, and the pursuit of happiness" but at the same time some two or three millions of people are held as slaves for life, because the spirit in them is covered with a darker skin than ours; . . .

The wisdom which ought to characterize the freest, wisest, and most noble nation of the nineteenth century, should, like the sun in his meridian spender, warm every object beneath its rays; and the main efforts of her officers, who are nothing more nor less than the servants of the people, ought to be directed to ameliorate the condition of all, black or white, bond or free; for the best of books says, "God hath made of one blood all nations of men for to dwell on the face of the earth."

Our common country presents to all men the same advantage; the same facilities, the same prospects, the same honors, and the same rewards; and without hypocrisy, the Constitution, when it says, "We, the people of the United States, in order to form a more perfect union, establish justice, ensure the domestic tranquility, provide for the common defense, promote the general welfare, and secure the blessings of liberty to ourselves and our posterity, [d]o ordain and establish this Constitution for the United States of America," meant just what it said without reference to color or condition, ad infinitum. . . .

A hireling pseudo priesthood will plausibly push abolition doctrines and doings, and "human rights," into Congress and into every other place where conquest smells of fame, or opposition swells to popularity. . . .

Petition, also, ye goodly inhabitants of the slave states, your legislators to abolish slavery by the year 1850, or now, and save the abolitionist from reproach and ruin, infamy and shame. Pray congress to pay every man a reasonable price for his slaves out of the surplus revenue arising from the sale of public lands, and from the deduction of pay from the members of Congress. Break off the shackles from the poor black man, and hire him to labor like other human beings; for "an hour of virtuous liberty on earth, is worth a whole eternity of bondage! . . ."

The southern people are hospitable and noble: they will help to rid so free a country of every vestige of slavery, whenever they are assured of an equivalent for their property. . . . .

"Wherefore, were I president of the United States, by the voice of a virtuous people, I would honor the old paths of the venerated fathers of freedom; I would walk in the tracks of the illustrious patriots, who carried the ark of the government upon their shoulders with an eye single to the glory of the people and when that people petitioned to abolish slavery in the slave states, I would use all honorable means to have their prayers granted; and give liberty to the captive; by paying the southern gentleman a reasonable equivalent for his property, that the whole nation might be free indeed! . . . [38]

3

Brigham Young, the Beginning of Black Priesthood Denial, and Legalization of Slavery in Utah, 1844–1877

General Introduction

The thirty-three years from 1844 to 1877, when Brigham Young served as Mormonism's principal leader, proved fateful for black Latter-day Saints. Under Young's leadership, African American Latter-day Saints were denied access to Mormon priesthood offices and sacred temple ordinances—restrictions that remained in force for some 126 years. The legalization of slavery in the Mormon-dominated Utah Territory also affected black Latter-day Saints—this done in 1852 at the urging of Brigham Young as territorial governor.[1]

Also by 1852, Young had implemented Mormonism's long-standing priesthood ban.[2] Several crucial developments motivated his action. First and most immediate was the controversial behavior of three noteworthy African Americans—at least two of whom were ordained to the Mormon priesthood. One was Joseph T. Ball, a resident of Boston, Massachusetts, an ordained high priest and close associate of William Smith—Joseph Smith's younger brother. Ball, under William's influence, engaged in polygamy without official authorization from Brigham Young. Such behavior notwithstanding, Ball served for a brief time as Boston branch president, becoming the first African American to preside over a Mormon congregation. Ball, however, soon found himself out of favor with Young when details of his earlier unauthorized polygamist practices reached church leaders in August 1845, at which point Ball's involvement with Mormonism apparently ceased.[3]

Less clear is the priesthood status of African American Mormon William (aka Werner) McCary, who associated with the Mormons for some two years, from 1845 to 1847. McCary encountered the wrath of Young and other Mormon leaders when he organized his own schismatic Mormon group. Among McCary's rituals was his own form of unauthorized polygamy, wherein he coaxed several of his white female followers to be "sealed" to him through sexual intercourse. Following disclosure of his unorthodox practices, McCary fled Winter Quarters. Apostle Parley P. Pratt proclaimed that "McCary had 'got the blood of Ham in him which lineage was cursed as regards [to] the priesthood.'"[4]

Also in 1847 the priesthood legitimacy of an African American Latter-day Saint came into question, namely Quock Walker Lewis, a resident of Lowell, Massachusetts. William L. Appleby, a Mormon official in charge of church activities in the eastern United States, expressed concern to Brigham Young, asking if "it was the order of God or tolerated, to ordain negroes to the Priesthood . . . If it is, I desire to know it as I have yet got to learn it."[5] Despite Appleby's confusion, Lewis had clearly been ordained to the priesthood—this by William Smith, the brother of the Mormon prophet.[6]

A second, more subtle factor prompted Young to deny blacks the priesthood. This involved what one scholar called "a retrospective construction of Mormon lineage" or "Mormon ethnicity."[7] Mormons emphasized their "ethnicity" as a divinely chosen people characterized by their "whiteness."[8] This emphasis on Mormon "whiteness" correlated with concurrent efforts to identify with certain Old Testament "chosen peoples," in particular the seed of Abraham through the Children of Israel. Brigham Young and his followers claimed a literal relationship between themselves and the "Seed of Abraham."[9] After 1844 Young emphasized Abrahamic descent as an essential prerequisite for church leadership, presenting himself and his Mormon followers as the pure and unmixed "seed of Abraham" or "Ephraim," a "royal lineage" through which they asserted priesthood authority.[10]

Such claims of priesthood authority through Abrahamic descent negatively impacted black Latter-day Saints, who, in contrast to their white counterparts, could not trace their lineage back to the "chosen seed" of Abraham, but were considered direct descendants of Ham—the accursed son of Noah. Latter-day Saints accepted such beliefs as divine truth. Of particular relevance was the *Book of Abraham*—Joseph Smith's penultimate scriptural work, first published in 1842. This work chronicled the deeds (or rather misdeeds) of African Americans' alleged biblical ancestors—Cain, the people of Canaan, and the idolatrous Egyptians. Of crucial importance was the volume's assertion that an Egyptian pharaoh as a "descendent of . . . Ham" and "partaker of the blood of the Canaanites cursed as pertaining to the priesthood." Thus the *Book of Abraham*, in proclaiming Abrahamic lineage an essential prerequisite for the Mormon priesthood, weakened black claims to such power and authority.[11]

The expansion of plural marriage in the church constitutes a third development motivating Young to prohibit black priesthood ordination—a process facilitated by Young and other Mormon leaders in the wake of Joseph Smith's death. As more Latter-day Saints embraced plural marriage during the period 1844–1852, Young and other church leaders sought, with varying degrees of success, to systematize and control this expanding practice, disciplining church members who married additional plural wives without official authorization. Young found repugnant, indeed intolerable, the polygamous practices of African American Mormons Joseph T. Ball and William McCary, given that such activities involved racial miscegenation. In sum, these developments prompted Young to redefine the church's racial policy by denying black people priesthood and temple privileges.[12]

1. GOVERNOR BRIGHAM YOUNG AND THE UTAH TERRITORIAL LEGISLATURE LEGALIZE SLAVERY IN UTAH IN 1852.

DOCUMENT INTRODUCTION

The legalization of slavery in Utah shortly after its creation as a federal territory underscored a decline in the status of black Latter-day Saints. Brigham Young, acting in his capacity as recently appointed territorial governor, requested such legislation. Young's action stood in sharp contrast to Joseph Smith's earlier call for the abolition of slavery. Smith's death, in fact, marked a sharp decline in Mormonism's antislavery impulse, particularly following the Mormon migration to the Great Basin.[13] Initially, Young and other Mormon leaders sought to remain aloof from the slavery controversy, evident during the period 1848–1850 as the nation faced a protracted sectional crisis over the status of slavery in western territories seized from Mexico in the Mexican-American War. The regions in question included the Mormon-dominated Great Basin along with California and New Mexico. Northern antislavery advocates argued for the prohibition of slavery in all three regions on the basis of the Wilmot Proviso, then pending in Congress. By contrast, southern politicians supported slavery throughout the region.

The Compromise of 1850 temporarily solved the crisis over slavery in the region. Under its provisions California became a free state—in compliance with the request of its residents largely drawn from the non-slaveholding North. New Mexico, with its majority Hispanic population and the Mormon-dominated Great Basin—ultimately known as Utah—became territories. Both regions handled the crucial question of slavery by appealing to "popular sovereignty"—that is, allowing territorial residents to decide the issue for themselves.[14]

Brigham Young's comments on slavery during the early 1850s appeared "a bundle of contradictions."[15] Young initially rejected slavery favoring "free soil," exclaiming: "Shall we lay a foundation for Negro slavery?" he rhetorically asked in a June 1851 sermon. "No God forbid!" Some six months later in early January 1852, in an address to the Utah Territorial Legislature as territorial governor, Young stated: "My own feelings are that no property can or should exist in slaves." In referring to Utah's small black population, he called for a moderate approach between making African Americans "beasts of the field," as he claimed the South had done, or elevating them to the same status of equality with white people, as called for by

Northern abolitionists. Young instead envisioned a form of benevolent indentured servitude.[16]

Some two weeks later, Young, in addressing this same body, proclaimed himself "a firm believer in slavery," urging territorial lawmakers to legalize its status. Initially the measure was titled an "act in relation to African slavery," but at Young's urging its title was changed to "An Act in Relation to Service." Four major factors motivated the Mormon leader in promoting this measure. First, Young acted in response to the presence of some sixty to seventy black slaves in the territory belonging to twelve Mormon slave owners. Among the most noteworthy were apostle Charles C. Rich; William H. Hooper—a prominent Mormon merchant—ultimately Utah's territorial delegate to Congress; and Abraham O. Smoot, a Salt Lake City mayor.[17]

Second, Young hoped to secure possible southern support for Utah statehood.[18] The Mormon leader sought to assure all southerners—both Mormon and non-Mormon—that their rights as slaveholders in Utah would be upheld by law. As Young noted, there were "many Bren. [brethren] in the South with a great amount [invested] in slaves" who might migrate to the Great Basin if their slave property was protected by law. The 1852 act, in fact, was addressed to those "persons coming into this Territory and bringing with them servants justly bound to them."[19]

Young's belief that blacks were inherently inferior to whites and thus fit for involuntary servitude constituted a third motive. Young accepted uncritically the so-called "traditional genealogy" that Africans came through the lineage of Canaan and Ham back to Cain, which in turn "gave divine sanction" to their "servile condition."[20]

A fourth, seemingly contradictory factor motivating Young's push of "An Act in Relation to Service" involved his desire to discourage *large-scale* slaveholding in the territory. A careful reading of its provisions indicates the act consisted primarily of rules to control and restrict slaveholders and only incidentally of proscriptions on the black slaves themselves. This statute required Utah slaveholders to prove that servile blacks had entered the territory "of their own free will and choice." Slaveholders, moreover, could not sell their slaves or remove them from the territory without the servants' explicit consent. In addition, the statute required masters to provide their servants "comfortable habitations, clothing, bedding, sufficient food, and recreation." It further restricted the master's right to "correct and punish his servant." The law also required the masters to "send their servant or servants to school [for] not less than eighteen months, between the ages of six and twenty years." Finally, in contrast to the prevailing practices in the slaveholding South, the act forbade masters from engaging in "sexual intercourse with any of the African race." A master found in violation of this provision was compelled "to forfeit all claims to said servant or servants" and subject to a fine ranging from $500 to $5,000 and/or a term of imprisonment from three to five years. The territorial probate courts enforced all such provisions.[21]

In general, "An Act in Relation to Service" contrasted sharply with southern slaveholding statutes, both in its tone and tenor. It was, in fact, more akin to the practice of black indentured servitude existing in the Latter-day Saints' one-time gathering place of Illinois.[22] In fact, "An Act in Relation to Service" discouraged any large slaveholding within the territory with Young himself, declaring that the act "nearly freed the territory of the colored population."[23]

Below are the provisions of the 1852 "An Act in Relation to Service."

DOCUMENT

From "An Act in Relation to Service," February 4, 1852, in Utah Territory, Legislative Assembly, *Acts Resolutions and Memorials* (Salt Lake City, 1852), chapter 17, pp. 160–162.

SEC. I. Be it enacted by the Governor and Legislative Assembly of the Territory of Utah: That any person or persons coming to this Territory, and bringing with them servants justly bound to them, arising from special contract or otherwise, said person or persons be entitled to such service or labor by the laws of loin territory, this Territory: Provided, that he shall file in the office of the probate court written and satisfactory evidence that such service or labor is due.

SEC. 2. That the probate court shall receive as evidence any contract properly attested in writing or any How contracts well proved agreement wherein the party or parties serving have received or are to 'receive a reasonable compensation for his, her, or their services: Provided, proviso. that no contract shall bind the heirs of the servant or servants to service for a longer period than will satisfy the debt due his, her, or their master or masters.

SEC. 3. That any person bringing a servant or servants, and his, her, or their children from any part . . . [in] the United States, or other country, and shall place in the office of the probate court the certificate of any . . . record under seal, properly attested that he, she, or they are entitled lawfully to the service of such servant or servants, and his, her, or their children, the probate justice shall record the same, and the master or mistress, or his, her, or their heirs shall be entitled to the services of the said servant or servants unless forfeited as hereinafter provided, if it shall appear that such servant or servants came into the Territory of their own free will and choice.

SEC. 4. That if any master or mistress shall have sexual or carnal intercourse with his or her servant or servants of the African race, he or she shall forfeit all claim to said servant or servants to the commonwealth; and if any white person shall be guilty of sexual inter- course with any of the African race, they shall be subject, on conviction thereof to a fine of not exceeding one thousand dollars, nor less than five hundred, to the use African race, of the Territory, and imprisonment not exceeding three years.

SEC. 5. It shall be the duty of masters or mistresses to provide for his, her, or their servants comfortable habitations, clothing, bedding, sufficient food, and recreation.

And it shall be the duty of the servant in return therefore, to labor faithfully all reasonable hours, and do such service with fidelity as may be required by his or her master or mistress.

SEC. 6. It shall be the duty of the master to correct and punish his servant in a reasonable manner when it be necessary, being guided by prudence and humanity; and if he shall be guilty of cruelty or abuse, or neglect to feed, clothe, or shelter his servants in a proper manner, the probate court may declare the contract between master and servant or servants void, or Transfer of servants. . . .

SEC. 7. That servants may be transferred from one master or mistress to another by the consent and approbation of the probate court, who shall keep a record of the same in his office; but no transfer shall be made without the consent of the servant given to the probate judge in the absence of his master or mistress.

SEC. 8. Any person transferring a servant or servants contrary to the provisions of this act, or taking one out of the Territory contrary to his, or her will, except by decree of court in case of a fugitive from labor, shall be on conviction thereof, subject to a fine, not exceeding five thousand dollars, and imprisonment, not exceeding five years, or both, at the discretion of the court, and shall forfeit all claims to the services of such servant or servants, as provided in the fourth section of this act.

SEC. 9. It shall further be the duty of all masters or mistresses to send their servant or servants to school, not less than eighteen months, between the ages of six, and twenty years.

2. BRIGHAM YOUNG'S 1852 SPEECH OUTLINING HIS RATIONALE FOR DENYING BLACKS THE MORMON PRIESTHOOD.

DOCUMENT INTRODUCTION

"An Act in Relation to Service" inspired Brigham Young's speech of February 5, 1852, to the Utah Territorial legislature outlining his rationale for black priesthood denial. Young's lengthy discourse represented the most thorough discussion on the topic up to that time.

This speech, however, was *not* the Mormon leader's first declaration on the topic. He had made strong statements concerning the status of blacks within the church as early as 1847. The precise date Young decreed blacks ineligible for the priesthood is unclear. The fateful decision was certainly made within the time frame 1847–1852. Evidence for its enactment as early as 1847 is suggested in apostle Parley P. Pratt's statement in April of that year, affirming that black schismatic leader William McCary "had 'got the blood of Ham in him which lineage was cursed as regards [to] the priesthood.'"[24] Lending validity to Pratt's statement is that it paraphrases a crucial verse in the *Book of Abraham* stating that the Egyptian pharaoh, as "a descendant of . . . Ham," was "cursed as pertaining to the priesthood."[25] Also supporting the 1847 date is Mormon leader William Appleby's inquiry questioning the priesthood status of black elder Quock Walker Lewis, asking if "it was the order of God or tolerated, to ordain negroes to the Priesthood . . . If it is, I desire to know it as I have yet got to learn it."[26] Missing, however, during this early period is any direct statement by Brigham Young himself. To the contrary, Young, in confronting William McCary at Winter Quarters in early 1847, reassured the African American Mormon "that race had no bearing on an individual's standing within the church." Young further opined that it had "nothing to do with the blood, for one blood has God made all flesh." He then added, "we have one of the best Elders an African in Lowell [Massachusetts] a barber" named Q. Walker Lewis."[27]

By February 1849, however, "Young's beliefs about the place of black people within the church [had] hardened" to the point that he rejected a proposal by apostle Lorenzo Snow that the church "unlock the door" to the African race so that this people "would have a chance of redemption." What Snow precisely meant is unclear. Perhaps the apostle desired "either an emphasis on missions to African Americans or allowing them access to sacred church rituals."[28] In response, Young stated "very lucidly" that blacks were under a curse because their biblical ancestor Cain had "cut off the wives of Abel to hedge up his way and take the lead but the Lord has given them [Cain's descendants] blackness so as to give the children of Abel an opportunity to keep his place with his descendants in the eternal worlds." Young further theorized that Cain as the murderer of Abel "had deprived both Abel and his wives of increasing their progeny" and for this "God had punished the 'seed of Cain' with blackness," emblematic of African Americans' "inferior position within society, the church, and ultimately" in the hereafter. Young did concede that at some future time "after Abel's posterity had received their blessings in full, God would remove the curse. Until then, Young insisted the church could not alter 'the true eternal principles the Lord Almighty had ordained.'"[29]

Three years later Young, in his February 5, 1852, speech to the Utah Territorial Legislature, formally declared blacks ineligible for the priesthood.[30] In doing so Young affirmed a direct link between priesthood denial and African American slavery, proclaiming the two practices intertwined and divinely sanctioned. Slavery, he asserted, had existed throughout the course of human history. He stated that when "Eve pertook [sic] of the forbidden fruit . . . this made a slave of her." Adam became a "slave" when he followed Eve's example. Young further proclaimed "that slavery would continue" into the indefinite future until the "righteous establishment of the kingdom of God" on earth.[31]

The Mormon leader then turned his discussion to the African race, proclaiming them the direct descendants of Cain. He stated that the

> Lord told Cain that he should not receive the priesthood nor his seed, until the last of the posterity of Able [sic] had received the priesthood, until the redemption of the earth. If there never was a prophet, or apostle of Jesus Christ spoke it before, I tell you, this people that are commonly called negroes are the children of old Cain. I know they are, I know that they cannot bear rule

in the priesthood, for the curse on them, until the resedue [sic] of the posterity of Michael and his wife receive the blessings, the seed of Cain would have received had they not been cursed.³²

Young further characterized black priesthood denial as "a true eternal [principle] the Lord Almighty has ordained," asserting that humankind could not remove it, "the angels cannot, and all the powers of earth and hell cannot take it off." He emphatically affirmed: "In the kingdom of God on the earth the Affricans [sic] cannot hold one partical [sic] of power in Government."³³

Young's fear of interracial marriage undergirded the priesthood ban. He issued two dire warnings to that effect. First, he asserted that "Where the children of God to mingle there [sic] seed with the seed of Cain it would not only bring the curse of being deprived of the power of the priesthood upon themselves, but entail it upon their children after them, and they cannot get rid of it." The only way to get rid of this sin, Young speculated, was by sacrifice through blood atonement.³⁴ Young also warned that "The moment we consent to mingle with the seed of Cain the Church must go to dessruction [sic]—we should receive the curse which has been placed upon the seed of Cain, and never more be numbered with the children of Adam who are heirs to the priesthood until that curse be removed."³⁵

Below is the entire text of Brigham Young's February 5, 1852, speech to the Utah Territorial Legislature.

DOCUMENT

From Brigham Young, "Speech in Joint Session of the Legislature," February 5, 1852, box 48, folder 3, Brigham Young Papers, LDS Church History Library.

I rise to make a few remarks. The Items before the house I do not understand.

The principle of slavery I understand, at least I have self confidence enough, and confidence enough in God to believe I do. I believe still further that a great many others understand it as I do. A great portion of this community have been instructed, and have applied their minds to it, and as far as they have, they agree precisely in the principles of slavery. My remarks in the first place will be upon the cause of the introduction of slavery. Long ago mama Eve our good old mother Eve partook of the forbiden fruit and this made a slave of her. Adam hated very much to have her taken out of the garden of Eden, and now our old daddy says I beleive I will eat of the fruit and become a slave too. This was the first introduction of slavery upon this earth; and there has been not a son or daughter of adam from that day to this but what where slaves in the true sense of the word.

That slavery will continue, untill there is a people raised up upon the face of the earth who will contend for righteous principles, who will not only beleive in but operate, with every power and faculty given to them to help to esstablish the kingdom of God, to overcome the devil, and drive him from the earth, then will this curse be removed. This was the starting point of slavery. Again after adam, and Eve had pertook of the curse, we find they had two sons Cain and Able, but which was the oldest I cannot positively say; but this I know, Cain was given more to evil practices than Abel, but whether he was the oldest or not matters not to me. Adam was commanded to sacrifise, and offer up his offerings to God, that placed him into the garden of Eden. Through the faith and obedience of Able to his heavenly father, Cain became jealous of him, and he laid a plan to obtain all his flocks; for through his perfect obedience to father he obtained more blessings than Cain; consequently he took it into his heart to put able of this mortal existance. after the dead was done, the Lord enquired to able, and made Caine own what he had done with him. Now says the grand father I will not distroy the seed of michal and his wife; and cain I will not kill you, nor suffer any one to kill you, but I will put a mark upon you. What is that mark? you will see it on the countenance of every African you ever did see upon the face of the earth, or ever will see. Now I tell you what I know; when the mark was put upon Cain, Abels children was in all probability young; the Lord told Cain that he should not receive the blessings of the preisthood nor his see, until the last of the posterity of Able had received the preisthood, until the redemtion of the earth. If there never was a prophet, or apostle of Jesus Christ spoke it before, I tell you, this people that are commonly called negroes are the children of old Cain. I know they are, I know that they cannot bear rule in the preisthood, for the curse on them was to remain upon the, until the resedue of the posterity of Michal and his wife receive the blessings, the seed of Cain would have received had they not been cursed; and hold the keys of the preisthood, until the times of the restitution shall come, and the curse be wiped off from the earth, and from michals seed. Then Cain's seed will be had in rememberance, and the time come when that curse should be wiped off.

Now then in the kingdom of God on the earth, a man who has has the Affrican blood in him cannot hold one jot nor tittle of preisthood; Why? because they are the true eternal principals the Lord Almighty has ordained, and who can help it, men cannot. the angels cannot, and all the powers of earth and hell cannot take it off, but thus saith the Eternal I am, what I am, I take it off at my pleasure, and not one partical of power can that posterity of Cain have, until the time comes the says he will have it taken away. That time will come when they will have the privilege of all we have the privelege of and more. In the kingdom of God on the earth the Affricans cannot hold one partical of power in Government. The the subjects, the rightfull servants of the resedue of the children of Adam, and the resedue of the children through the benign influence of the Spirit of the Lord have the privilege of seeing to the posterity of Cain; inasmuch as it is the Lords will they should receive the spirit of God by Baptisam; and that is the end of their privilege; and there is not power on earth to give them any more power . . .

But let me tell you further. Let my see mingle with the seed of Cain, that brings the curse upon me, and upon my generations, - - we will reap the same rewards with Cain. In the preisthood I will tell you what it will do. Where the children of God to mingle there seed with the seed of Cain it would not only bring the curse of being deprived of the power of the preisthood upon themselves but the entail it upon their children after them, and they cannot get rid of it. If a man in an ungaurded moment should commit such a transgression, if he would walk up and say cut off my head, and kill man woman and child it would do a great deal towards atoneing for the sin. Would this be to curse them? no it would be a blessing to them. -it would do them good that they might be saved with their Bren. A man would shuder should they here us take about killing folk, but it is one of the greatest blessings to some to kill them, allthough the true principles of it are not understood . . .

I am as much oposed to the principle of slavery as any man in the present acceptation or usage of the term, it is abused. I am opposed to abuseing that which God has decreed, to take a blessing, and make a curse of it. It is a great blessing to the seed of Adam to have the seed of Cain for servants, but those they serve should use them with all the heart and feeling, as they would use their own children, and their compassion should reach over them, and round about them, and treat them as kindly, and with that humane feeling necessary to be shown to mortall beings of the human species. Under these sercumstances there blessings in life are greater in proportion than those who have to provide the bread and dinner for them

We know there is a portion of inhabitants of the earth who dwell in Asia that are negroes, and said to be jews. The blood of Judah has not only mingled almost with all nations, but also with the blood of Cain, and they have mingled there seeds together; These negro Jewes may keep up all the outer ordinenances of the jewish releigeon, they may have there sacrifices, and they may perform all the releigeous seremonies any people on earth could perform, but let me tell you, that the day they consented to mingle their seed with Cannan, the preisthood was taken away from Judah, and that portion of Judahs seed will never get any rule, or blessings of the preisthood until Cain gets it . . .

. . . Therefore I will not consent for one moment to have an african dictate me or any Bren. with regard to Church or State Government. I may vary in my veiwes from others, and they may think I am foolish in the things I have spoken, and think that they know more than I do, but I know I know more than they do. If the Affricans cannot bear rule in the Church of God, what buisness have they to bear rule in the State and Government affairs of this Territory or any others? . . .

But say some, is there any thing of this kind in the Constitution, the U.S. has given us? If you will allow me the privilege telling right out, it is none of their damned buisness what we do or say here. What we do it is for them to sanction, and then for us to say what we like about it. It is written right out in the constitution, "that every free white male inhabitant above the age of twenty one years" &c. My mind is the same to day as when we where poreing over that constitution; any light upon the subject is the same, my judgement is the same, only a little more so. Prahapes I have said enough upon this subject. I have given you the true principles and doctrine. No man can vote for me or my Bren. in this Territory who has not the privilege of acting in Church affairs. Every man, and woman, and Child in this Territory are Citizens; to say the contrary is all nonsense to me. The indians are

Citizens, the Africans are Citizens, and the jews than come from Asia, that are almost entirely of the blood of Cain, It is our duty to take of them, and administer to them in all the acts of humanity, and kindness, they shall have the right of Citizenship, but shall not have the right to dictate in Church and State matters. The abolishonists of the east, have cirest them them, and their whol argument are callculated to darken Counsel, as it was here yesterday . . .

What the Gentiles are doing we are consenting to do. What we are trying to do to day is to make the Negro equal with us in all our privilege. My voice shall be against all the day long. I shall not consent for one Moment I will call them a counsel. I say I will not consent for one moment for you to lay a plan to bring a curse upon this people. I shall not be while I am here.

3. BRIGHAM YOUNG DISCUSSES HIS VIEWS ON SLAVERY WITH NEW YORK JOURNALIST HORACE GREELEY IN 1859.

DOCUMENT INTRODUCTION

In 1859, some seven years after his landmark 1852 speech to the Utah Territorial legislature, Brigham Young provided yet another perspective on his pro-slavery convictions. The occasion was a personal meeting between the Mormon leader and Horace Greeley—the nationally known editor of the *New York Herald*, outspoken reformer, and ardent antislavery advocate. In a question-and-answer session that dealt with a wide range of topics, Young responded forthrightly to Greeley's inquiry concerning slavery. He frankly stated that the LDS church considered it a "Divine institution, and not to be abolished until the curse pronounced on Ham shall have been removed from his descendants."[36] Young further acknowledged the presence of slaves within the Utah Territory, claiming that slavery was legal under existing territorial statutes.

The interview took an unexpected turn when Greeley questioned Young concerning the fate of Utah slavery should the territory be admitted to the Union. Pointedly he asked the Mormon leader: would Utah "be a slave state?" Young bluntly replied: "No; she will be a free state," further stating that "Slavery here would prove useless and unprofitable." Utah, he added "is not adapted to slave labor." He further pronounced it "generally . . . a curse to the masters." He then discussed his own situation: "I myself hire many laborers and pay them fair wages; I could not afford to own them [as slaves]."[37]

Young's unvarnished comments reflected the legal status of Utah slavery. By 1859 the number of slaves local Mormons held was small, declining from what it was when first legalized in 1852. The 1860 Utah Census recorded a mere twenty-nine black slaves and twelve owners.[38] Young himself never held slaves, despite his status as the territory's wealthiest resident. The Mormon leader did, however, hire two noteworthy black Mormon laborers—namely Isaac James, who served as his coachman, and Isaac's wife, Jane Manning, a housekeeper. Young also upheld enforcement of the 1850 Fugitive Slave Law, returning runaway blacks to their owners on at least two occasions during the 1850s.[39]

Young's comments concerning the unsuitability of Utah's climate for large-scale slaveholding is also striking. Utah was not "slave country," Young proclaimed on more than one occasion. He did not want "Slavery entailed upon our young, vigorous, and thriving Territory." "Neither our climate, soil, productions, nor minds of the people are congenial to African Slavery."[40] Young, moreover, accepted the arguments of Hinton Rowan Helper as outlined in his stridently antislavery *The Impending Crisis of the South*—a book that Horace Greeley himself promoted. Helper argued that slavery had retarded the South's economic progress and thus the prosperity of most of its white citizens. Young himself suggested that if the South "would abolish slavery and institute free labor they would be much richer than they are."[41]

Below are portions of Young's interview with Greeley.

DOCUMENT

From Horace Greeley, "Two Hours with Brigham Young," *New York Herald*, August 24, 1859.

H.G.—What is the position of your church with respect to slavery?
B.Y.—We consider it of Divine institution, and not to be abolished until the curse pronounced on Ham shall have been removed from his descendants.
H.G.—Are there any slaves now held in this Territory?
B.Y.—there are.
H.G.—Do your Territorial laws uphold slavery?
B.Y.—Those laws are printed—you can read them for yourself. If slaves are brought here by those who owned them in the States, we do not favor their escape from the service of those owners.
H.G.—Am I to infer that Utah, if admitted as a member of the federal Union, will be a slave State?
B.Y.—No; she will be a free State. Slavery here would prove useless and unprofitable. I regard it generally as a curse to the masters. I myself hire many laborers and pay them fair wages; I could not afford to own them. I can do better than subject myself to an obligation to feed and clothe their families, to provide and care for them, in sickness and health. Utah is not adapted to slave labor.

4. BRIGHAM YOUNG ON SLAVERY, THE CIVIL WAR, AND INTERRACIAL MARRIAGE, 1863.

DOCUMENT INTRODUCTION

In early March 1863, Brigham Young delivered a hard-hitting sermon to a throng of Latter-day Saints assembled in the Mormon Tabernacle on Temple Square. The Mormon leader, expressing extreme frustration and anger, vented his views concerning slavery, interracial marriage, and the state of the Union ravaged by two years of civil war.

In particular, the ongoing national crusade by Protestant leaders and government officials against the Mormon practice of plural marriage rankled Young. On the national level, political leaders within both the Democratic and Republican parties, along with federal government officials, zeroed in on the Mormons' "peculiar institution."[42] The Republican Party expressed strong hostility, labeling polygamy and southern slavery the "twin relics of barbarism," with crusading Republicans calling for the eradication of both in their platforms of 1856 and 1860. Not to be outdone, Democratic president James Buchanan in 1857 dispatched a 2,500-man federal army to Utah, declaring the Latter-day Saints "in a state of rebellion." One of the casualties of this almost bloodless conflict known as the "Utah War" was the removal of Young as Utah territorial governor.[43] In 1862 the U.S. Congress passed the punitive Morrill Act, which prohibited plural marriage in the territories, disincorporated the LDS church, and restricted the church ownership of property.[44] Even worse, President Abraham Lincoln, in the fall of 1862, dispatched to Utah an armed force known as the Third California Volunteers, intended to monitor the Mormons.[45]

Not surprisingly, Young lashed out at Republican Party activists, whom he labeled "rank, rabid abolitionists" and "black hearted," blaming them for starting the Civil War, thus setting "the whole national fabric on fire." Also Young stated twice in his discourse: "I am no abolitionist, neither am I a pro-slavery man," thereby revealing his continuing ambivalence toward slavery.[46]

Young then focused his wrath on northern Republicans, specifically their treatment of the Mormons through passage of the 1862 Morrill Act. He scolded the party for its hypocrisy, stating: "If the government of the United States, in Congress assembled, had the right to pass an anti-polygamy bill, they had also the right to pass a law that slaves should not be abused as they have been." Young called for legislation mandating that "negroes should be used like human beings, and not worse than dumb brutes," and he appeared to project his own idealized image of how Utah's small slave population had been treated.[47]

Young also lashed out against black-white racial intermixture, reiterating his continuing, deep-seated abhorrence: "Shall I tell you the law of God in regard to the African race? If the white man who belongs to the chosen seed mixes his blood with the seed of Cain, the penalty, under the law of God, is death on the spot." This stark pronouncement reflected his long-standing position dating back to the mid-1840s when confronted with the situation of African American Mormon Enoch Lovejoy Lewis, married to a white woman with whom he fathered a biracial child. At the time the Mormon leader called for the death of all three through divinely sanctioned blood atonement. In specific, he proclaimed that if the Lewis family were not so "far away" in Massachusetts "they would all have to be killed—when they mingle seed it is death to all. If a black man &white woman come to you & demand baptism can you deny them? The law is that there seed shall not be amalgamated." Young further observed, albeit incorrectly: "Mulattoes are like mules they can't have children, but if they will be Eunuchs for the Kingdom of Heaven's sake they may have a place in the Temple."[48]

Young's bleak discourse also reflected a sense of Mormon millenarianism anticipating the apocalyptic End Times and Second Coming of Jesus Christ, particularly strong during the Civil War.[49] The Mormon leader lamented that "The nations of the earth have transgressed every law that God has given." Young then turned his remarks to an American society in the midst of Civil War, pleading: "I say to all men and women, submit to God, to his ordinances and to His rule; and cease your quarrelling, and stay the shedding of each other's blood."[50]

Below is the text of Brigham Young's March 8, 1863, sermon.

DOCUMENT

From Brigham Young speech, March 8, 1863, in Franklin D. Richards and Stephen W. Richards, eds., *Journal of Discourses*, 26 vols. (Liverpool, Eng., 1855–1887), 10:110–111.

The rank, rabid abolitionists, whom I call black-hearted Republicans, have set the whole national fabric on fire. Do you know this, Democrats? They have kindled the fire that is raging now from the north to the south, and from the south to the north. I am no abolitionist, neither am I a pro-slavery man; I hate some of their principles and especially some of their conduct, as I do the gates of hell. The Southerners make the negroes and the Northerners worship them; this is all the difference between slaveholders and abolitionists. I would like the President of the United States and all the world to hear this.

Shall I tell you the law of God in regard to the African race? If the white man who belongs to the chosen seed mixes his blood with the seed of Cain, the penalty, under the law of God, is death on the spot. This will always be so. The nations of the earth have transgressed every law that God has given, they have changed the ordinances and broken every covenant made with the fathers, and they are like a hungry man that dreameth that he eateth, and he awaketh and behold he is empty . . .

If the government of the United States, in Congress assembled, had the right to pass an anti-polygamy bill, they had also the right to pass a law that slaves should not be abused as they have been; they had also a right to make a law that negroes would be used like human beings, and not worse than dumb brutes. For their abuse of that race, the whites will be cursed, unless they repent.

I am neither an abolitionist nor a pro-slavery man. If I could have been influenced by private injury to choose one side in preference to the other, I should certainly be against the pro-slavery side of the question, for it was pro-slavery men that pointed the bayonet at me and my brethren in Missouri, and said, "Damn you we will kill you." I have not much love for them, only in the Gospel. I would cause them to repent, if I could, and make them good men and a good community. I have no fellowship for their avarice, blindness, and ungodly actions. To be great, is to be good before the Heavens and before all good men. I will not fellowship the wicked in their sins, so help me God.

4

Justifying and Perpetuating Black Priesthood Denial, 1877–1949

General Introduction

During the seventy-two-year period from 1877 to 1949, a succession of Latter-day Saint church leaders and spokesmen affirmed the divine legitimacy of denying black Mormons the priesthood and access to sacred temple ordinances.[1] These restrictions occurred in the aftermath of the Civil War, when antiblack violence peaked, white supremacy proliferated, and Jim Crow and antimiscegenation laws became legal and acceptable. This period, the "nadir of American race relations," also saw the reemergence of the Ku Klux Klan, whose terror on black families led to the establishment of the National Association for Colored People in 1909.[2]

Mormon racial attitudes dovetailed with these larger efforts to deny African Americans their rights, facilitating church efforts to prohibit black people from priesthood and temple privileges. Several critical factors accounted for this development. First and perhaps most important was the acceptance of Mormon church founder Joseph Smith as the author of the priesthood ban. The effort to link Smith directly to the ban commenced in 1879, two years following the death of Brigham Young. Apostle John Taylor, about to succeed Young as Mormon church president, was anxious to determine the precise origins of the ban.[3]

A second important development reinforced the practice of black priesthood denial—LDS canonization of the *Pearl of Great Price* in 1880, followed by its use as scriptural "proof text." This work, containing the *Books of Moses* and *Abraham*, produced by Joseph Smith during the 1830s and early 1840s, had been originally published in book form in 1851 but not accorded the same canonized status as Smith's earlier writings—the *Book of Mormon* and *Doctrine and Covenants*.

A third factor encouraged the affirmation of priesthood denial—an increased sense of the Mormons' own ethnic self-identity as an "Israelite people." Church leaders averred that Mormons were direct descendants of the tribe of Joseph through Ephraim. Further enhancing the Mormons' self-identity as a royal, Israelite chosen people was their embrace of "British Israelism and Anglo-Saxon triumphalism"—this trend taking root during the half century following Brigham Young's death.[4] All this, one scholar perceptively noted, "postulated a divine rank-ordering of lineages with the descendants of ancient Ephraim (son of Joseph) at the top (including the Mormons); the 'seed of Cain' (Africans) at the bottom and various other lineages in between."[5]

A Latter-day Saint tendency to identify with the former Confederate states, particularly during the late nineteenth century, constituted a fourth factor facilitating the development of the ban. Radical Republicans, including Schuyler Colfax of Indiana and Benjamin F. Wade of Ohio, assailed both polygamous Mormons and white southerners. Such crusading Republicans called for restrictions on the polygamous Mormons while promoting legislation upholding the political and civil rights of newly emancipated southern blacks. Thus church spokesmen, through the official publication *Millennial Star*, excoriated northern Republicans for reversing "the social, political, and civil relations of the blacks and whites" by placing "the white man's head under the nigger's heel" and describing such blacks as "utterly unprepared, unfit, and incapable" of self-government.[6] Church leaders John Taylor and Franklin D. Richards defended the South, lamenting that the region's whites had been "ground under the heel of sectional injustice" and condemning northern Republicans for their "deprivations and arbitrary rule."[7]

At the same time, Mormon leaders sought to discourage missionary efforts among blacks both within the United States and abroad. In 1908 the First Presidency and the Council of Twelve, under the leadership of Joseph F. Smith, ordered missionaries "not [to] take the initiative in proselyting among the Negro people . . . or [to those] people tainted with Negro blood."[8] Two years later, the First Presidency gave scriptural legitimacy to this position by referring to the *Pearl of Great Price*. Quoting this work they declared: "We learn that Enoch in his day called upon all the people to repent, save the people of Canaan, and it is for us to do likewise."[9] The Mormon policy avoiding missionary contacts with blacks would remain in effect for the next fifty years.[10]

1. ABRAHAM SMOOT AND ZEBEDEE COLTRIN, MEMBERS OF THE FIRST QUORUM OF SEVENTY, RECALL JOSEPH SMITH AS THE ORIGINATOR OF THE PRIESTHOOD BAN, 1879.

DOCUMENT INTRODUCTION

It was an important church meeting on May 31, 1879, when "Ordaining Negro's [*sic*] to the Priesthood" was the subject under consideration, according to the minutes by Leonard John Nuttal, private secretary to apostle John Taylor. Also in attendance was Taylor himself, who apparently called the meeting. Taylor, president of the Quorum of the Twelve at the time, had taken control of Mormon church affairs in the wake of Brigham Young's death two years earlier. In fact, Brigham Young Jr., the deceased leader's namesake and himself a church apostle, was among those in attendance. Abraham O. Smoot, at whose home the meeting was held, and Zebedee Coltrin were also present. Both men, elderly church members, had personally known and interacted with Joseph Smith years earlier. Coltrin claimed that the priesthood ban had come up in 1834 during his sojourn in Missouri as the result of a discussion with another early church member, John P. Greene. Coltrin and Greene had disagreed, with Greene asserting that black Mormon males had "a right to the priesthood." Coltrin, by contrast, maintained they had no such right. The debate became so heated that Green accused Coltrin of "preaching false doctrine" and threatened to report him to Joseph Smith once they both returned to Ohio. Coltrin further recalled:

> And when we got to Kirtland, we both went to Brother Joseph's office together to make our returns, and Brother Green[e] was as good as his word and reported to Brother Joseph that I said the Negro could not hold the priesthood. Brother Joseph kind of dropped his head and rested it on his hand for a minute and then said. "Brother Zebedee is right, for the spirit of the Lord saith the Negro has not right nor cannot hold the Priesthood." He made no reference to Scripture at all, but such was his decision.[11]

Coltrin then acknowledged that African American Elijah Abel had been "ordained a Seventy because he had labored on the Temple," going on to claim that when Joseph Smith "learned of his lineage he was dropped from the quorum and another was put in his place."[12]

Abraham Smoot in his recollections claimed that the question of black ordination arose in 1835–1836 while he was "laboring in the Southern States" as a missionary along with three other Mormons, namely David W. Patten, Warren Parish, and Thomas B. Marsh and in conjunction with some "Negro's [sic] who made Application for Baptism." Smoot, along with the others, decided to hold off conferring the priesthood until after they had consulted with Joseph Smith. The Mormon leader declared that these blacks "were not entitled to the Priesthood, nor yet to be baptized without the consent of their masters."[13]

In a meeting of the Council of Twelve, just four days later, the accuracy of the Coltrin-Smoot testimonies came into question. Apostle Joseph F. Smith pointed out certain inconsistencies and expressed skepticism that Joseph Smith had inaugurated black priesthood denial. Elijah Abel's case compounded apostle Smith's doubts. After carefully examining Abel's situation, the apostle concluded that Joseph Smith had continued to recognize Abel's priesthood authority right up to the time of his death in 1844. In rationalizing the conflicting accounts, the Council of the Twelve declared that Abel had "been ordained before the word of the Lord was fully understood."[14]

Below is the complete text of the Coltrin-Smoot testimonies.

DOCUMENT

From L. John Nuttal Journal, May 31, 1879, vol. 1, pp. 171–177, L. Tom Perry Special Collections, Harold B. Lee Library, Brigham Young University Special Collections. Used by permission of Brigham Young University. (Spelling and punctuation have been retained from the original.)

After meeting Prest Taylor [he] invited me to accompany him to Bro Smoots where with others, the subject of the Negro being ordained to the Priesthood was considered—whereupon I wrote the following statements.

Saturday May 31st 1879 At the house of Prest A.O. Smoot. Provo City. Utah County Utah—5 P.M.—President John Taylor, Elders Brigham Young, A.O. Smoot, Zebedee Coltrin and L. John Nuttal [m]et and the subject of Ordaining Negro's to the Priesthood was presented. Prest Taylor said [s]ome parties have said to me that Zebedee Coltrin had talked to the Prophet Joseph Smith on this subject, and they said that he (Coltrin) thought it was not right for them to have the Priesthood whereupon Joseph Smith said to him that Peter on a certain occasion had a vision wherein he "saw heaven opened and a certain vessel descended unto him as it had been a great sheet Knit at the four corners and let down to the earth wherein all manner of four footed beasts of the earth, and wild beasts, and creeping tings, and fowls of the Air. And there came a voice to him, "Rise, Peter! Kill and eat. But Peter said, Not so Lord; for I have never eaten any thing that is common or unclean, and the voice spake unto him again the second time. What God hath cleansed, that call not thou common." And that the Prophet Joseph then said to Bro Coltrin as the Angel said to Peter, "What God hath cleansed, that call not thou common" (speaking of the Gentiles). Prest Taylor asked Bro Coltrin—Did the Prophet Joseph Smith ever make such a statement to you? Bro C., No sir, he never said anything of the Kind in his life to me. Pres T.—What did he say? Bro C.—The spring that we went up in Zion's camp in 1834 Bro Joseph sent Bro J.P.Green and me out south to gather up means to assist in gathering out the Saints from Jackson County, Mo. On our return home we got in conversation about the Negro having a right to the Priesthood and I took the side he had no right. Bro Green argued that he had; the subject got so war[m] between us that he would report me to Bro Joseph when we got home for preaching false doctrine, which doctrine that I advocated was that the Negro could not hold the Priesthood. All right said I, I hope you will and when we got home to Kirkland we both went in to Bro Joseph's office together to make our returns and Bro Green was as good as his word and reported to Bro Joseph that I had said that the Negro could not hold the Priesthood. Bro Joseph kind of dropt his head and rested it on his hand for a minute and then said, Bro Coltrin is right, for the Spirit of the Lord saith the Negro has no right nor cannot hold the Priesthood. Bro Coltrin further said, Bro Abel was ordained a Seventy because he had labored on the Temple (it must have been into the 2nd Quorum) and when the Prophet Joseph learned of his lineage he was dropped from the quorum and another was put in his place. . . .

In the washing and Anointing of Bro Abel at Kirkland I anointed him and while I had my hands upon his head I never had such unpleasant feelings in my life, and I said I never would again Anoint another person who had Negro blood in him unless I was commanded by the Prophet to do so. Prest A.O. Smoot said, W.W. Patten, Warren Parish and Thomas B. Marsh were laboring in the Southern States in 1835 & 1836 [and] there were Negro's who made Application for Baptism and the question arose with them whether Negro's were entitled to hold the Priesthood, and by those brethren it was decided they would not confer the Priesthood until they had consulted the Prophet Joseph, and subsequently they communicated with him and his decision as I understood, was they were not entitled to the Priesthood, nor yet to be baptized without the consent of their Masters. In [later] years . . . I became acquainted with Joseph myself in Far West about the year 1838. I received from Joseph substantially the same instructions. It was on my application to him what should be done with the Negro in the South as I was preaching to them. He said I could baptize them by the consent of their Masters, but not to confer the Priesthood upon them. These two statements were duly signed by each of these brethren.

2. BRIGHAM H. ROBERTS, A MEMBER OF THE FIRST QUORUM OF SEVENTY AND NOTED LDS SCHOLAR, INSTRUCTS CHURCH YOUTH WHY BLACKS CAN'T HOLD THE PRIESTHOOD, 1885.

DOCUMENT INTRODUCTION

Among the most noteworthy Mormon writers to draw extensively on the *Pearl of Great Price* as a scriptural "proof text," upholding black priesthood denial, was Brigham Henry Roberts, doing so in an essay entitled "To the Youth of Israel" and published in *The Contributor*—a church magazine designed for young Latter-day Saints.

Roberts, born in 1857 in Great Britain, had immigrated to Utah with his parents when they converted to Mormonism. He served as a church missionary and embraced polygamy, marrying three wives fathering fifteen children. Rising through the Mormon ranks, he eventually became a member of the church's First Council of Seventy. A prolific scholar and writer, Roberts authored some twenty books dealing with a wide range of Mormon historical and theological topics.[15]

Brigham H. Roberts's "To the Youth of Israel" was among his earliest published works. In affirming black priesthood denial to be a divinely sanctioned practice, he made extensive use of a variety of scriptural works, specifically the Old and New Testament, the *Doctrine and Covenants*, and particularly the recently canonized *Pearl of Great Price*. Central to Roberts's arguments was the importance of the preexistence, or humankind's premortal state, in determining the inferior status of blacks. This involved a war in heaven between the forces of good and of evil. Roberts stated that those who "wickedly rebelled and were adjudged to deserve banishment from heaven . . . [became] the devil and his angels."[16]

Directly affecting the status of blacks was the fate of "others... who may not have rebelled against God, and yet were so indifferent in the support of the righteous cause of our Redeemer, that they forfeited certain privileges and powers granted to those who were more valiant for God and correct principle." Roberts further paraphrased the *Pearl of Great Price*: "We have... a demonstration of this in the seed of Ham. The first Pharaoh—patriarch-king of Egypt—was a grandson of Ham ... *cursed* ... *as pertaining to the Priesthood*. He being of that lineage by which he could not have right to the Priesthood, notwithstanding the Pharaoh's [*sic*] would fain claim it from Noah through Ham."[17]

Roberts described why "the seed of Ham was cursed as pertaining to the Priesthood." Again paraphrasing the *Pearl of Great Price*, Roberts stated that the proscription stemmed from the fact that "Ham's wife was named 'Egyptus,' which signifies that which is forbidden; and thus from Ham sprang that race which preserved the curse in the land." Roberts also asserted that Egyptus was "a descendant of Cain who was cursed for murdering his brother..." Then returning to his discussion of the preexistence, Roberts concluded: "I believe that race [black Africans] is the one through which it is ordained those spirits that were not valiant in the great rebellion in heaven should come; who, through their indifference or lack of integrity to righteousness, rendered themselves unworthy of the Priesthood and its powers, and hence it is withheld from them to this day."[18]

Below are portions of Brigham H. Roberts "To the Youth of Israel."

DOCUMENT

From B. H. Roberts, "To the Youth of Israel," *The Contributor* 6 (1885): 296–297 (excerpts).

... From the Pearl of Great Price (pp. 7 and 32) we learn it was for seeking to destroy the agency of man, and for rebellion, that Lucifer and his followers were cast out of heaven. The contest was a severe one, and during its progress all degrees of integrity were manifest. Those who stood with Christ and the plan He favored for the salvation of man, formed one extreme, while those who stood with Lucifer and for the plan of salvation devised by him, which was destructive of man's agency, formed the other extreme; between these two extremes every shade of faith, fullness and indifference was exhibited. Only those, however, who wickedly rebelled against God were adjudged to deserve banishment from heaven, and become the devil and his angels. Others there were, who may not have rebelled against God, and yet were so indifferent in their support of the righteous cause of our Redeemer, that they forfeited certain privileges and powers granted to those who were more valiant for God and correct principle. We have, I think, a demonstration of this in the seed of Ham. The first Pharaoh—patriarch-king of Egypt—was a grandson of Ham; and "being a righteous man, established his kingdom, and judged his people wisely and justly all his days, seeking earnestly to imitate that order established in the first generation, in the days of the first patriarchal reign, even in the reign of

Adam, and also of Noah, his father, who blessed him with the blessings of wisdom, but who *cursed him as pertaining to the Priesthood*. He being of that lineage by which he could not have right to the Priesthood, notwithstanding the Pharaoh's would fain claim it from Noah through Ham." (*Pearl of Great Price*, p. 28.)

Now, why is it that the seed of Ham was cursed as pertaining to the Priesthood? Why is it that his seed "could not have right to the Priesthood? Ham's wife was named "Egyptus, which signifies that which is forbidden; and thus from Ham sprang that race which preserved the curse in the land." (*Pearl of Great Price*, p. 28.) Was the wife of Ham, as her name signifies, of a race with which those who held the Priesthood were forbidden to intermarry? Was she a descendant of Cain, who was cursed for murdering his brother? And was it by Ham marrying her, and she being saved from the flood in the ark, that "the race which preserved the curse in the land" was perpetuated? If so, then I believe that race is the one through which it is ordained those spirits that were not valiant in the great rebellion in heaven should come; who, through their indifference or lack of integrity to righteousness, rendered themselves unworthy of the Priesthood and its powers, and hence it is withheld from them to this day.

The point, then, is clear that among those spirits which have been appointed to obtain bodies upon this planet are some who were more faithful, noble and intelligent than others. . . .

I have not set forth this conclusion for the purpose of flattering the vanity of the youth of Israel, to whom this address is made . . .

I have merely pointed out what I believe may reasonably be regarded as a great truth, that by drawing the attention of our youth to the fact that their spirits were among heaven's nobility, I may incline them to the continual performance of noble deeds.

B.H. Roberts

3. AFRICAN AMERICAN MORMON JANE ELIZABETH MANNING JAMES'S CONTINUING APPEAL TO LATTER-DAY SAINT LEADERS FOR PERMISSION TO RECEIVE HER TEMPLE ENDOWMENTS, 1885–1905.

DOCUMENTS INTRODUCTION

Among the most noteworthy early African American Mormons was Jane Elizabeth Manning James, whose life experiences as a Latter-day Saint underscore the subordinate status imposed on black church members from the late nineteenth century until well into the twentieth.[19] Born in the 1810s or 1820s in Wilton, Connecticut, to free black parents, Jane was introduced to Mormonism by missionaries proselytizing in that region. In the early 1840s she, along with several other members of her immediate family, joined the church. Shortly thereafter, Jane, along with nine other members of her family, migrated from Connecticut to Nauvoo, Illinois.

Upon her arrival, Joseph Smith Jr. hired her as a domestic servant. Meanwhile she met and married Isaac James, also a free black Mormon. In the wake of Joseph Smith's death, Jane and her husband cast their lot with Brigham Young and were, in fact, among the first Latter-day Saints to arrive in the Great Basin in September 1847.

Following Jane and Isaac James's arrival, they obtained a parcel of land near central Salt Lake City, where they earned sufficient income to be considered moderately wealthy. Together they had six children. But their "relative prosperity evaporated" when Isaac abandoned the family, resulting in divorce in late 1869 or early 1870.[20] Compelled to move to a smaller residence, Jane supported her family as a domestic and by manufacturing soap. By 1874 she married a second time, to Frank Perkins—also an African American Mormon, originally brought to Utah as a slave of Latter-day Saint Ruben Perkins. Jane's marriage to Perkins, however, was short-lived and by 1876 the two had separated. In 1890, Jane's first husband, Isaac, returned to Utah shortly before his death one year later in November 1891. The two apparently reconciled, because church officials conducted Isaac's funeral service in her home.

Despite her marital difficulties, Jane "remained a steadfast member of the Mormon church throughout her life." Much of her activity focused on the Woman's Relief Society—a church auxiliary whose major activity was charitable work. She supported the organization's numerous special drives, including funds she donated towards the construction of the St. George, Logan, and Manti Temples. She also contributed to the Lamanite (Indian) Mission, an Old Folks' Excursion at nearby Liberty Park, and a fair on behalf of the Deseret Hospital.[21]

Her religious devotion notwithstanding, "the racial practices of her church were a test of Jane's faith," most evident in her repeated, persistent requests for temple ordinances—rituals considered essential for Mormon exaltation.[22] Motivating her was "a sense of millennial expectation, combined with anxiety for her future salvation." Jane, moreover, "was also aware of apparent inconsistencies in past practices" involving African American Mormons, most notably Elijah Abel and Q. Walker Lewis, although she was "sufficiently circumspect not to mention" these directly.[23]

In December 1884 Jane directed her first request for temple admittance to President John Taylor, in which she made reference to an earlier conversation she had had with the church leader concerning her "future salvation." She confessed that "I realize my race and color & cant expect my Endowments as others who are white," further stating that her "race was handed down through the flood & God promised Abraham that in his seed all the nations of the earth should be blest & as this is the fullness of all dispensations is there no blessing for me." She then referred to a conversation she had had with Emma Smith, prior to the Martyrdom, in which James claimed that Smith had offered to adopt her into their family "as a Child," with James further pleading that "If I could be adopted to him as a child my Soul would be satisfied."²⁴ Taylor denied James's request, although there is no record of his reply.

Four years later, in June 1888, Angus M. Cannon, president of the Salt Lake Stake, gave Jane permission "to enter the Temple to be babtized [sic] and confirmed" on behalf of her deceased ancestors, with Cannon cryptically adding the following: "You must be content with this privilege, awaiting further instructions from the Lord to his servants."²⁵

Not satisfied, Jane, in February 1890, once more sought her temple endowments, addressing her request to Joseph F. Smith, at the time a member of the Quorum of Twelve. On this occasion, she took a somewhat different tack, asking that she be sealed to Q. Walker Lewis, the black elder who had been ordained in the 1840s prior to the imposition of the priesthood ban. She claimed that Lewis himself "wished me to be Sealed to Him." Jane made two subsequent requests, in which she sought Temple Endowments for her dead ancestors for whom she had "the privilege of being baptized earlier." She also renewed her desire to "be adopted" into Joseph Smith's family.²⁶

Four years later in January 1894, the ever-persistent Jane James made yet another request that she "be adopted into Joseph Smith's family as a child." She asked that her first husband, Isaac James, along with her brother Isaac Manning, also be included in such a request.²⁷ This latest query provoked extensive discussion involving President Wilford Woodruff, who firmly rejected her request to "have her Endowments in the Temple. . . . This I Could not do as it was against the Law of God," further adding, "All the seed of Cain would have to wait for Redemption until all the seed that Abel would have had that may Come through other men Can be redeemed."²⁸ And the following year, President Woodruff, in apparent response to yet another request, "told her that they could see in no way by which they could accede to her wishes."²⁹

Despite this, President Wilford Woodruff allowed Jane to "be adopted into the family of Joseph Smith as a servant," for which "a special ceremony" was "prepared for the purpose." But Jane, "not satisfied . . . applied again after this for sealing blessings, but of course in vain."³⁰ In August 1903, she made yet one final request, this one to President Joseph F. Smith, specifically asking for her "endowments and also [to] finish the work I have begun for my dead" ancestors.³¹

Some five years later on April 16, 1908, Jane Elizabeth Manning James died at her home, burdened by the infirmities of old age and weakened by a severe fall.³² Below are portions of the correspondence between Jane Manning James and various LDS officials pertaining to Jane's repeated requests to receive her temple ordinances.³³

DOCUMENTS

Correspondence between Jane Manning James and various LDS church officials from originals as contained in the LDS Church History Library.

JUSTIFYING AND PERPETUATING BLACK PRIESTHOOD DENIAL · 53

a. **From Jane E. James to President John Taylor, 1884 (excerpts)**

Salt L City Dec 27, 1884
Pres John Taylor

Dear Brother

I cauled at your house last Thursday to have conversation with you concerning my future salvation [.] . . .

You know my history & according to the best of my ability I have lived to all of the requirements of the Gospel [.] when we reached Nauvoo we were 9 in the family & had traveled 9 hundred miles on foot [.] Bro Joseph Smith took us in & we staid with him until a few day [s] of his death [.]

Sister Emma came to me & aksed me how I would like to be adopted to them as a Child [.] I did not comprehend her & she came again [.] I was so green I did not give her a decided answer & Joseph died & [I] remain as I am [.] if I could be adopted to him as a child my Soul would be satisfied [.] I had been in the Church one year when we left for the East that was 42 years the 14th of last Oct [.]

Br Taylor I hope you . . . will be able to lay my case before Br Cannon & Br Jos F Smith & God in mercy grant my reques [t] in being adopted to Br Joseph as a Child [.]

I remain yor Sister in the Gospel of Christ

Jane E James

b. **From Angus M. Cannon, President of Salt Lake Stake to Jane E. James, 1888 (excerpts)**

Salt Lake City
June 16, 1888

Mrs. Jane James,

I enclose your recommend properly signed,—which will entitled you to enter the Temple to be baptized and confirmed for your dead kindred.

You must be content with this privilege, awaiting further instructions from the Lord to his servants. I am your servant and brother in the Gospel.

Angus M. Cannon

c. **From Jane E. James to Apostle Joseph F. Smith, 1890 (excerpts)**

Salt Lake City
February 7, 1890

Dear Brother—

I am anxious for my Welfare for the future- . . . Hoping you will please show kindness to me—by answering my questions- . . .—

First a Coloured Brother, Brother Lewis wished me to Be Sealed to Him, He has been dead 35 or 36 years- Can I be sealed to him- . . .

Second, - Can I obtain Endowments for my Dead [.] Also, I had the privilege of being babtised for My Dead, in October Last,—Third, Can I also be adopted in

Brother Joseph Smiths the prophet ['s] family, . . . Emma Said Joseph told her to tell me—I could be adopted In their family, she ask me if I should Like to. I Did not understand the Law of adoption the- but Understanding it now. Can that be Accomplished and When—

I have heard you attend to the prophets Business in those matters-And so have Written to you for information . . .

I remain
Your Sister In the Gospel
Jane E James, Elizabeth
I am Couloured
Jane E James
529- 2 East
S L C

d. From Zina D. H. Young to Apostle Joseph F. Smith, 1894 (excerpts)

S. L. City Jan 15th 1894

Jane E. James, says, Sister Emma Smith asked her if she would like to be adopted into Joseph Smith's family as a child, & not understanding her meaning said no

Jane was Born

Wilton Fairfield, Co. Conn

Jane also asked me to ask if Isaac James & her Brother could also be adopted

Zina D. H. Young

e. Entry of October 16, 1894 from Journals of Wilford Woodruff (excerpts)

We had a Meeting with several individuals among the rest *Black Jane* wanted to know if I would not let her have her *Endowments* in the Temple [,] this I could not do as it was against the *Law of God* As *Cain killed Abel* All the seed of Cain would have to wait for redemption until all of the seed that Abel would have had that may come through other me can be redeemed.

f. Minutes of a meeting of the Council of the Twelve, August 22, 1895 (excerpts)

President Woodruff informed the Council that Sister Jane James, a negress of long standing in the Church, had asked him for permission to receive her endowments, and the he and his counselors, had told her that they could see no way by which they could accede to her wishes; . . .

g. Minutes of a meeting of the Council of the Twelve, January 2, 1902 (excerpts)

The wife of Isaac James (know[n] as Aunt Jane) asked to receive her own endowments and to be sealed; but Presidents Woodruff, Cannon, and Smith decided that this could not be done, but decided that she might be adopted into the family of Joseph Smith as a servant, was done, a special ceremony having been prepared for the purpose. But Aunt Jane was not satisfied with this, and as a mark of her dissatisfaction she applied again and after this for sealing blessings, but of course in vain.

h. From Jane E. James to President Joseph F. Smith, August 31, 1903 (excerpts)

Mrs. Jane Elizabeth James
529 S. 2nd East St
Salt Lake City
Aug 31st 1903

President Joseph F. Smith

Dear Brother

I take this opportunity of writing to ask you if I can get my endowments and also finish the work I have begun for My dead . . .

Your sister in the Gospel
Jane E James
I have enclosed a stamped Envelope for reply [.]

4. AN ARTICLE ON "THE NEGRO AND THE PRIESTHOOD" READ BY MORMON MISSIONARIES, 1908.

DOCUMENT INTRODUCTION

"The Negro and the Priesthood," appearing some twenty years after Brigham H. Roberts's publication "To the Youth of Israel," constituted a second important church-sanctioned article affirming black priesthood denial. The article, whose author is unknown, was published in *Liahona: The Elder's Journal*—the official publication for all North American Latter-day Saint missions. It had commenced publication just one year earlier. In its prime, the journal boasted some twenty thousand subscribers.[34] "The Negro and the Priesthood" appeared concurrent with the First Presidency's 1908 statement instructing church missionaries to avoid "proselyting among the Negro people."[35]

"The Negro and the Priesthood" quoted extensively from the *Pearl of Great Price*, while carefully elaborating the divinely mandated rationale behind the inferior status of black people. Thus the author acknowledged Cain as the father of "the negro race [which] flourished before the flood," further stating that following the flood, Ham, the son of Noah, "married a women of this race" in violation of "the law of God"—this a "shocking crime" reflective of Ham's "depraved proclivities." "The curse of Noah rested upon Canaan, the son of Ham and it was he who became ancestor of the black race." "It thus appears," the article explained, "that the original inhabitants of Egypt were descendants of Ham through Canaan, and hence were black."[36]

The article discussed "the double curse of a black skin and a condition of perpetual servitude" placed by Noah upon Canaan as "the sole ancestor of the negro race" and "his seed." Its unique definition of "perpetual servitude" linked the practice directly to black priesthood denial. It stated: "Now the priesthood is divine authority to preside, and to say of a race that they shall be servants forever is equivalent to saying that they shall not hold authority, especially divine authority. Hence the curse of Noah necessarily means that the race upon which it rests cannot hold the priesthood."[37]

"The Negro and the Priesthood" then turned "to the pre-existent state of mankind" providing "a more comprehensive explanation." It further claimed that certain "strains of lineage" have been allowed "to hold the priesthood" and others denied this privilege. "A few [spirits] by their faithful devotion to truth, won the promise" that they would come to earth "through a lineage that would entitle them to the priesthood . . . while some [spirits] were predestined to come to earth through a parentage that would deprive them of this honor." In particular, "the spirits that appear in mortality as negroes were of this latter class, and a lineage had to be provided for them which would accord with their deserts; hence the dealings of God with Cain, Ham, Canaan, etc."[38]

And finally, "the present writer" of this essay claimed to have

> . . . heard President Brigham Young quoted as offering a still further explanation of the reason why negroes are not ordained to the priesthood. It was to the effect that they did not possess sufficient innate spiritual strength and capacity to endure the responsibility that always goes with the priesthood, and to successfully resist the powers of darkness that always oppose men who hold it; and that, were they to be clothed with it, evil agencies would harass and torment them, frighten them with spiritual manifestations from a wrong source, and so destroy their rest and peace that the priesthood instead of being a blessing to them would be the reverse.[39]

Below are excerpts of "The Negro and the Priesthood."

DOCUMENT

From "The Negro and the Priesthood," *Liahona: The Elder's Journal* 5 no. 2 (April 18, 1908): 1164–1167 (excerpts).

THE NEGRO AND THE PRIESTHOOD

We learn from the Pearl of Great Price that the gospel, including animal sacrifice foreshadowing the atonement of Christ, was taught to Adam and his immediate descendants. Abel, the righteous son of Adam, offered sacrifice "of the firstlings of his flock," thus obeying the law and honoring the Savior who was to come. Of Cain and his offering the Bible says:

And in process of time it came to pass that Cain brought of the fruit of the ground an offering unto the Lord. (Gen. 4:3.)

The following verse from the Pearl of Great Price, page 21, throws more light on Cain's sacrifice:

And Cain loved Satan more than God, and Satan commanded him saying: Make an offering unto the Lord.

Cain's offering was made in obedience to a command of Satan, and consisted of fruits of the ground instead of a living animal whose life could be taken, thus typifying the atonement of a Messiah who should come in the "meridian of time." Here we have "a changing of the ordinances," a rebelling against God, a denial of the Christ, an apostasy. God had respect for Abel's offering—his religion—but for Cain's He had no respect. We learn from the Pearl of Great Price, pages 22–3, that Cain was angry and made a compact with Satan under which Satan was to deliver Abel into Cain's hands, and Cain was to obey the commands of Satan. This compact was carried out, and Cain slew Abel. His motive was double: To gain possession of the dead man's flocks, and gratify a jealous hate. The murderer became the head of a secret cabal whose object was to murder for gain. God cursed him and "set a mark" upon him so that no one finding him should kill him, and he became a fugitive and a vagabond. Still he begot many sons and daughters and builded a city. His seed were black, and did not mix with the other descendants of Adam. (page 39.)

It is thus clear that the negro race flourished before the flood, and it is probable that the law of God forbade admixture with them. The theory that Ham, in violation of this law, married a woman of this race is, we think very reasonable. The shocking crime which he committed after the flood could hardly have been his first offense, and proves him to have been a man of depraved proclivities, at least when under a wrong spirit, although at one time, before the flood, he was a righteous man, for he "walked with God" in company with his father and two brothers (page 49.)

That the negroes are descended from Ham is generally admitted, not only by Latter-day Saint writers but by historians and students of the scriptures. That they are also descended from Cain is also a widely accepted theory, although sacred history does not record explicitly how this lineage bridged the flood. In our opinion the best explanation of this difficulty is the hypothesis that Ham's wife was a descendant of Cain. The curse of Noah rested upon Canaan, the son of Ham, (see below) and he it was who became ancestor of the black race. That all of the descendants of Ham were black is not shown by the record. He had four sons (Gen. 10:6) and at least one daughter who had children (Pearl of Great Price, page 37). But that all of the posterity of Canaan were black is made plain (Pearl of Great Price, page 37):

And there was a blackness came upon all the children of Canaan, that they were despised among all people.

Abraham, referring to a king of Egypt of his day, says (Pearl of Great Price, page 55):

Now this king of Egypt was a descendant from the loins of Ham, and as a partaker of the blood of the Canaanites by birth.

From this descent sprang all the Egyptians, and thus the blood of the Canaanites was preserved in the land.

It thus appears that the original inhabitants of Egypt were descendants of Ham through Canaan, and hence were black. It also appears that a king of Egypt, known to Abraham, and presumably contemporary with him, was of the same race. But were the Egyptians, that is the ruling class in that country, during the period from Joseph to Moses, negroes? Without undertaking to discuss this question fully, we will suggest that between Abraham and Moses there was plenty of time for such political changes as would place a different race in power; and that, if the taskmasters of the children of Israel were descendants of Canaan, the prophetic curse pronounced upon him was reversed. The children of Israel were the descendants of Shem, and under the curse of Noah, Canaan was to be a servant to Shem, instead of his master. He was also to be a servant to Japheth. . . .

So far as any record in our possession shows, Canaan was the sole ancestor of the negro race, and upon Canaan and his seed Noah placed the double curse of a black skin and a condition of perpetual servitude. Now the priesthood is divine authority to preside, and to say of a race that they shall be servants forever is equivalent to saying that they shall not hold authority, especially divine authority. Hence the curse of Noah necessarily means that the race upon which it rests cannot hold the priesthood. . . .

By reading the Book of Abraham and Paul's epistle to the Hebrews, not to mention many other portions of sacred writ, we see that it was the design of the Almighty to confine the priesthood to a certain lineage which ran from Shem to Noah, and from him to Abraham, and thence down through certain strains of blood to the end of the world. Deprivation of the priesthood was part of the curse placed upon Canaan and his seed by Noah, who held the keys that "bind on earth that it may be bound in heaven." From the Pearl of Great Price, page 55, we learn that "the first government of Egypt was established by Pharaoh, the eldest son of Egyptus, the daughter of Ham;" that this Pharaoh was a righteous man, and that Noah "blessed him with the blessings of the earth, and with the blessings of wisdom, but cursed him as pertaining to the priesthood." That is, forbade him and his posterity to hold the priesthood. Noah had authority from the Almighty to designate which branches of his posterity should, and which should not, hold the priesthood; and he was undoubtedly directed in the matter by revelation.

A more comprehensive explanation of the reason why certain strains of lineage have been chosen to hold the priesthood, while certain others have been forbidden to do so, is found by going back to the pre-existent state of mankind . . . A few by their faithful devotion to truth, won the promise that they should receive their mortal bodies through a lineage that would entitle them to the priesthood; but to the great mass of spirits this promise was not given, while some were predestined to come to earth through a parentage that would deprive them of this honor. The spirits that appear in mortality as negroes were of this latter class, and a lineage had to be provided for them which would accord with their deserts; hence the dealings of God with Cain, Ham, Canaan, etc.

The present writer has heard President Brigham Young quoted as offering a still further explanation of the reason why negroes are not ordained to the priesthood. It was to the effect that they did not possess sufficient innate spiritual strength and capacity to endure the responsibility that always goes with the priesthood, and to successfully resist the powers of darkness that always oppose men who hold it; and that, were they to be clothed with it, evil agencies would harass and torment them, frighten them with spiritual manifestations from a wrong source, and so destroy their rest and peace that the priesthood instead of being a blessing to them would be the reverse....

5. JOSEPH FIELDING SMITH, GRAND-NEPHEW OF MORMON FOUNDER JOSEPH SMITH AND MEMBER OF THE QUORUM OF THE TWELVE APOSTLES, EXPLAINS WHY BLACKS WERE DENIED THE PRIESTHOOD, 1931.

DOCUMENT INTRODUCTION

Even more noteworthy discussing the rationale behind the priesthood ban was Joseph Fielding Smith, whose *The Way to Perfection: Short Discourses on Gospel Themes*, published in 1931 went through numerous printings over the following half century. The author's explicitly stated, lucidly written arguments on blacks and race in general, received widespread exposure among the LDS faithful. But at the same time his concepts generated controversy both within and outside of Mormonism.[40]

Joseph Fielding Smith was a controversial figure during his long, eventful life.[41] He was born in 1876 to Joseph F. Smith, after whom he was named. Of patrician Mormon stock, the younger Smith was the grand-nephew of founding Mormon prophet Joseph Smith. His father, Joseph F. Smith, served initially as a Mormon apostle and then as LDS church president from 1901 until his death in 1918. In 1910, Joseph Fielding Smith, just thirty-three years old, was made a church apostle in the midst of his father's tenure as LDS leader—this generating charges of nepotism both from inside and outside the church.[42]

As a member of the Quorum of Twelve, Smith developed a reputation as Mormonism's foremost doctrinal authority. This was reflected in his numerous published books and articles, as well as the First Presidency's reliance on him to answer difficult gospel questions.[43] In addition, Smith willingly tackled controversial topics, as evidenced in his *Blood Atonement and the Origins of Plural Marriage* (1905) denouncing post-Manifesto polygamy; *Origins of the "Reorganized" Church* (1907), wherein he dismissed the claims of the rival RLDS church; and *Man: His Origin and Destiny* (1954), wherein he condemned scientific evolution postulating as an alternative a form of Mormon creationism. Smith was sustained as president of the LDS church in January 1970 at the age of ninety-three, serving in that position for a mere two and a half years, until his death in July 1972.[44]

Smith's discussion of blacks and the rationale behind their denial of the priesthood in *The Way to Perfection* represented the most extensive discussion on the topic up to that time. He presented the topic in engaging storybook fashion, effectively capturing the attention of even the most casual reader. Smith's telling began with a detailed biographical account of Cain, which the author labeled "The Saddest Story in History." Cain was "born heir to an everlasting inheritance in righteousness with the promise of a crown of glory that would never fade . . . and he threw it all away!" Smith theorized that Cain "No doubt held the Priesthood; otherwise his sin could not make of him Perdition. He sinned against the light. And this he did . . . because he loved Satan more than he loved God." Smith, in outlining these facts along with other details of "Cain's Unholy Ambition," quoted extensively from the *Pearl of Great Price*, specifically the Book of Moses.[45]

Among the most controversial aspects of Smith's narrative was his discussion of "The Curse Upon Cain and His Descendants," again drawing from the Book of Moses, wherein Smith asserted: "Not only was Cain called upon to suffer, but because of his wickedness . . . became the father of an inferior race. A curse was placed upon him and that curse has continued through his lineage and must do so while time endures." Smith provocatively added: "Millions of souls have come into this world cursed with a black skin and have been denied the privilege of priesthood and fullness of the blessings of the Gospel." They have, moreover "been made to feel their inferiority and have been separated from the rest of mankind from the beginning." "Their black covering," Smith further added, was "emblematical of eternal darkness." He continued with a discussion of "The Seed of Cain After the Flood," noting that the "Curse continued through Ham's Posterity," drawing such information again from the *Pearl of Great Price*, specifically the Book of Abraham.[46]

Smith also dealt with the topic of "When the Curse will Be Removed," suggesting that this would occur in the far distant future. He quoted Brigham Young stating: "When all the other children of Adam have had the privilege of receiving the Priesthood, and coming into the kingdom of God, and of being redeemed from the four quarters of the earth, and have received their resurrection from the dead, then it will be time enough to remove the curse from Cain and his posterity."[47] The apostle concluded the essay by linking the ban directly to Joseph Smith. As the LDS church's chief doctrinal expositor for much of the twentieth century, Smith's views tying the ban to the founding prophet remained in favor among general authorities until church officials officially repudiated this position in 2013.[48]

Below is a discussion on blacks and the priesthood excerpted from Joseph Fielding Smith's *The Way to Perfection*.

DOCUMENT

From Joseph Fielding Smith. *The Way to Perfection: Short Discourses on Gospel Themes*, 5th ed. (orig. pub., 1931; Independence, MO: Genealogical Society of Utah, Zion's Printing and Publishing Co., 1945), 97, 99, 101–103, 107–108, 110–111 (excerpts).

The saddest story in all history is the story of Cain. Born heir to an everlasting inheritance in righteousness, with the promise of a crown of glory that would never fade away, and that too, in the morning of creation when all things were new—and he threw it all away . . . !

And the scriptures say, "And Cain loved Satan more than God. And Satan commanded him, saying: Make an offering unto the Lord." So we see it was not because the Lord had commanded him that prompted Cain to make his offering, but because Satan had commanded him. Naturally, then, we expect that the Lord would have respect for the offering of righteous Abel, but would have no respect for the offering of Cain. . . .

Cain chose knowingly, but not intelligently. He killed his brother, not so much for his flocks as for the glory of being Master Mahan. Not so much with the expectancy of obtaining his brother's worldly possessions, but to cut off without posterity that righteous brother, and, because Satan commanded him . . . !

Not only was Cain called upon to suffer, but because of his wickedness he became the father of an inferior race. A curse was placed upon him and that curse has been continued through his lineage and must do so while time endures. Millions of souls have come into this world cursed with a black skin and have been denied the privilege of Priesthood and the fullness of the blessings of the Gospel. These are the descendants of Cain. Moreover, they have been made to feel their inferiority and have been separated from the rest of mankind from the beginning. . . . In justice it should be said that there have been among the seed of Cain many who have been honorable and who have lived according to the best light they had in this second estate. Let us pray that the Lord may bless them with some blessing of exaltation, if not the fullness, for their integrity here.

But what a contrast! The sons of Seth, Enoch and Noah honored by the blessings and rights of Priesthood! The sons of Abraham made rightful heirs to all the blessings of the fathers! And the sons of Cain, denied the Priesthood; not privileged to receive the covenants of glory in the kingdom of God! What could be more sad than this . . . ? In the spirit of sympathy, mercy and faith, we will also hope that blessings may eventually be given to our negro brethren, for they are our brethren—children of God—notwithstanding their black covering emblematical of eternal darkness. . . .

The question has been asked, "what evidence do we have that the negro of the present day is the descendant of Cain, and why is it he cannot have the Priesthood?" There is no definite information on this question in the Bible, and profane history is not able to solve it. From the Pearl of Great Price and the teachings of Joseph Smith and the early elders of the Church who were associated with him, we do obtain some definite instruction in regard to this matter. . . .

It is generally believed that the curse place on Cain was continued in his posterity and that through the seed of Ham this curse was brought through the flood. Since Ham was the son of Noah, we must conclude that it was not Ham who had the black skin and was a descendant of Cain. However, there is in the Church the general belief that Ham married a woman who was a descendant of Cain, and in this way the curse of Cain was continued after the flood in Ham's posterity. Some of the brethren who were associated with the Prophet Joseph Smith have declared that he taught this doctrine. . . .

It was well understood by the early elders of the Church that the mark which was placed on Cain and which his posterity inherited was the black skin. The Book of Moses informs us that Cain and his descendants were black. Enoch taught the Gospel among all the people everywhere, except the people of Canaan. The people of Canaan lived before the flood, and were descendants of Cain. Is it not probable that Ham named his son Canaan after Cain or one of the descendants of Cain, who gave his name to the land in which the posterity of Cain lived before the flood . . . ?

From these references we discover that the children of Cain were in all respects very much like the children of Ham. The Canaanites before the flood preserved the curse in the land; the gospel was not taken to them, and no other people would associate with them. The Canaanites after the flood also preserved the curse in the land and were denied the rights of Priesthood. Abraham informs us that through Egypt, daughter of Ham—who evidently bore the same name as her mother—Egypt was inhabited and named, and that her sons could not hold the Priesthood . . .

The name of Ham is also rather significant, for it means "swarthy" or "black." It is possible that this is an appellation given to the third son of Noah because of the part he played in preserving through his lineage—and that most likely, as we have tried to show, through his wife Egyptus—the race of blacks upon whom the curse was placed. Piecing together the evidence as we discover it in holy writ and in tradition, we are brought to the conclusion that Ham, through Egyptus, continued the curse which was placed upon the seed of Cain. Because of that curse this dark race was separated and isolated from all the rest of Adam's posterity before the flood, and since that time the same condition has continued, and they have been "despised among all people."

This doctrine did not originate with President Brigham Young but was taught by the Prophet Joseph Smith. . . .

Joseph Smith has left very little on record in his own words outside of the Pearl of Great Price. . . . But we all know it is due to his teachings that the negro today is barred from the Priesthood. The negro may be baptized and enter the Church; and some of these unfortunate people have been baptized and have proved their faithfulness and worthiness before the Lord, in this their second estate, setting examples in righteousness which many of the sons of Shem and Japheth could emulate with everlasting profit. Surely the Lord will remember their faithfulness and reward them accordingly.

5

Church Growth, Confronting Civil Rights, and Official Affirmations of Black Priesthood Denial, 1945–1970

General Introduction

Two pivotal developments during the twenty-five-year period from 1945 until 1970 directly impacted Mormon attitudes and related practices involving African Americans both within and outside of the LDS church. The first was the church's demographic and geographic growth. Total church membership dramatically increased threefold, from slightly less than one million members in 1945 to just under three million by 1970.[1] Equally dynamic was the geographic expansion of Mormonism, involving its ethnic transformation from a relatively isolated Intermountain West–based, overwhelmingly white denomination to an increasingly international religion drawing a significant number of new converts from nonwhite, non-European parts of the world, particularly Latin America, Asia, and the South Pacific.[2]

In the 1950s, church leaders announced temples in England, Switzerland, and New Zealand, in addition to expanding efforts in South Africa, a country that had recently adopted apartheid as a policy of racial segregation. The church's presence in South Africa caused David O. McKay, then second counselor in the First Presidency, considerable anxiety, for he expressed concern "about the present practice in South Africa of not conferring the priesthood" on black Africans, who constituted about 68 percent of the population.[3] This perplexing color question, he wrote, proved to be a stumbling block for the church in that it proved difficult to determine who had "negro" blood and who did not.[4]

Concurrently, a second pivotal development impacted the LDS church—its confrontation with the fledgling civil rights movement, which emerged immediately following World War II and reached its climax during the turbulent decade of the 1960s. As early as the 1940s, activist Catholic, Jewish, and Protestant spokesmen engaged in the struggle for black equality, with several denominations officially endorsing the fledgling civil rights movement.[5] By contrast, the LDS church held back. A number of church leaders, in fact, strongly condemned the quest for black equality. In 1946 J. Reuben Clark, a member of the First Presidency, warned that "at the end of the road" of the struggle "to break down all race prejudice . . . is intermarriage."[6]

At the same time, LDS leaders struggled to maintain the priesthood ban despite intense opposition from civil rights groups, Mormon politicians and intellectuals, and crusading journalists who sought change. This pressure manifested intense conflict within the LDS hierarchy over racial policies and the place of blacks within the church. Most prominent in arguing for an end to the priesthood ban was Hugh B. Brown, a counselor in the First Presidency. Brown pushed for a change despite the overwhelming majority of general authorities who favored the status quo. A defining moment occurred in 1969 and 1970 when dozens of universities protested the church's racial policies by boycotting BYU athletic contests. Brown's vision of a racially inclusive church would not be fulfilled until years later, when LDS president Spencer W. Kimball ended the ban in 1978.

1. FIRST PRESIDENCY ISSUES FIRST OFFICIAL STATEMENT AFFIRMING BLACK PRIESTHOOD DENIAL AS CHURCH DOCTRINE, 1949.

DOCUMENT INTRODUCTION

Racial issues arising from possible church expansion into Cuba prompted the LDS church to issue its 1949 official statement affirming black priesthood denial. The First Presidency asked Heber Meeks, president of the Southern States Mission, to explore the possibility of sending missionaries into Cuba, a country with a robust Afro-Cuban population. Concerned with the challenges of his new assignment, Meeks turned to his friend, Lowry Nelson, for advice. Nelson, a PhD-trained sociologist at the University of Wisconsin, had deep roots in LDS culture. A native of Ferron, Utah, and lifelong member of the Mormon church, Nelson had taught at both Brigham Young University and Utah State Agricultural College (now Utah State University) before joining the faculty at the University of Minnesota in 1937. His seminal study, entitled *Mormon Village*, enhanced his credentials as a leading scholar of rural sociology in the United States, and his research travels to Cuba made him a valuable asset to Meeks.[7]

In June 1947, Meeks wrote to Nelson requesting help. "I would appreciate your opinion as to the advisability of doing missionary work particularly in the rural sections of Cuba, knowing, of course, our concept of the Negro and his position as [to] the Priesthood." Specifically, Meeks wanted to know if "there [are] groups of pure white blood in the rural sections . . . in the small communities. If so," he asked, "are they maintaining segregation from the Negroes? The best information we received was that in the rural communities there was no segregation of the races and it would probably be difficult to find, with any degree of certainty, groups of pure white people."[8]

Stunned at Meeks's "disturbing letter," Nelson responded a week later informing his old friend that "the attitude of the church in regard to the Negro" made him "very sad." Meeks's letter was the "first intimation" he had "that there was a fixed doctrine on this point." Nelson had "always known that certain statements had been made by authorities regarding the status of the Negro, but [he] had never assumed that they constituted an irrevocable doctrine. I hope no final word has been said in this matter," he explained to Meeks.[9]

On the same day he wrote Meeks, Nelson penned an impassioned letter to church president George Albert Smith, condemning the priesthood restriction. He told Smith that he was writing "out of strong conviction . . . and with the added impression that there is no irrevocable church doctrine on this subject." Nelson, not aware of any fixed doctrine denying blacks the priesthood, became concerned "that the doctrine was finally crystallized."[10]

The First Presidency dismissed Nelson's concerns. The governing body, which consisted of church president George Albert Smith and counselors J. Reuben Clark Jr. and David O. McKay, maintained in a letter of July 17 that "some of God's children were assigned to superior positions before the world was formed. Higher critics do not accept this, but the church does." The First Presidency, moreover, reaffirmed the priesthood ban, declaring that Nelson's position "seems to lose sight of the revelations of the Lord touching the preexistence of our spirits, the rebellion in heaven, and the doctrines that our birth into this life and the advantages under which we may be born, have a relationship in the life heretofore." The First Presidency concluded with a statement excoriating interracial marriage.[11]

Nelson responded with another penetrating letter. He expressed shock at the First Presidency's letter, as he later recalled in his *Memoir*.[12] In a missive of October 8, 1947, he scolded the First Presidency for advancing an ethnocentric view of race that was demeaning to blacks as well as to whites. He further lamented, "I am now confronted with this doctrine of my own church which says in effect that white supremacy is part of God's plan for his children," adding that such a possibility made Mormons "nominal allies" with southern bigots.[13] Nelson vowed to fight the issue.

The First Presidency showed little patience for the professor's frank opinions. In a letter of November 12, church leaders informed Nelson that his "worldly learning" had led him away from gospel principles and urged him to fall in line "with the revealed word of God."[14] Nelson's recalcitrance set the stage for the first official statement affirming black priesthood denial as an essential church doctrine and practice. This statement, dated August 17, 1949, asserted that Mormon racial policy was indeed a "doctrine" founded on revelation and a practice since the earliest days of the church.[15] It further stated that God had cursed blacks and that they lacked spiritual valor in a premortal existence.

This statement gave the priesthood ban a canonical status it had previously lacked.[16] The statement of 1949, appended below, provided a doctrinal guide for LDS apostles and educators when asked about the priesthood ban. During the following two decades it was widely distributed in response to queries over the policy.[17] Not until the mid-1960s, during the height of the civil rights era, did the church begin to distance itself from the 1949 statement.[18]

DOCUMENT

From "LDS Church First Presidency Statement," August 17, 1949, LDS Church History Library, Salt Lake City, Utah.

August 17, 1949

The attitude of the Church with reference to Negroes remains as it has always stood. It is not a matter of the declaration of a policy but of direct commandment from the Lord, on which is founded the doctrine of the Church from the days of its organization, to the effect that Negroes may become members of the Church but that they are not entitled to the priesthood at the present time. The prophets of the Lord have made several statements as to the operation of the principle. President Brigham Young said: "Why are so many of the inhabitants of the earth cursed with a skin of blackness? It comes in consequence of their fathers rejecting the power of the holy priesthood, and the law of God. They will go down to death. And when all the rest of the children have received their blessings in the holy priesthood, then that curse will be removed from the seed of Cain, and they will then come up and possess the priesthood, and receive all the blessings which we now are entitled to."

President Wilford Woodruff made the following statement: "The day will come when all that race will be redeemed and possess all the blessings which we now have."

The position of the Church regarding the Negro may be understood when another doctrine of the Church is kept in mind, namely, that the conduct of spirits in the premortal existence has some determining effect upon the conditions and circumstances under which these spirits take on mortality and that while the details of this principle have not been made known, the mortality is a privilege that is given to those who maintain their first estate; and that the worth of the privilege is so great that spirits are willing to come to earth and take on bodies no matter what the handicap may be as to the kind of bodies they are to secure; and that among the handicaps, failure of the right to enjoy in mortality the blessings of the priesthood is a handicap which spirits are willing to assume in order that they might come to earth. Under this principle there is no injustice whatsoever involved in this deprivation as to the holding of the priesthood by the Negroes.

The First Presidency

2. APOSTLE MARK E. PETERSEN DISCUSSES CIVIL RIGHTS AND AFFIRMS THE DIVINELY-SANCTIONED NATURE OF RACIAL SEGREGATION, 1954.

DOCUMENT INTRODUCTION

In 1954, apostle Mark E. Petersen delivered a landmark address condemning the fledgling civil rights movement and affirming the inferior place of blacks within Mormonism. This address, given to LDS religious educators at a symposium at Brigham Young University, substantiated the "Church's position on the negro question."[19] In "Race Problems—As They Affect the Church," Petersen posited a link between segregation and theology, stating that segregation was biblically sanctioned and that God had favored whites over blacks. He specifically denounced civil rights legislation then pending in Congress and warned the rank-and-file of the church "not to be led astray by the philosophies of men on this subject."[20]

The timing of Petersen's address was not accidental. It came just two months after the United States Supreme Court delivered a stunning blow to racial segregation in the historic case *Brown v. the Board of Education*. The High Court, under the energetic leadership of Chief Justice Earl Warren, averred that segregation was unconstitutional in public schools, in that it violated the rights of black Americans. Southerners, outraged by the decision, mounted a vigorous protest. They closed schools, petitioned Congress, and otherwise condemned anyone who supported the *Brown* ruling. They feared that blacks would "dumb down" the curriculum and sexually harass white students.[21]

The court's ruling set in motion a cascade of unintended consequences in Utah and in the LDS church. Even though Utah did not have segregated schools, the state had very strict segregation laws, particularly with regard to housing, theaters, restaurants, and employment. Like the rest of the country, the *Brown* decision threatened these laws by calling into question the propriety of racial exclusion in an age of racial inclusiveness. Nearly 50 percent of Utah's employers refused to hire blacks. In Salt Lake, the state's largest city, blacks could not eat at white lunch counters, frequent white bowling alleys, or lodge in white hotels.[22] This caused considerable embarrassment to the LDS church when black scholars and musicians visited the University of Utah to speak or perform. The LDS-owned and -operated Hotel Utah enforced a policy of racial exclusion against visiting black dignitaries, by requiring them to eat alone in their rooms and ride in the freight elevator. Similarly, blacks were prohibited from performing in the LDS Tabernacle and were not allowed to appear in photographs with whites on the pages of the *Deseret News*, the church-owned and -operated newspaper.[23]

Black Mormons were also shunned. Along with the obvious temple and priesthood ban, they were not permitted to speak at priesthood meetings or at firesides— the latter ban decreed by church president David O. McKay in 1952.[24] Likewise, LDS leaders countenanced segregation in sacrament meetings by instructing blacks and whites to separate seating when white members complained about having to mingle with "coloreds" at church. In one instance, leaders prohibited a black family from attending church altogether, after white members complained about their presence.[25]

Church authorities also advocated segregating blood banks at hospitals—a practice enforced in certain places in the United States until the 1960s and in Utah until the late 1970s. Mormon leaders feared that if white members received blood transfusions from blacks it would pollute the "purity of the blood streams," thereby disqualifying them from the priesthood.[26] More conspicuously, Mormon officials fought to prevent blacks from moving into white neighborhoods. Ignoring a 1948 Supreme Court decision barring the courts from enforcing racial covenants in housing,[27] they urged white members to join civic groups and to use LDS chapels "for meetings to prevent Negroes from becoming neighbors." Church leaders, moreover, counseled members to "control the colored situation" by purchasing property that would prevent blacks from buying homes in white neighborhoods near LDS chapels.[28] Lastly, they warned against interracial marriage, "which the Lord has forbidden."[29]

The leading proponents of segregation within the LDS hierarchy were church president David O. McKay, First Presidency counselor J. Reuben Clark, and apostles Henry D. Moyle, Ezra Taft Benson, Joseph Fielding Smith, Harold B. Lee, and Mark E. Peterson.[30]

Mark E. Petersen, born in 1900 in Salt Lake, came of age in a city where blacks were few and far between.[31] He was called as an apostle in 1944, serving until his death in 1984. Prior to his church service, he worked as the general manager of the *Deseret News* and also wrote scores of books and articles on many theological subjects, including for the *Ensign*, the church-owned magazine. Petersen was a gruff man with a prickly personality.[32] Like his colleague Bruce R. McConkie, he favored doctrinal orthodoxy over theological speculation and distrusted LDS intellectuals, whom he sometimes targeted for church sanction.[33]

Thus Petersen, as a proponent of segregation, condemned the fledgling civil rights movement. He believed that the civil rights discussion had "blinded the thinking of some of our own people."[34] Moreover, he wanted to preserve the purity of the white race fearing that blacks would not be satisfied until they had accomplished complete "absorption with the white race."[35]

Petersen's reasoning rested on a long-held Mormon belief in the hierarchy of lineages, a theory promoted by fellow apostle Harold B. Lee, among others.[36] Petersen affirmed that whites were blessed with a "favored lineage" and that God had cursed blacks because of their moral failings in a premortal life. He conceded that black Mormons could still inherit a celestial glory in heaven, albeit not on an equal basis with whites. Their status would be that of "servant."[37]

The apostle's views caused considerable controversy and embarrassment. One critic, LDS sociologist Kendall White, noted that Peterson's "position was so extreme that it is reminiscent of the Klan." Another critic, LDS religious educator Lowell Bennion, asked Petersen if it was "fair, either from a human or divine perspective . . . to brand blacks as somehow deserving their exclusion because of undocumented choices in the pre-existence."[38] Others circulated the speech, which angered Petersen.[39] In 1966, *New York Times* journalist Wallace Turner published a book on the Mormons, part of which berated Petersen for teaching that segregation was inspired by God.[40] Indeed, over time Petersen denied giving the talk, clearly embarrassed by what he had said.[41]

The address, nevertheless, is significant for two reasons. First, it was widely circulated in the 1950s and 1960s by BYU religion faculty.[42] Second, it demonstrates the church's ambivalence toward civil rights in the 1950s while also illustrating how certain high church officials viewed such issues within the context of ongoing Mormon racial practices.

Excerpts of the address appear below.

DOCUMENT

From Mark E. Petersen, "Race Problems—As They Affect the Church," address given to Religious educators at Brigham Young University, August 27, 1954, LDS Church History Library, Salt Lake City, Utah (excerpts).

I think I have read enough to give you an idea of what the Negro is after. He is not just seeking the oppor[t]unity of sitting down in a cafe where white people sit. He isn't just trying to ride on the same streetcar or the same Pullman car with white people . . . [I]t appears that the Negro seeks absorption with the white race. He will not be satisfied until he achieves it by intermarriage. That is his objective and we must face it. We must not allow our feelings to carry us away, nor must we feel so sorry for Negroes that, we will open our arms and embrace them with everything we have. Remember the little statement that they used to say about sin, "First we pity, then endure, then embrace. . . ."

What should be our attitude as Latter-day Saints toward Negro and other dark races? Does the Lord give us any guidance? Is there any Church policy in this matter? Is segregation in and of itself a wrong principle? Just where should we stand? . . .

Was segregation a wrong principle? When the Lord chose the nations to which the spirits were to come, determining that some would be Japanese and some would be Chinese and some Negroes and some Americans, He engaged in an act of segregation. When He permitted the banishment of Hagar and Ishmael again He indulged in segregation. In the case of Jacob and Esau, He engaged in segregation. When He preserved His people Israel in Egypt for 400 years, He engaged in an act of segregation, and when He brought them up out of Egypt and gave them their own land, He engaged in an act of segregation. . . . In placing a curse on Laman and Lemuel, He engaged in segregation. When He placed the mark upon Cain, He engaged in segregation. When he told Enoch not to preach the gospel to the descendants of Cain who were black, the Lord engaged in segregation. When He cursed the descendants of Cain as to the Priesthood, He engaged in segregation. When He forbade intermarriages as He does in Deuteronomy, Chapter 7, He established segregation....

Who placed the Negroes originally in darkest Africa? Was it some man, or was it God? And when He placed them there, He segregated them. Who placed the Chinese in China? The Lord did. It was an act of segregation. When He placed only some of His chosen people in the tribe of Judah, the royal tribe, wasn't that an act of segregation? And when He gave the birthright only to Ephraim, wasn't that an act of segregation?

The Lord segregated the people both as to blood and place of residence, at least in the bases of the Lamanites and the Negroes we have the definite word of the Lord himself that He placed a dark skin upon them: as a curse—as a sign to all others. He forbade inter-marriage with them under threat of extension of the curse (2 Nephi 5:21) And He certainly segregated the descendants of Cain when He cursed the Negro as to the Priesthood, and drew an absolute line. You may even say He dropped an iron curtain there. The Negro was cursed as to the Priesthood, and therefore, was cursed as to the blessings of the Priesthood. Certainly God made a segregation there....

Think of the Negro, cursed as to the Priesthood. Are we prejudiced, against him? Unjustly, sometimes we're accused of having such a prejudice. But what does the mercy of God have for him? This Negro, who in the pre-existence life lived the type of life which justified the Lord in sending him to the earth in the lineage of Cain with a black skin, and possibly being born in darkest Africa - if that Negro is willing when he hears the gospel to accept it, he may have many of the blessings of the gospel. In spite of all he did in the pre-existent life, the Lord is willing, if the Negro accepts the gospel with real, sincere faith, and is really converted, to give him the blessings of baptism and the gift of the Holy Ghost. If that Negro is faithful all his days, he can and will enter the Celestial Kingdom. He will go there as a servant, but he will get a Celestial resurrection....

Now what is our policy in regard to intermarriage? As to the Negro, of course, there is only one possible answer. We must not intermarry with the Negro....

Now we are generous with the negro. We are willing that the Negro have the highest kind of education. I would be willing to let every Negro drive a Cadillac if they could afford it. I would be willing that they have all the advantages they can get out of life in the world. but let them enjoy these things among themselves. I think the Lord segregated the Negro and who is man to change that segregation? It reminds me of the scripture on marriage, "what God hath joined together, let not man put asunder." Only here we have the reverse of the thing—what God hath separated, let not man bring together again....

3. APOSTLE BRUCE R. MCCONKIE AFFIRMS THE INFERIOR STATUS OF BLACK PEOPLE IN A BESTSELLING WORK, 1958.

DOCUMENT INTRODUCTION

Bruce R. McConkie's *Mormon Doctrine* is one of the most widely read LDS books ever published. It sold thousands of copies and went through seven reprint editions over some fifty-two years from 1958 to 2010—when it went out of print. The volume established McConkie as a premier doctrinal authority in the church during the latter half of the twentieth century, and it provided a ready market for his later books.[43] Rank-and-file members of the church quoted from *Mormon Doctrine* for years, utilizing its teachings in general church meetings, Sunday school classes, and missionary discussions. In the 1980s, the general membership of the church rated it among their top ten favorite books authored by a general authority.[44]

Bruce Redd McConkie, born in 1915 in Ann Arbor, Michigan, was ordained to the First Council of the Seventy in 1946 at the age of thirty-one. He served in that body until 1972, when then president Harold B. Lee elevated him to the Quorum of the Twelve Apostles, where he served until his death in 1985. He developed a particularly close relationship with Joseph Fielding Smith, his father-in-law, who presided over the Quorum of the Twelve during much of McConkie's tenure as a Seventy. As previously noted, Smith himself was also a leading doctrinal authority and, in turn, strongly influenced McConkie's own theological development.[45] In *Mormon Doctrine*, McConkie referenced Smith's various works 178 times, second only to church founder Joseph Smith.[46] McConkie's training as a lawyer at the University of Utah also influenced his development, particularly his formal, legalistic writing style. In addition, McConkie embraced his role as a guardian of doctrinal orthodoxy, correcting dissidents who he felt erred in their doctrinal understanding of core Mormon beliefs.[47]

Mormon Doctrine achieved instant notoriety from the moment of its publication in 1958, in accordance with McConkie's claim that it represented "the first major attempt to digest, explain, and analyze all of the important doctrines in the kingdom."[48] McConkie's hefty tome included over two thousand entries, each alphabetized beginning with "Aaron," the Old Testament figure, and concluding with "Zoramites"—the people descended from Zoram, a Book of Mormon counterfigure. Controversy marked the book from the beginning. LDS church president David O. McKay described the volume "a source of concern to the Brethren."[49] McKay pointed to errors of fact that numbered in the hundreds, affecting "most of the 776 pages of the book."[50] Also the book's tone, language, and doctrinal zeal caused McKay and his counselors additional unease. *Mormon Doctrine* violated established church custom and practice, wherein grassroots members looked to the church president himself as the sole arbiter of Mormon doctrine.[51]

Such problems alarmed President McKay, prompting him to convene a committee to look into the volume's alleged errors. This committee, consisting of senior apostles Mark E. Petersen and Marion G. Romney, found 1,067 doctrinal errors, prompting their recommendation that the book not be republished. The First Presidency and other apostles concurred, and thus McConkie allowed *Mormon Doctrine* to go out of print, albeit reluctantly. Seven years later, however, the ever-persistent McConkie approached McKay requesting permission to republish a revised version of the book. The aged McKay, by this time ninety-two and in failing health, granted permission to allow its republication.[52]

McConkie removed and softened certain controversial entries in the reissued 1966 edition.[53] But his entries dealing with blacks, specifically on the "Negro," "Caste System," "Cain," and "Ham," remained as originally written, given that his initial treatment of these topics caused no controversy among church leaders. In fact, McConkie's views on the priesthood ban mirrored those of Joseph Fielding Smith and other church spokesmen.[54] Indeed, neither President McKay nor apostles Petersen and Romney expressed criticisms of McConkie's entries on black lineage or on his discussion of the rationale for the priesthood ban. It was simply a nonissue.

In a later edition of *Mormon Doctrine*, published in 1979, the only revisions McConkie made to the "Negro" entry was inclusion of the 1978 black priesthood revelation. McConkie's entry on the "Negro," however, remained intact, affirming "the curse," segregation, and racial inequality. Moreover, his continuing assertion equating black worthiness with a preexistent life appeared passé and theologically unsound, particularly to African American Mormon converts who joined the church in ever-increasing numbers during this period. The apostle's assertion of segregation as God-inspired was particularly offensive. Finally, in 2010, the book slipped quietly out of print, marking the end of a controversial work that had encapsulated Mormon racial doctrine for decades.[55] Included below are excerpts from some of the most prominent entries.

DOCUMENT

From Bruce R. McConkie, *Mormon Doctrine* (Salt Lake City: Bookcraft, 1958), 102, 107–108, 314, 476–477 (excerpts).

CAIN. See Devil, Ham, Master Mahan, Negroes, Perdition, Sons of Perdition.

Though he was a rebel and an associate of Lucifer in preexistence, and though he was a liar from the beginning whose name was Perdition, Cain managed to attain the privilege of mortal birth.... He understood the gospel plan of salvation, was baptized, received the priesthood, had a perfect knowledge of the position of God, and talked personally with Deity. Then he came out in open rebellion, fought God, worshipped Lucifer, and slew Abel....

As a result of his rebellion, Cain was cursed with a dark skin; he became the father of the Negroes, and those spirits who are not worthy to receive the priesthood are born through his lineage....

CASTE SYSTEM. See Bondage, Pre-existence, Slavery, Tribes of Israel.

... [I]n a broad general sense, caste systems have their root and origin in the gospel itself, and when they operate according to the divine decree, the resultant restrictions and *segregation* are right and proper and have the approval of the Lord. To illustrate: Cain, Ham, and the whole negro race have been cursed with a black skin, the mark of Cain, so they can be identified as a caste apart, a people with whom the other descendants of Adam should not intermarry....

All this is not to say that any race, creed, or caste should be denied any inalienable rights. But it is to say that Deity in his infinite wisdom, to carry out his inscrutable purposes, has a caste system of his own, a system of segregation of races and peoples. The justice of such a system is evident when life is considered in its true eternal perspective. It is only by a knowledge of [the] pre-existence that it can be known why some persons are born in one race or caste and some in another....

Segregation and caste systems will continue on in a future eternity; the righteous will go to paradise and the wicked to hell; and finally all men will be segregated into kingdoms—each separate from the others—according as their works have been.

HAM. See Cain, Egyptus, Negroes, Pre-existence, Priesthood.

Through Ham (a name meaning *black*) 'the blood of the Canaanites was reserved' through the flood, he having married Egyptus, a descendant of Cain. (Abra. 1:20–27.) Negroes are thus descendants of Ham, who himself also was cursed, apparently for marrying into the forbidden lineage.... These descendants cannot hold the priesthood.

NEGROES. See Cain, Ham, Pre-existence, Priesthood, Races of Men.

In the pre-existence eternity various degrees of valiance and devotion to the truth were exhibited by different groups of our Father's spirit offspring.... Of the two-thirds who followed Christ, however, some were more valiant than others.... Those who were less valiant in [the] pre-existence and who thereby had certain spiritual restrictions imposed upon them during mortality are known to us as the *negroes*. Such spirits are sent to earth through the lineage of Cain, the mark put upon him for his rebellion against God and his murder of

Abel being a black skin. (Moses 5:16–41; 7:8, 12, 22.) Noah's son Ham married Egyptus, a descendant of Cain, thus preserving the negro lineage through the flood. (Abra. 1:20–27.)

Negroes in this life are denied the priesthood; under no circumstances can they hold this delegation of authority from the Almighty (Abra. 1: 20–27.) The gospel message of salvation is not carried affirmatively to them. . . .

The present status of the negro rests purely and simply on the foundation of the pre-existence. Along with all races and peoples[,] he is receiving here what he merits as a result of the long pre-mortal probation in the presence of the Lord. . . .

The negroes are not equal with other races where the receipt of certain spiritual blessings are concerned, particularly the priesthood and temple blessings that flow therefrom, but this inequality is not of man's origin. It is the Lord's doing, is based on his eternal laws of justice, and grows out of the lack of spiritual valiance of those concerned in their first estate. . . .

4. FIRST PRESIDENCY COUNSELOR HUGH B. BROWN STATEMENT ON CIVIL RIGHTS IN GENERAL CONFERENCE, 1963.

DOCUMENT INTRODUCTION

The LDS church remained silent on racial equality in the 1950s and early 1960s until First Presidency counselor Hugh B. Brown read a statement in general conference in 1963 indicating the church's support for civil rights. His words marked a dramatic moment, because a majority of his colleagues in the church hierarchy were reluctant to support civil rights, most notably church president David O. McKay whose exposure to blacks was limited as he grew up in the small farming community of Huntsville, Utah. While McKay declared that "the relationship of the church to the colored person was one of the most pressing problems that had to be faced and resolved,"[56] he did not support racial integration, affirming instead a separation of the races. He further declared "colored people [as] better off" in the South than in the integrated North. Moreover, he supported segregation practices at the church-owned Hotel Utah.[57]

McKay also had the support of the Quorum of the Twelve, a majority of whom opposed the fledgling civil rights movement. A notable exception was Hugh B. Brown, who did not fit the typical profile of a general authority.[58] Although born in Granger, Utah, in 1883, Brown came of age and spent the majority of his adult life in Canada, where he embraced that nation's liberal political and social ideals. He was ordained an Assistant to the Twelve in 1953 and an apostle in 1958, where he served until his death in 1975. Strong in his convictions and something of a maverick, he favored racial equality and also hoped to abolish the church policy on black priesthood denial.[59] By 1961, Brown found himself in a position to exert his influence after McKay named him a counselor in the First Presidency.[60] Later that same year McKay sustained him as second counselor and two years later he elevated him to first counselor.

Timing also aided Brown. The election of John F. Kennedy in 1960 marked a dramatic change, with the new president making civil rights a major priority. Following Kennedy's assassination, Lyndon Johnson continued that agenda, pushing through the 1964 Civil Rights Act and the Voting Rights Act of 1965.[61] Meanwhile, the LDS church remained silent, despite Brown's pleading for the church to affirm official support for racial equality.

By 1963, LDS leaders faced considerable criticism for their failure to endorse, let alone comment on, the still pending civil rights legislation. Journalists wrote unflattering articles critiquing LDS attitudes toward blacks. At the same time, concerned Mormons themselves pressed their leaders.[62] Stewart L. Udall, then secretary of the interior in the Kennedy administration and a lifelong Mormon, wrote Brown expressing his disgust with Mormon racial policy. He believed that the church's racial policies reflected badly on the church and its members, as did Michigan governor George Romney, an emerging Republican presidential contender, who himself strongly supported civil rights. Udall expressed abhorrence at the extreme right-wing views of apostle Ezra Taft Benson, the latter asserting that communist agents provoked the civil rights movement. Brown, by contrast, suggested that the church's position on civil rights might change. Ongoing church efforts to commence missionary activity in the African nation of Nigeria prompted Brown's optimism.[63]

Just weeks before the church's October 1963 general conference, external pressures forced the church to express itself on civil rights. The NAACP, upset that Utah "was the only western state that had not passed laws guaranteeing basic civil rights for minority groups,"[64] threatened to protest the upcoming LDS general conference. Alarmed at this development, Brown and fellow First Presidency counselor N. Eldon Tanner met with local NAACP leaders, including Albert Fritz, president of the Salt Lake chapter. Brown assured the NAACP that "a statement would be made" at the forthcoming conference affirming LDS support for civil rights. Brown, acting on his own, sought the help of Sterling McMurrin, a University of Utah philosophy professor and a former U.S. commissioner of education.[65]

Brown found securing approval from his fellow apostles for such a statement much more challenging. He had often tussled with apostles Ezra Taft Benson, Joseph Fielding Smith, and Harold B. Lee on issues involving racial equality.[66] The timing was in his favor. When President McKay learned that the NAACP would protest at the conference, he agreed to let Brown read the statement. Though McKay refused to let Brown present it as "an official pronouncement of the First Presidency"—undoubtedly out of deference to those apostles opposed to civil rights—he instructed his counselor to read the pronouncement as part of his talk. Brown craftily ignored the president's wishes by reading the statement, pausing, then proceeding with his talk, "giving the impression," Sterling McMurrin later recalled, that this was ... an official statement of church policy from the First Presidency."[67]

The statement had its desired effect. The NAACP decided not to protest at the conference. NAACP president Fritz approved the statement, acknowledging that it "makes it possible for all of us to work in harmony for a better state." In the statement, Brown pledged the church's support for full citizenship rights for blacks and stated "that it is a moral evil for any person or group of persons to deny any human being the right to gainful employment, to full education opportunity, and to every privilege of citizenship."[68] The full statement is included below.

DOCUMENT

From Hugh B. Brown General Conference address, October 4–6, 1963, in *Conference Report* (Salt Lake City: Published by the Church of Jesus Christ of Latter-day Saints, 1963), 91.

During recent months, both in Salt Lake City and across the nation, considerable interest has been expressed in the position of The Church of Jesus Christ of Latter-day Saints on the matter of civil rights. We would like it to be known that there is in this Church no doctrine, belief, or practice, that is intended to deny the enjoyment of full civil rights by any person regardless of race, color, or creed. We say again, as we have said many times before, that we believe that all men are the children of the same God, and that it is a moral evil for any person or group of persons to deny any human being the right to gainful employment, to full education opportunity, and to every privilege of citizenship, just as it is a moral evil to deny him the right to worship according to the dictates of his own conscience . . . We call upon all men, everywhere, both within and outside the Church, to commit themselves to the establishment of full civil equality for all of God's children. Anything less than this defeats our high ideal of the brotherhood of man.

5. APOSTLE EZRA TAFT BENSON LINKS THE CIVIL RIGHTS MOVEMENT WITH COMMUNISM, 1965.

DOCUMENT INTRODUCTION

Two years after the general conference statement endorsing civil rights, apostle Ezra Taft Benson delivered a stinging address in conference linking the civil rights movement to communism. The speech "revealed sharp and bitter differences among [the LDS church's] leadership on civil rights," a reporter observed. Benson "speaks for himself," Brown "tartly" noted, when asked if Benson's address offered a new direction on civil rights. The 1963 statement on civil rights, Brown carefully added, "is the official church position. It was personally approved by President McKay."[69]

Benson had always been his own man. Born in 1899 in a small farming community in Whitney, Idaho, he had developed an independence that carried over into his service as an apostle from 1943 to 1985 and as U.S. secretary of agriculture under President Dwight Eisenhower from 1953 to 1961. After eight years in the latter position, Benson resumed his full-time duties as an apostle. He harbored further political ambitions when former Alabama governor George C. Wallace asked him to be his vice presidential running mate on the segregationist American Independent Party ticket in 1968, but President McKay refused to approve the request. And in the 1970s Benson briefly toyed with running for president on an ultra-right-wing third-party ticket.⁷⁰

Benson's fierce political views were often indistinguishable from his religious ones. "He talks of his service in the government, condemns communism, and preaches that no one can be a good Mormon who is either a socialist or a communist," BYU president Ernest Wilkinson observed.⁷¹ Benson's experience in the Eisenhower administration hardened his views of government. He "denounced Democrat officeholders and intellectuals as socialists and Communist sympathizers" and also praised the John Birch Society as "the most effective non-church organization," fighting against "creeping socialism and Godless Communism."⁷² Benson condemned government programs, labor unions, and liberals, whom he saw as being soft on communism. He also assailed government leaders, in particular President Eisenhower and Supreme Court Chief Justice Earl Warren, both of whom he believed betrayed the constitution and had become "a tool of the worldwide communist conspiracy."⁷³

Benson, moreover, embraced the ultra-right-wing views of Robert Welch and his John Birch Society.⁷⁴ Accordingly, Benson embarked on a passionate crusade to warn Mormons about the ills of communism. In church meetings, civic gatherings, and in public speeches, he decried the dangers of communism, the civil rights movement, and the evils of the welfare state. Throughout the late 1950s and into the 1960s and 1970s, Benson's indefatigable zeal denouncing these "threats to freedom" aroused the ire of his colleagues, particularly Hugh B. Brown, Joseph Fielding Smith, Harold B. Lee, N. Eldon Tanner, Mark E. Petersen and Spencer W. Kimball, who felt Benson's anticommunist crusade detracted from his responsibilities as an apostle.⁷⁵

Grassroots members of the church, also concerned that Benson's views were too extreme, wrote dozens of letters to church headquarters complaining that Benson had abused his authority.⁷⁶ In response to such letters, Brown and other leaders warned members that Benson's views on communism did not represent the church. "You are no more disturbed, and may I say, disgusted, than I am with the attitude taken by some of our friends in connection with the John Birch Society," Brown explained to a BYU religion professor. "I feel sure" the president of the church "feels as I do that some disciplinary action [on Benson] should be taken."⁷⁷ Though Benson never officially joined the Birch Society, he sympathized with the society's extreme anticommunist leanings and occasionally spoke at public gatherings with Robert Welch. Benson's son Reed served as a John Birch regional director, taking cues from his father about the evils of communism.⁷⁸

Despite warnings from leaders to temper his views,⁷⁹ Benson continued preaching his extreme anticommunist, anti–civil rights, and antigovernment beliefs. Just weeks after Brown endorsed civil rights in the fall 1963 general conference,

Benson, in a series of speeches delivered at various venues in Utah and Idaho, asserted that the civil rights movement had been "fomented almost entirely by the Communists."[80] This rhetoric reached a crescendo that fall when Idaho Democratic Congressman Ralph Harding, himself a Latter-day Saint, assailed Benson in a powerful speech on the floor of the United States Congress.[81] Harding, along with other concerned LDS politicians and intellectuals, felt that Benson was an embarrassment whose public criticisms of Eisenhower and Warren crossed the lines of acceptable propriety. Harding, moreover, believed that Benson's affiliation with the John Birch Society besmirched the church as an organization and implied LDS support of an extreme right-wing agenda.[82]

In November 1963, just two months after Harding's House speech assailing Benson, the First Presidency announced the appointment of apostle Benson to preside over the European states mission.[83] In commenting on Benson's appointment, Joseph Fielding Smith, president of the Quorum of the Twelve Apostles, told the media that the move had nothing to do with Benson's extreme political views as publicly expressed. In private, however, Smith offered a different view, frankly confiding to Congressman Harding, "I am glad to report to you that it will be some time before we hear anything from Brother Benson, who is now on his way to Great Britain where I suppose he will be, at least for the next two years. When he returns I hope his blood will be purified."[84]

When Benson returned to Utah in 1965, his views had not moderated in the least, nor his desire to express them publicly. In the April 1965 session of general conference, he branded "communism [as] the greatest threat to the Church," further stating that "communists were using the Civil Rights movement to promote revolution and eventual take-over of this country." Ominously, he further warned that there were "traitors in the church"—a not-too-subtle reference to Hugh B. Brown. He admonished the faithful to remain vigilant and alert to avoid "temptations and avenues of apostasy."[85]

The First Presidency and Benson's fellow apostles were dismayed by both the tone and content of Benson's speech. They ordered removed the most inflammatory portions from the published versions in both the conference report and the *Improvement Era*, the church's magazine.[86] Benson remained undeterred, continuing his anticommunist crusade and his relentless criticism of the civil rights movement.[87] Below are Benson's unexpurgated remarks as delivered at the October 6, 1965, general conference.

DOCUMENT

From Ezra Taft Benson general conference address, "Not Commanded in All Things," October 6, 1965, unaltered version in David O. McKay Scrapbook #79, David O. McKay Papers, Special Collections, Marriott Library, University of Utah (used by permission of Special Collections, Marriott Library, University of Utah).

For our day President David O. McKay has called communism the greatest threat to the Church—and it is certainly the greatest mortal threat this country has ever faced. What are you doing to fight it? Before I left for Europe I warned how the communists were using the Civil Rights movement to promote revolution and eventual take-over of this country. When are we going to wake up? What do you know about the dangerous Civil Rights Agitation in Mississippi? Do you fear the destruction of all vestiges of state government?

Now brethren, the Lord has never promised there would not be traitors in the Church. We have the ignorant, the sleepy and the deceived who provide temptations and avenues of apostasy for the unwary and the unfaithful. But we have a prophet at our head and he has spoken. Now what are we going to do about it . . . ?

6. FIRST PRESIDENCY OFFICIAL STATEMENT REAFFIRMING BLACK PRIESTHOOD DENIAL AS DOCTRINE, 1969.

DOCUMENT INTRODUCTION

The second official church statement reaffirming black priesthood denial was issued in late 1969 at the peak of the civil rights movement. By this time, the church faced increasing pressure both from within and without to change its policies. In 1968 Sterling McMurrin, coauthor of the church's 1963 statement affirming civil rights, addressed the NAACP and excoriated the church for what he labeled its "crude superstitions about negroes." McMurrin's critique made national headlines.[88]

Meanwhile, the church faced criticism on a new front in the form of protests directed against Brigham Young University. Such protests, occurring between 1968 and 1971, generated an abundance of media attention. In 1968, athletes on the University of Texas–El Paso track team chose not to compete against BYU in conference play. In 1969, fourteen members of the University of Wyoming football team were suspended from that school for protesting the church's racial policy.[89] That same year Stanford University severed all ties with BYU, citing the LDS church's view on blacks.[90]

In 1970, students at the University of Washington demanded that their university administration condemn BYU "as a racist institution."[91] That same year the protests turned violent at Colorado State University in Fort Collins, Colorado, during a basketball contest between that institution and BYU.[92] Athletes also staged protests at Arizona State University, San Jose State University, the University of New Mexico, and other universities.[93] By early 1970, *Sports Illustrated* characterized BYU as a school under assault, stating that "as much as the [BYU] Cougars would like to ignore them, the protests have grown in intensity to the point where they have almost transcended all else."[94]

Church officials and BYU administrators immediately tried to counter the negative publicity. BYU president Ernest Wilkinson denied charges of discrimination claiming that the church school did not spurn African Americans. Undertaking a public-relations blitz, Wilkinson ordered a "full text" statement to be published "in full-page [newspaper] ads" in some states where the protests occurred. In such ads, he countered the so-called "misinformation concerning the practices and beliefs of BYU and the Mormon Church" appearing in the national media. He addressed the issue of the almost complete absence of African Americans on the campus. "Blacks do not attend BYU . . . for their own reasons," not because they faced discrimination. Wilkinson then denied any connection between the priesthood ban and the church stand on civil rights.[95]

From within the church hierarchy, Hugh B. Brown sought to defend the church and quell emotions in this super-charged atmosphere. At the same time he actively sought to have the priesthood ban lifted. Some six years earlier, Brown, in a 1963 interview with *New York Times* reporter Wallace Turner, had intimated that a change was imminent, prompting Turner to report that "The top leadership of the Mormon church is seriously considering the abandonment of its historic policy of discrimination against Negroes," albeit erroneously.[96]

In December 1969 Brown claimed once more that the ban was about to be lifted, basing his assumption on the fact that he had secured support from a majority of the Council of Twelve Apostles, who concurred that a change was necessary. Church president David O. McKay, who was ill, did not attend the proceedings. Senior apostle Harold B. Lee was also absent and out of the country on church assignment, as was Alvin R. Dyer, a First Presidency counselor, both of whom strongly opposed lifting the ban.[97] Seizing the moment, Brown secured the majority support from those present. However, when Lee and Dyer returned to Salt Lake, they rejected what Brown had done and prevailed upon the majority of the apostles, along with First Presidency counselor N. Eldon Tanner, to withdraw their support from Brown's proposal. Lee then drew up his own proposal, the official 1969 statement reaffirming black priesthood denial as doctrine. He and other church officials then pressured the seventy-nine-year-old Brown to sign it, thereby clearing up any confusion that had been caused in the national media regarding the church's position on blacks and the priesthood.[98]

Brown reportedly wept when he signed the official declaration. In private, he said he was forced to do so to maintain the appearance of unanimity in the church.[99] At least one apostle, Spencer W. Kimball, came to him later "crying" and said Brown was right and "we're wrong." Kimball lamented that he did not "have the courage to stand up to Lee," who was then acting as the interim president of the Quorum of Twelve given senior apostle Joseph Fielding Smith's advanced age.[100]

The 1969 statement represents the second time in LDS history when church leaders had affirmed black priesthood denial as officially sanctioned church doctrine. Dated December 15, 1969, it was signed by only two members of the First Presidency, namely Hugh B. Brown and N. Eldon Tanner. Failing to sign it was ailing church president David O. McKay, who died just one month later on January 18, 1970. The Mormon hierarchy distributed copies of the statement to media outlets throughout the United States and asked local leaders to read it over the pulpit in Mormon meetinghouses. It was also published in the *Improvement Era* and *Church*

News.[101] Its most salient points note that God is "discriminatory" to those whom he grants the priesthood and that the church supports civil rights, an admission that Brown insisted be added as a precondition for his signature.[102] There is nothing about the divine curse or anything linking blacks with a pre-earth life—expressions that marked the 1949 statement. Instead, the statement indicated that it was not clear why God had denied blacks the priesthood. These were "reasons which we believe are known to God, but which He has not made fully known to man."[103]

Portions of the statement are contained below.

DOCUMENT

From First Presidency statement of December 15, 1969, published in "Church Section," *Deseret News*, January 10, 1970, 12.

December 15, 1969

To General Authorities, Regional Representatives of the Twelve, Stake Presidents, Mission Presidents, and Bishops.

Dear Brethren:

In view of confusion that has arisen, it was decided at a meeting of the First Presidency and the Quorum of the Twelve to restate the position of the Church with regard to the Negro both in society and in the Church.

First, may we say that we know something of the sufferings of those who are discriminated against in a denial of their civil rights and Constitutional privileges. Our early history as a church is a tragic story of persecution and oppression. Our people repeatedly were denied the protection of the law. They were driven and plundered, robbed and murdered by mobs, who in many instances were aided and abetted by those sworn to uphold the law. We as a people have experienced the bitter fruits of civil discrimination and mob violence.

We believe that the Constitution of the United States was divinely inspired, that it was produced by "wise men" whom God raised up for this "very purpose," and that the principles embodied in the Constitution are so fundamental and important that, if possible, they should be extended "for the rights and protection" of all mankind.

In revelations received by the first prophet of the Church in this dispensation, Joseph Smith (1805–1844), the Lord made it clear that it is "not right that any man should be in bondage one to another." These words were spoken prior to the Civil War. From these and other revelations have sprung the Church's deep and historic concern with man's free agency and our commitment to the sacred principles of the Constitution.

It follows, therefore, that we believe the Negro, as well as those of other races, should have his full Constitutional privileges as a member of society, and we hope that members of the Church everywhere will do their part as citizens to see that these rights are held inviolate. Each citizen must have equal opportunities and protection under the law with reference to civil rights.

However, matters of faith, conscience, and theology are not within the purview of the civil law. The first amendment to the Constitution specifically provides that "Congress shall make no law respecting an establishment of religion, or prohibiting the free exercise thereof."

The position of the Church of Jesus Christ of Latter-day Saints affecting those of the Negro race who choose to join the Church falls wholly within the category of religion. It has no bearing upon matters of civil rights. In no case or degree does it deny to the Negro his full privileges as a citizen of the nation.

This position has no relevancy whatever to those who do not wish to join the Church. Those individuals, we suppose, do not believe in the divine origin and nature of the church, nor that we have the priesthood of God. Therefore, if they feel we have no priesthood, they should have no concern with any aspect of our theology on priesthood so long as that theology does not deny any man his Constitutional privileges.

A word of explanation concerning the position of the Church.

The Church of Jesus Christ of Latter-day Saints owes its origin, its existence, and its hope for the future to the principle of continuous revelation. "We believe all that God has revealed, all that He does now reveal, and we believe that He will yet reveal many great and important things pertaining to the Kingdom of God."

From the beginning of this dispensation, Joseph Smith and all succeeding presidents of the Church have taught that Negroes, while spirit children of a common Father, and the progeny of our earthly parents Adam and Eve, were not yet to receive the priesthood, for reasons which we believe are known to God, but which He has not made fully known to man.

Our living prophet, President David O. McKay, has said, "The seeming discrimination by the Church toward the Negro is not something which originated with man; but goes back into the beginning with God. . . .

"Revelation assures us that this plan antedates man's mortal existence, extending back to man's pre-existent state."

President McKay has also said, "Sometime in God's eternal plan, the Negro will be given the right to hold the priesthood."

Until God reveals His will in this matter, to him whom we sustain as a prophet, we are bound by that same will. Priesthood, when it is conferred on any man comes as a blessing from God, not of men.

We feel nothing but love, compassion, and the deepest appreciation for the rich talents, endowments, and the earnest strivings of our Negro brothers and sisters. We are eager to share with men of all races the blessings of the Gospel. We have no racially segregated congregations.

Were we the leaders of an enterprise created by ourselves and operated only according to our own earthly wisdom, it would be a simple thing to act according to popular will. But we believe that this work is directed by God and that the conferring of the priesthood must await His revelation. To do otherwise would be to deny the very premise on which the Church is established.

We recognize that those who do not accept the principle of modern revelation may oppose our point of view. We repeat that such would not wish for membership in the Church, and therefore the question of priesthood should hold no interest for them. Without prejudice they should grant us the privilege afforded under the Constitution to exercise our chosen form of religion just as we must grant all others a similar privilege. They must recognize that the question of bestowing or withholding priesthood in the Church is a matter of religion and not a matter of Constitutional right.

We extend the hand of friendship to men everywhere and the hand of fellowship to all who wish to join the Church and partake of the many rewarding opportunities to be found therein.

We join with those throughout the world who pray that all of the blessings of the gospel of Jesus Christ may in due time of the Lord become available to men of faith everywhere. Until that time comes we must trust in God, in His wisdom and in His tender mercy.

Meanwhile we must strive harder to emulate His Son, the Lord Jesus Christ, whose new commandment it was that we should love one another. In developing that love and concern for one another, while awaiting revelations yet to come, let us hope that with respect to these religious differences, we may gain reinforcement for understanding and appreciation for such differences. They challenge our common similarities, as children of one Father, to enlarge the out-reachings of our divine souls.

Faithfully your brethren,
The First Presidency
By Hugh B. Brown
N. Eldon Tanner

7. BLACK LATTER-DAY SAINTS PRESSURE CHURCH LEADERS TO END THE PRIESTHOOD BAN, 1967, 1971.

DOCUMENTS INTRODUCTION

Notwithstanding the LDS church's claim that "we have more to offer the negro than any other church,"[104] black Latter-day Saints often expressed anguish with the priesthood ban.[105] In 1967, David Gillispie, a black man from Ogden, Utah, penned an emotional three-page letter to church president David O. McKay articulating his frustration with the church's racial policies. "I often felt left out because [white men] had the brotherhood of the Priesthood," lamenting that the older he had gotten, the more he "sometimes sensed a feeling of distance on the part" of his friends who did not have the restriction.

Gillispie's frustration increased dramatically during his adolescent years, when his friends were ordained to the Aaronic and Melchizedek Priesthood, allowing them to serve in leadership positions in the church, including that of missionary, one of the pivotal moments in a Mormon male's life.[106] Gillispie's angst continued when he married a Latter-day Saint woman, not in the LDS temple for "time and all eternity," but in a Mormon meetinghouse, where he was married "until death do us part." He expressed his profound anguish to McKay on this point.

Three other factors compounded and added to his growing dissatisfaction. The first occurred when he could not give his newborn son a "father's blessing," the latter performed by a white man who stood in for Gillispie by proxy, giving Gillispie "a feeling of sadness" and "bitterness." The second was when Gillispie's second child died unexpectedly, a tragedy further exacerbated by the Mormon teaching that they could not raise their child in the hereafter, because they had not been "sealed" as a family in the temple. A third factor occurred when the Gillispies's son was baptized knowing that the ban would exclude him from receiving the priesthood.

These factors led Gillispie to pointedly ask McKay whether the ban was "the will of God or the will of man," clearly suggesting that it be lifted. The aging McKay, by then in frail health, did not respond himself, but instructed Gillispie's bishop to do so—to "give [Gillispie] encouragement as [he] deem[ed] appropriate." A. Hamer Reiser, the First Presidency secretary, also reached out to Gillispie, acknowledging receipt of his letter to President McKay but also to express his "deep respect" for the "valiancy" and "faith" of black people in the church.[107]

Other blacks also felt a profound sense of displacement and pressured church leaders to end the ban. In 1971, three black men—Ruffin Bridgeforth, Darius Gray, and Eugene Orr—petitioned church headquarters to form a branch of black Latter-day Saints. Church leaders broached a similar idea in 1955 when Quorum of the Twelve president Joseph Fielding Smith recommended to the First Presidency that "all the Negro members in the [Salt Lake] area be organized into a unit and made a part of one of the stakes of Zion, an independent unit which would function somewhat the same as the Deaf Branch or the Spanish-American Branch." Smith candidly acknowledged that of the "144 Negroes in this area, very few of them are active, undoubtedly because our program has not met their needs."[108]

The First Presidency rejected Smith's proposal, but when Smith became church president in 1970, he later approved the establishment of the "Genesis Group," a black Latter-day Saint support group designed to provide enrichment to black LDS families. The timing was right. Coming on the heels of the BYU athletic protests where the church's racial policies had become a target of intense scorn in the national news media, it was part of a larger church effort to reach out to the black Mormon community and integrate them into "the mainstream of the church."[109] In doing so, church leaders sought to avoid "anything that looks like segregation," not wanting to leave themselves open to criticism in the media. Accordingly, the Genesis Group served as an auxiliary unit to the Liberty Stake in Salt Lake, and met monthly to share testimony and to provide outreach to the black LDS community.[110]

Approximately 200 black Mormons lived in the Salt Lake Valley in 1971 and roughly "70 to 80" took part in the initial Genesis Group meetings.[111] Apostles Gordon B. Hinckley, Thomas S. Monson, and Boyd K. Packer were called to oversee the group and provide edification and instruction. The group convened in 1971 when the apostles called Ruffin Bridgeforth, a forty-nine-year-old truck driver, as president, KSL-TV journalist Darius Gray as first counselor, and Eugene Orr, a University of Utah library employee, as second counselor.[112] Apostle Packer cautioned them to keep a "low profile." He wanted them to avoid talking to the media, asserting that this "was not a tourist attraction." "Things that are young and tender need room to grow," Packer instructed. "Those who don't belong [should] stand back, give them room."[113]

Packer's instruction notwithstanding, the group presidency was emphatic in its desire for priesthood ordination. "Main objective is to get the Priesthood and then do missionary work among the Black both in America and throughout the world," read one account. Another said that the "cards were laid on the table and the Apostles were told that the Blacks in the Church wanted the Priesthood." When pressed, the apostles indicated that on June 24, 1971, "the First Presidency and the Twelve [had] prayed in the Temple about whether Black members... should hold the Priesthood," but the "First Presidency and Twelve were not in agreement on the question." The Genesis presidency said that this "was the first time" that the First Presidency had prayed about the issue in the temple.[114]

The church's refusal to grant blacks the priesthood in 1971 caused friction in the group. Bridgeforth recalled that the group experienced "dissention" and people who were "dissatisfied." "Trying to keep them calm was a constant challenge. We had the general authorities come and speak, but the dissenters would come and try to create problems." He continued: "Some of them would come to the meetings and not make any outright disturbance, but would talk privately to our people. Some, of course[,] were vulnerable" and left the church. Others stayed, though dissatisfied that they could not hold the priesthood.[115]

Dissention in the Genesis Group continued throughout the 1970s. Gray recalled that "one of our members, Gene Orr, was really pressing hard for the priesthood being made available to blacks," characterizing him a "young firebrand." When Spencer W. Kimball lifted the ban in 1978, Hinckley, Monson, and Packer each called Bridgeforth to share the news—perhaps as a gesture of good faith to acknowledge that the group's aspirations for priesthood ordination had been finally granted.[116] After the ban was lifted, the Genesis meetings fizzled for a brief period but then reconvened in the mid-1990s under the leadership of Darius Gray. In 2014 the Genesis Group continues to serve as a support group for "black Latter-day Saints" and "their families and friends."[117]

Included below are excerpts of two interviews that Michael Marquardt conducted with Eugene Orr, an inaugural member of the Genesis Group presidency. Also included is David Gillispie's letter to LDS church president David O. McKay.

DOCUMENTS

From David Gillispie letter to LDS church president David O. McKay, June 4, 1967, box 4, folder 16, John W. Fitzgerald Papers, Special Collections, Merrill-Cazier Library, Utah State University (used by permission of Special Collections, Merrill-Cazier Library, Utah State University); H. Michael Marquardt notes from his interview with Eugene Orr, November 7 and 14, 1971, box 6, folder 3, H. Michael Marquardt Papers, Special Collections, Marriott Library, University of Utah (used by permission of Special Collections, Marriott Library, University of Utah).

a. Letter from David Gillispie to David O. McKay, 1967

Ogden, Utah
June 4, 1967

Dear Beloved, President McKay:

I too, have been born of goodly parents and have been taught to love The Lord and to live as He wants us to. I have spent many wonderful and happy hours attending Sunday School, Primary and other church activities with my friends. There we have been taught of the love of Christ for little children and those who love The Lord. I remember what great joy and happiness filled me when I reached my eighth year and was taken into the waters of baptism. I remember talking with some of my friends, that day, as we waited for it to happen. Some of them expressed fear at the thought of being held under the water, yet I had no such feeling because, I could remember so strongly the teaching of my mother and Sister Wilson, my Primary teacher. They had taught me that Jesus loved me and I knew that if Jesus loved me there was nothing to fear in this whole, wide, wonderful world as long as I loved Him in return.

After my baptism, I remember, I was so happy I thought I heard angels singing. Then, the even more wonderful feeling that came to me as I sat and felt Bishop Jensen's hands on my head as he confirmed me a member of the church and promised me the gift of the Holy Ghost, if I would do what was right in the sight of God. The years that followed have been wonderful and happy ones as I have felt myself grow in the Gospel under the wise teaching of my parents and others.

As I now look back and recall how quick the time passed and I was twelve years old, this age is a mile stone in the life of most Mormon Boys. It is an age when a whole new life begins to open up. I soon passed my twelve year of life, I saw my friends receiving the Aaronic Priesthood and become active in their Deacon's Quorum, but for some reason I was not there with these friends with whom I had enjoyed Primary so much. They were able to learn their new duties in the Church by passing the Sacrament, the emblems of Christ's suffering on the Cross of Crucifixion for me, yet, I couldn't join my friends in this. They were able to bring the

Fast Offerings of the faithful ward members to the Bishop, this I could not do. I could still go to Sunday School and MIA where I joined the Boy Scout Troop and there had the association of my friends.

I saw my friends advancing through the quorums of the Priesthood, learning more ways of service. Although I was in Sunday School and advancing through the ranks of scouting, I often felt left out because they had the brotherhood of the Priesthood. As I grew older I sometimes sensed a feeling of distance on the part of these, my friends, who had been so dear to me in my earlier years.

As the years passed I found myself attending fewer Sunday Schools and MIA meetings. Soon I was nineteen and I saw my lifelong friends being prepared to receive the Melchizedek Priesthood as well as preparing to go on missions for the Church. I sensed disappointment as I realized I could not be a missionary and carry the wonderful knowledge of Christ to others who don't know Him as I had learned to know Him in my childhood.

As these my friends left to serve The Lord as missionaries, I lost my last real ties with the Church and I began drifting away, I seemed to have the feeling that I had reached a spiritual 'dead end.'

I continued my education in college, where I made many new friends. I tried to be active in Institute even as I had been in Seminary, but it all seemed so different. I guess it was because those childhood friends were no longer with me. I found myself associating more and more with young people who did not have the same ideals as my Mormon heritage had given to me. But, at least, there was no gulf between us because I didn't hold the priesthood, since they didn't either. As much as I seemed to enjoy these new found friends, life with them was lacking something. It just wasn't like it used to be when I was active in church.

One day, quite by chance, I met Lisa, a wonderful girl and we seemed to have so much in common. As we got better acquainted we found that both of us had been taught much the same when it came to an understanding of the love of Christ and His great sacrifice made to open the way whereby we can come back into his presence. The months passed and my heart filled with happiness and thanksgiving for having found such a wonderful girl as Lisa. We began to make plans for our marriage. Some of those old friends who had by now returned from their missions and completed a couple of quarters of college work, were also making plans for marriage. But, what different plans they were. Oh, to be sure, we had Bishop Thomas perform our ceremony, but my old friends were taking their brides to the Temple, where dressed in the robes of the Holy Priesthood they were sealed for all time and eternity, by the power and authority of God. Bishop Thomas, by the power invested in him under the laws of the State of Utah married us for 'until death do you part.' Why the difference? I knew because I had been taught that the Temple Sealing is reserved for holders of the Melchizedek Priesthood, and that I did not have.

As my old friends continued to return, Lisa and I renewed old friendships and soon we attended church more frequently. I saw these old friends bearing their testimonies and relating the wonderful experiences of their missions. Their personalities glowed with fine qualities of leadership and I saw them being called to positions in the ward and the stake. On the other hand my spiritual progress seemed slow. At times I seemed to be at a standstill. Lacking the priesthood made it impossible for me to be called to serve in any responsibility of leadership in the Church. Because I was an Eagle Scout I did have an assignment with the Scouts in MIA which brought me great joy.

The day approached when my wonderful and faithful wife, Lisa, gave birth to our first child. After the birth of our son she became very ill. The Elders were called in. They administered to her, while all I could do was stand at the foot of the bed and watch and pray. Because of our faith, the mercy of God and the power of the priesthood, of these friends, exercised in her behalf, she was healed and soon took her place in our home again. She has been the type of mother to our children as mine was to me, teaching them to pray and trust in the Lord.

The day arrived when our first born son, David, was to receive his name and a father's blessing. What a dark cloud seemed to hang over me as I realized I could not give him that blessing reserved for the Priesthood holder. Our wonderful Ward Teacher, Brother Drayton, carried our son to the front of the chapel. In the circle were friends holding my son, and a lifelong friend giving him a Father's blessing by proxy. I was denied the privilege that some fathers have had since the dawn of creation, because I lacked the Holy Priesthood. I could sense, written upon my face, a feeling of sadness and yes, for the first time, some bitterness.

With the passing of time a second child, a beautiful girl, was given to us. She was a lovely child and because of her beauty and cheerful nature many were the friends who sought her companionship as she grew. Little did we realize the short life she was to share with us and others. At the age of six she was suddenly taken from us. A cold chill coursed down my spine as one day my wife said: "We will not be able to raise our little Jill in the hereafter, as will the Randall family who lost their daughter last year." They were sealed in the Temple and their children were sealed to them. Since our marriage will dissolve when we die, we'll not have need for children and our family life.

Nearly eight years have elapsed since our son was born. He is now ready for baptism. He has been faithful in his attendance at Sunday School and Primary, and I see in him a reflection of my own happy childhood. I contemplate and wonder about his future, will it be like mine has been? I find myself praying that he will not lack the blessings of the Priesthood as I have. Again, as it has so many times in the past, my friends will substitute for me in the baptism and confirmation of my son, again I will stand on the outside.

Now, I feel developing within me a spirit of bitterness the likes of which I have never felt before. I find myself on my knees, again and again, asking God to free my soul of this canker. But it persists. I see others who have recently been baptized into the Church, and after a few short weeks receive the Priesthood. Now we have

'Project Temple' organized in our stake and I see men with whom I have worked and associated for years being given special lessons and concessions. Men who have been indifferent to the Church, men who have had their nasty little jokes about the Word of Wisdom, about Tithing and many of the things that have meant so much to me. Men who had received the Priesthood in their youth but who denied its power and through their own ignorance had damned themselves far more than I who had not received the Priesthood. Men, who though they held the Melchizedek Priesthood had thought so little of the women they loved that they denied them the blessings of a Temple Sealing. Yes, and some who had scoffed so much at the Church that they were married by a justice of the peace. Now, I see these men suddenly so swept up in a wave of religious revival that after twelve short weeks of special lessons are to be given the Holy Melchizedek Priesthood and take their wives and children to the Temple where they will be endowed and sealed. This, in spite of my faithfulness, I am denied.

I begin to wonder of the justice of such things and as I wonder the realization strikes me like ten thousand bolts of lightning. I see myself a man, a child of God, one who knows of the great love and mercy of God, one who knows of the great redemptive powers of Jesus Christ, one who knows of the tremendous power embodied in the Holy Priesthood of God. Yes, one who knows that without the Holy Priesthood there can be no Church, nor can man reach perfection, eternal life and Celestial Exaltation.

As these truths dawn on me, even as they have many times before, I find myself shocked out of this nightmarish day dream with the realization that it is not merely a bad dream, but it is the truth. I realize more fully than ever before that as things stand now, I cannot receive the Holy Priesthood nor can my son for we are black, and the blood of Cain courses through and contaminates our mortal bodies. One question stands foremost in my mind, is this the will of God or the will of man?

Sincerely yours,
David Gillispie

b. Michael Marquardt notes from his interview with Eugene Orr, Nov. 7, 1971

[Eugene Orr], Second counselor in the presidency of the Genesis Group of the Liberty Stake of Zion.

[The Genesis Group was] set up for Black missionary work. There are at present about 240 baptized members of the church who are Black. Of these 40 are active. The Group hopes to reactivate Black members in the Salt Lake Area. Main objective is to get the Priesthood and then do missionary work among the Black both in America and throughout the world. The Group couldn't be called a branch but something like an independent branch of the Church. Mention was made of the film *Man's Search for Happiness* with member[s] of the Church who are Black in it. This was made about Jan. 1969. It is now playing at the Visitor's Center on Temple Square in Salt Lake City, Utah.

The Genesis Group meets in the same chapel with the Danish and Norwegian Branches of Liberty Stake. June 24, 1971 was the first time that the First Presidency and the Twelve have prayed in the Temple about whether Black members of the Church should hold the Priesthood. The First Presidency and Twelve were not in agreement on the question. But they did agree that the Genesis Group should be formed.

Concerning the Nigerian Mission: Brother LaMar Williams went to Nigeria and baptized members of the Reorganized Church into the LDS Church. He didn't tell them that they could not hold the Priesthood. About 1,000 joined the Church and Civil War broke out and after the Civil War these members of the Church baptized about 3,000 and they sen[t] their reports to Church headquarters in Salt Lake City, Utah. The total number of members of the LDS Church in Nigeria is about 4,000 (?). They call the Church "The Mormon Church of Nigeria."

Apostles Boyd K. Packer, Thomas S. Monson and Gordon B. Hinckley are in charge of Black members of the Church. Meeting first held June 8, 1971. Mr. Eugene Orr knows a man who is part black who was given special permission by President David O. McKay to be ordained to the Priesthood. Abraham 1:26–27 was discussed but nothing of importance became of it. He said that Ham held the Priesthood and that verses 26 and 27 referred to Pharoah.

c. Michael Marquardt notes from his interview with Eugene Orr, Nov. 14, 1971

We talked for 2.5 hours. A boy David Smith who was part Black was adopted into a family without the parents' knowing it. They were told that he could not hold the Priesthood. They were very disturbed about it and went to President David O. McKay and he gave special permission so that he could be ordained a Deacon. This man, David Smith, is at the present time on a mission for the Church.

Elijah Abel was a member of the 10th Ward. In 1879 the position of the Church that Negroes could not hold the Priesthood was reaffirmed.

Meeting with the Apostles [Thomas S.] Monson, [Gordon B.] Hinckley and [Boyd K.] Packer took place on June 8, 1971 at 8 a.m. The cards were laid on the table and the Apostles were told that the Blacks in the Church wanted the Priesthood. The group fasted and prayed before going and wanted to see the "Prophet" but they were told that the Prophet had appointed the three of them as a committee on the Blacks in the Church.

Eugene Orr rejects the idea that sin was committed in the pre-existence. Through baptism your sins are remitted and yet you are told that you have a sin which was not remitted which was committed before earth life.

We talked on many places of the problem of the Blacks not having the Priesthood.

There are about 3,000 members in Nigeria. The man who incorporated the Church in Nigeria is attending BYU in Provo, Utah. The name of the Church is "The Mormon Church of Nigeria."

Eugene Orr received his patriarchal blessing from Eldred G. Smith. [I]n it he was given no lineage. Later when asked why he was told by Patriarch Smith that the lineage came from him (Patriarch Smith) and that when he receives a burning in his bosom then he knows that it is correct. He was asked—then you denied yourself of the right to receive the burning of the bosom?

Brother Bridgeforth patriarchal blessing said that he was a descendant of Abraham but when it was written down it wasn't included.

Earl Jones who is part Black was ordained a Priest.

John Taylor had a Negro mistress, children might have come from her; also Brigham Young.

We talked about the Book of Abraham in regard to the curse mentioned. Eugene Orr stated that Ham had the Priesthood and that the reason for denial of the Priesthood was idolatry. Abraham 1:26 and mainly verses 27 refer to the Pharaoh.

I [Marquardt] talked about some notes which I had made a number of years ago. Then I showed them some material concerning Elijah Abel and son and grandson: that they held the Priesthood. Finally[,] I showed them a photo of a portrait of Elijah Abel, [and] Mr. and Mrs. Orr [were] very interested in it and expressed that they would like an enlargement to place in the Chapel so that everyone could see what they could achieve—Priesthood!

I thought the meeting was very fruitful and enjoyable.

6

The 1978 Revelation and Its Implications

General Introduction

The decision to lift Mormonism's long-standing priesthood ban has a complicated history. During the 1960s and 1970s, the church faced tremendous pressure from both within and outside of the Mormon community to admit blacks into full fellowship. Indeed, such discussions dominated nearly every public event where high-ranking church leaders appeared. Lawsuits and potential legal action constituted another concern. The church's expanding presence in countries with a significant black population was another factor, particularly in Brazil, where the church had announced a temple in 1975. Likewise, by the late 1960s and early 1970s, scholars began probing the church's racial past, finding contradictory evidence concerning the precise origins of the ban. Finally, the church's genealogy department became overwhelmed with the large number of requests to determine temple and priesthood eligibility for "dark-skinned" converts. All such factors hastened the demise of LDS racial policy by creating a cultural milieu in which the ban could be lifted.[1]

1. LDS SCHOLARS AVER THAT PRIESTHOOD BAN IS A POLICY, NOT A DOCTRINE, 1970, 1973.

DOCUMENT INTRODUCTION

The chances for reversing the ban increased by the early 1970s as liberal LDS scholars effectively questioned its legitimacy as church doctrine. Sociologist Armand Mauss's 1967 pathbreaking study pointed out the speculative nature of the divine curse and the unsustainable proposition that blacks were less valiant in a premortal life.[2] Subsequent writers also rejected such claims, characterizing the church's priesthood ban as a tradition devoid of scriptural support.[3] The carefully documented findings of Stephen Taggart and Lester Bush raised probing ethical and moral questions concerning the ban.

Stephen G. Taggart, a PhD student in sociology at Cornell University and a lifelong Mormon, heightened the controversy with his *Mormonism's Negro Policy: Social and Historical Origins* in 1970—this the most comprehensive work on the topic up to that time. Taggart theorized that the priesthood ban originated in the mid-1830s when Mormons experienced conflict with Missouri residents over slavery. As a slave state, Missourians grew resentful of the Mormons' favorable treatment of blacks—specifically their pro-abolitionist views. Taggart asserted that church founder Joseph Smith implemented a priesthood exclusion policy to appease pro-slavery Missourians.[4]

This policy, in Taggart's words, represented "a historical anachronism—an unfortunate and embarrassing survival of a once expedient institutional practice," given its emergence within the context of sociohistorical conditions in the nineteenth century. Thus Taggart saw priesthood denial not as a doctrinal matter but as a policy that demanded change. Such change, Taggart further averred, need not come by revelatory decree but by simple administrative fiat—which he considered possible if church leaders had the courage to act.[5]

Officials at both Brigham Young University and at LDS church headquarters lambasted Taggart's book. BYU Academic Vice President Robert K. Thomas fumed that Taggart's book "puts himself in a rather long and motley line of those who must find a 'rational' explanation for all Church doctrine and practices."[6] Chauncey C. Riddle, dean of the BYU Graduate School, commented that Taggart "rejects the actuality of direct personal revelation as the basis of Church operation," further asserting that "he rationalizes freely," linking "as fact what can only be pure conjecture." Daniel H. Ludlow, BYU dean of religious instruction, found "Taggart's arguments worthless." He "has absolutely no new information on this aspect of the subject, and he has not used any sources which have not already been published in one form or another."[7]

The book generated animated discussion at the highest levels of church leadership. The First Presidency discussed it in their regular meetings. Doctrinal hardliner and First Presidency counselor Alvin R. Dyer denounced the book as "one of the most vicious, untrue [accounts] that has ever been written about the Church. . . . It was filled with untruths and vilifications." Dyer, moreover, vowed to set the record straight by revealing "what the true facts are." By contrast, counselor Hugh B. Brown, also in the First Presidency, expressed praise for Taggart's meticulous research and careful analysis. He found it a plausible explanation for the underpinnings of the ban, how it was established, and, more clearly, why it should end.[8]

Church president David O. McKay was more circumspect in his response, perhaps due to his increasingly frail health. Nevertheless, he discussed it with his sons, Lawrence and Llewelyn. Of particular interest was Taggart's claim that President

McKay had told University of Utah educator Sterling McMurrin in 1954 that the priesthood ban was a custom and not a doctrine. McKay confirmed the accuracy of Taggart's account, thereby implying that he had sanctioned Taggart's work.[9]

In the meantime, an incensed Alvin Dyer produced a ten-page position paper in which he challenged Taggart's thesis. It was a hastily constructed summary of seminal scriptural passages "for our position with regard to the Negro." Dyer further reported that Brown "had tried twice of late to get President McKay to withdraw the withholding of the Priesthood from the Negro, but President McKay had refused to move on it."[10]

Taggart's book also generated attention in the news media and in scholarly journals. *Salt Lake Tribune* reporter Roger Porter, quoting Taggart, noted that the "weight of the evidence suggests that God did not place a curse upon the Negro— that His white children did."[11] Wallace Turner, in the *New York Times*, observed that "Mr. Taggart's research tends to show that Joseph Smith began his church organization with members drawn from abolitionist country, and so was able to urge equal treatment before God for all mankind in his first writings about Negro slaves."[12]

Strongly critical of Stephen Taggart's book, albeit from a scholarly perspective, was Lester E. Bush, a medical doctor and practicing Mormon whose interest in the black issue developed in the 1960s owing to inconsistent statements by church leaders.[13] Bush's own research into Mormon racial history went further than that of Taggart. Bush, unimpressed with what he felt to be Taggart's superficial research, dismissed Taggart's central argument that Joseph Smith initiated black priesthood denial during the Missouri period in the 1830s. Bush, in fact, had argued that the ban began with Smith's successor, Brigham Young, evident in the fact that Smith had allowed certain black men to be ordained to the priesthood during his lifetime.[14]

Bush developed his arguments further in a seminal article titled "Mormonism's Negro Doctrine: An Historical Overview," published in 1973 in *Dialogue*, an independent Mormon journal. This fifty-seven-page article, with some 219 footnotes, constituted by far the most thorough and comprehensive examination of Mormon racial policy written up to that time. It was, the editors later recalled, "the most important thing ever [published] in *Dialogue*."[15] Bush's article drew heavily upon his massively researched collection in Mormon archives, which he labeled "Compilation on the Negro in Mormonism." This four-hundred-page work contains First Presidency minutes, Quorum of the Twelve meeting minutes, and important published accounts from general authority interviews and writings. In his research, Bush found minimal evidence that priesthood denial resulted from divine revelation.[16] Like Taggart, he ascribed the ban to sociohistorical forces emerging in nineteenth-century America.

Bush made several important points. Joseph Smith, he asserted, had a favorable disposition toward blacks and thereby did not originate the exclusionary policy. He found no evidence linking the church founder to the ban.[17] By contrast, Brigham Young opined that the blacks' lineage through Ham prevented them from priesthood ordination. Bush asserted that Young proposed a ban as early as 1847, which was publicly endorsed by 1852. Subsequent church leaders amplified Young's views by interpreting certain Mormon scripture passages as proof texts denying blacks the priesthood. By the mid-twentieth century, Bush argues, LDS leaders created an additional rationale for the exclusion: blacks lacked moral rectitude in a preexistent life.[18]

When Bush submitted his manuscript to *Dialogue*, the editors immediately recognized its controversial potential. Proceeding with caution, they asked a number of Mormon scholars to submit critiques in an effort to minimize potential repercussions from church leaders. Hugh W. Nibley, a prominent BYU professor and noted scholar, penned "a scriptural and personal response"; Eugene England, a liberal English professor at BYU, provided "a theological interpretation of Bush's findings"; and Gordon C. Thomasson, an independent historian, evaluated it from a historical perspective.[19] Other scholars refused to participate—it was too controversial. Robert Rees, *Dialogue* editor, said that one scholar, popular BYU professor Truman G. Madsen, became "very frightened by the whole thing." Madsen thought that Bush's work "was a tar baby and he didn't want to get stuck."[20]

Church leaders were no less concerned. Upon completing his article, Bush sent a copy to newly called apostle Boyd K. Packer. Packer then alerted his superiors to Bush's study and indirectly implied that he should not publish it, although the apostle did not want to acknowledge that on record.[21] At the same time, BYU Academic Vice President Robert K. Thomas called Rees, informing him that church leaders were incensed with the journal's decision to move ahead with its publication. Thomas feared that such a publication might jeopardize the church's tax exemption status by exposing the church's racial discrimination, particularly in temples "where only whites can attend." Moreover, Thomas feared that the general authorities might seek retribution over the publication—that then church historian "Leonard Arrington would probably lose his job."[22]

Thomas's alarmist assertions shocked Bush. Even so, Bush pushed ahead. Publication of the article in 1973 caught the attention of Mormon leaders. Church president Spencer W. Kimball allegedly "annotated and virtually underlined the entire article in his own copy of *Dialogue*." Upon reading it, apostle Bruce R. McConkie denounced it as "crap." Apostle Mark E. Petersen wanted Bush excommunicated for his controversial views.[23] All the sound and fury notwithstanding, Bush's work "had far more influence than the Brethren would ever acknowledge," one general authority frankly noted years later. "It started to foment the pot."[24]

What follows below are excerpts from the two important works of Stephen G. Taggart and Lester E. Bush challenging the historical and doctrinal legitimacy of the priesthood ban. Both works inspired church president Spencer W. Kimball, albeit indirectly, to end the ban in 1978. As Kimball's son Edward later observed, these "independent scholars had weakened the traditional idea" that the ban was divine in origin. They "cast a shadow on the policy's purported scriptural justifications."[25]

DOCUMENTS

From Stephen G. Taggart, *Mormonism's Negro Policy: Social and Historical Origins* (Salt Lake City: University of Utah Press, 1970), 1–3, 5–8, 11, 43, 76–77, 81–82; Lester E. Bush Jr., "Mormonism's Negro Doctrine: An Historical Overview," *Dialogue: A Journal of Mormon Thought* 8 (Spring 1973): 11–13, 20–23, 25–26, 31, 34–37, 39, 48–49.

a. Taggart, *Mormonism's Negro Policy*, 1970 (excerpts)

The current policy and practice of the Church of Jesus Christ of Latter-day Saints is to withhold the priesthood from Negroes and to exclude them from the essential rites of the temple. The priesthood—conceived by Mormons as the authority to act in God's name—is the prerogative of all male non-Negro members of the Church in good standing, and the temple rites are the privilege, on condition of recommendation, of all non-Negro members in good standing. For a Negro to be denied these means that although he can be a member of the Church, he cannot be a full-fledged participant.

This policy has drawn considerable national attention in recent years, and has become an issue which polarizes the opinions of Church members. Many Mormons can no longer agree with their church on this crucial matter, and some openly declare that Church policy should be changed. Others say that such an attitude is presumptuous and seek justifications for the present Church policy. Despite the increased attention the subject is currently receiving, an important element is still missing from the discussion—an understanding of how the Church Negro policy came into being. The Church has never provided such an explanation, nor is the answer to be found in Mormonism's recorded revelations. The Church appears to be simply perpetuating a precedent of unspecified origin. To settle for no explanation at all is to be stifled into inaction on a subject which cries for a positive and moral resolution. Consequently, this study turns to an examination of Mormonism's social history—particularly the conflicts concerning Negroes and slavery which impinged upon the Church during its formative years—with the hope that the explanation for the present Mormon posture toward Negroes may be discovered in the Church's past experiences. . . .

When the early Saints were called to move to Missouri, they were being called to Zion; an everlasting inheritance was to be purchased. Consequently, when persecution at the hands of Missouri's mobs was imminent, the Saints were threatened with more than just the loss of homes and property. They were threatened with the loss of Zion.

The strength of the Mormon desire to remain in Missouri allows the inference of a willingness on the part of the Church to alleviate, where possible, the conflicts with the old settlers which were threatening to drive the Church from the state. This inference raises two questions: (1) What were the sources of conflict? and (2) What could the Church do to meliorate them?

Three major factors account for the arousal of most of the Missourian hostility: First was the simple demographic fact of rapid Mormon migration into northeastern Missouri.... Second was the rapidly emerging Mormon belief system and its corresponding style of life.... The third factor was the larger sectional conflict between the North and the South over slavery.... Church membership... tended to hold views on the question of slavery which were in opposition to those of the old settlers.

Now that the points of conflict between Mormons and the old settlers have been identified, we must consider what, if anything, could have been done by the Church to meliorate the causes of conflict....

Joseph Smith, concerned for the safety of the Southern membership, appears to have begun informally advising individuals in about 1834 not to ordain Negroes to the priesthood. He appears from all recorded instances to have advised only members who approached him on the subject and who were concerned with the Southern Church...

The present analysis nullifies the underlying assumption of divine origin of this argument by showing that the Negro policy and its attendant teachings all developed on an informal basis in response to historical circumstance rather than through revelation. Mormonism's Negro policy is shown to be a historical anachronism—an unfortunate and embarrassing survival of a once expedient practice....

This conclusion—that the action of social forces explains the present Mormon posture toward Negroes—suggests that Mormonism's practices regarding Negroes should be viewed as matters of policy rather than as points of doctrine....

The weight of the evidence suggests that God did not place a curse upon the Negro—that his white children did. The evidence also suggests that the time for correcting the situation is long past due.

b. Bush, "Mormonism's Negro Doctrine," 1973 (excerpts)

There once was a time, albeit brief, when a "Negro problem" did not exist for The Church of Jesus Christ of Latter-day Saints. During those early months in New York and Ohio no mention was even made of Church attitudes towards blacks. The Gospel was for "all nations, kindreds, tongues and peoples," and no exceptions were made. A Negro, "Black Pete," was among the first converts in Ohio, and his story was prominently reported in the local press. W. W. Phelps opened a mission to Missouri in July, 1831, and preached to "all the families of the earth," specifically mentioning Negroes among his first audience. The following year another black, Elijah Abel, was baptized in Maryland....

The Jackson County experience demonstrated the need for a clear statement of Church policy on slavery. In December, 1833, immediately following the expulsion from Jackson County, Joseph Smith received a revelation that seems to bear directly on this question. In part it declared that "it is not right that any man should be in bondage to another...."

In favoring "equal rights" for Negroes, Joseph Smith did not wish to remove all legal restrictions on that race. Nor should the impression be conveyed that he was completely free of nineteenth century prejudices. The aversion to miscegenation apparent in the articles in 1836 was later incorporated into the laws of Nauvoo; and in the same breath that the Prophet advocated "national equalization" for Negroes, he expressed a desire that they be confined "by strict law to their own species."

In fourteen years Joseph Smith led the Church from seeming neutrality on the slavery issue through a period of anti-abolitionist, pro-slavery sentiment to a final position strongly opposed to slavery. In the process he demonstrated that he shared the common belief that Negroes were descendants of Ham, but ultimately his views reflected a rejection of the notion that this connection justified Negro slavery. There is no contemporary evidence that the Prophet limited priesthood eligibility because of race or biblical lineage; on the contrary, the only definite information presently available reveals that he allowed a black to be ordained an elder, and later a seventy, in the Melchizedek priesthood....

After the Prophet's death, most of his philosophy and teachings were effectively canonized. There was one significant subject on which this does not appear to have been the case—the status of the Negro. A measure of the influence of Joseph Smith's personal presence in shaping early Mormon attitudes on this subject can be obtained by contrasting the Church position prior to his death with the developments which followed....

Though no law authorized or prohibited slavery in Utah, there were slaves in the territory.... In fact the first group of Mormons to enter the Salt Lake valley were accompanied by three Negro "servants." By 1850 nearly 100 blacks had arrived, approximately two thirds of whom were slaves.... The official acceptance of slavery in the Mormon community extended fully to slave owners as well. Bishops, high councilmen, and even an apostle were ordained from their small number....

Though Brigham Young clearly rejected Joseph Smith's manifest belief that the curse on Ham did not justify Negro slavery, possibly an even greater difference of opinion is reflected in the importance Young ascribed to the alleged connection with Cain. "The seed of Ham, which is the seed of Cain descending through Ham, will, according to the curse put upon him, serve his brethren, and be a 'servant of servants' to his fellow creatures, until God removes the curse; and no power can hinder it...."

Brigham Young derived a second far-reaching implication from the genealogy of the Negro. Asked what "chance of redemption there was for the Africans," Young answered that "the curse remained upon them because Cain cut off the lives of Abel.... [T]he Lord had cursed Cain's seed with blackness and prohibited them the Priesthood." The Journal History account of this conversation, dated February 13, 1849, is the earliest record of a Church decision to deny the priesthood to Negroes. At the time practical implications of the decision were limited. Though reliable information is very scanty, there appear to have been very few Negro Mormons in 1849. Only seven of the twenty thus far identified were men, and three of these were slaves; two of the four freemen had already been given the priesthood.

Though Brigham Young reaffirmed his stand on priesthood denial to the Negro on many occasions, by far the most striking of the known statements of his position was included in an address to the Territorial legislature, January 16, 1852. ... In this gubernatorial address, Young appears to both confirm himself as the instigator of the priesthood policy, and to bear testimony to its inspired origin:

> ... any man having one drop of the seed of [Cain] ... in him cannot hold the priesthood and if no other Prophet ever spake it before I will say it now in the name of Jesus Christ I know it is true and others know it ...

This clearly is one of the most important statements in the entire history of this subject....

Through three decades of discourses, Brigham Young never attributed the policy of priesthood denial to Joseph Smith, nor did he cite the Prophet's translation of the Book of Abraham in support of this doctrine. Neither, of course, had he invoked Joseph Smith on the slavery issue. Nor had any other Church leader cited the Prophet in defense of slavery or priesthood denial. It is perhaps not surprising then that shortly after the departure of President Young's authoritative voice, questions arose as to what Joseph Smith had taught concerning the Negro....

When John Taylor assumed the leadership of the Church there was no real question as to the basic Mormon policy towards Negroes. Brigham Young had made it quite clear that blacks, as descendants of Cain, were not entitled to the priesthood. It shortly became apparent, however, that all the related questions had not been resolved. In fact, decisions made during the next four decades were nearly as critical for modern Church Negro policy as those made by Brigham Young....

A second emerging theme can be traced almost in parallel with the beliefs concerning Joseph Smith. Writing in the *Contributor* in 1885, B. H. Roberts had speculated on the background of the priesthood restriction on blacks, and drew heavily on the recently canonized Pearl of Great Price....

How ... was the Pearl of Great Price put to such ready use in defense of the policy of priesthood denial to Negroes? Very simply, the basic belief that a lineage could be traced from Cain through the wife of Ham to the modern Negro had long been accepted by the Church, independently of the Pearl of Great Price. It was a very easy matter to read this belief into that scripture, for if one *assumes* that there was a unique continuous lineage extending from Cain and Ham to the present, and that this is the lineage of the contemporary Negro, then it must have been accomplished essentially as B. H. Roberts proposed. . . .

The most important of the new developments were the incorporation of Joseph Smith and the Pearl of Great Price into the immediate background of the Negro policy. . . .

One additional area of doctrinal import was considered during this period. In spite of Brigham Young's statement to the contrary, the notion that the curse on Negroes was somehow related to their relative neutrality in the War in Heaven had gained in popularity. . . .

Though most studies of the Church's Negro policy ignore the decades from 1880 to 1920, it is apparent that few periods have been as important for modern Church teachings. During this time the Church adjusted to the effective loss of two external rationales for the priesthood policy—the general acceptance of the Negro's biblical lineage and his inherent inferiority. In their place were introduced the much more substantial evidences of the Pearl of Great Price, and the increasing weight . . . of Church rulings that could now be traced through six presidents to the very earliest days of the Restoration. In addition the policy had been elaborated and refined to such a point that no real modifications were felt necessary for nearly fifty years. . . .

Mormon attitudes towards blacks have thus followed an unexpectedly complex evolutionary pattern. When first apparent, these beliefs were sustained by the widely accepted connection of the Negro with Ham and Cain, the acknowledged intellectual and social inferiority of the Negro, his black skin, and the strength of Brigham Young's testimony and/or opinion. With the unanticipated termination of the curse of slavery on Canaan, the death of Brigham Young, increased evidence of Negro capability, and the decline of general support for the traditional genealogy of the blacks, justification of Church policy shifted to the Pearl of Great Price . . . and the belief that the policy could be traced through all the presidents of the Church to the Prophet Joseph Smith. By the middle of the twentieth century little evidence remained for the old concepts of racial inferiority; skin color had also lost its relevance, and the Pearl of Great Price alone was no longer considered a sufficient explanation. Supplementing and eventually surpassing these concepts was the idea that the blacks had somehow performed inadequately in the pre-existence. Most recently all of these explanations have been superseded by the belief that, after all, there is no specific explanation for the priesthood policy. Significantly this progression has not weakened the belief that the policy is justified, for there remains the not inconsiderable evidence of over a century of decisions which have consistently denied the priesthood to blacks. . . .

2. DETERMINING LINEAGE AND BUILDING AN LDS TEMPLE IN BRAZIL PROMPTS THE CHURCH TO CONSIDER ITS PRIESTHOOD BAN, 1975.

DOCUMENT INTRODUCTION

Sustaining the priesthood ban had become more complicated by 1975 when LDS leaders announced a new temple in São Paulo Brazil. Church president Spencer W. Kimball and his counselors were heartened by the groundswell of support among black members in Brazil who had sacrificed their time and resources to help construct the temple—a space traditionally off-limits to black members. Kimball, moreover, was moved by his experiences there over the years in seeing black members remain loyal to the church despite the obvious challenge restricting them from full participation in sacred temple rites.[26]

This matter became particularly acute in the mid-1970s when Kimball met Helvécio Martins, a Brazilian destined to become Mormonism's first black general authority. He was "the strongest negro . . . in the whole church," apostle David B. Haight commented.[27] Martins joined the church in 1972 and had remained faithful even though neither he nor his family could hold the priesthood or experience temple privileges. Indeed, the "Martins family presented an interesting dilemma for Church leaders," Martins's friend Mark Grover candidly explains.

> They completely accepted the Church doctrines, including the restrictions on their activities. They became a model Latter-day Saint family, attending most Church functions and doing all they were asked to do, seemingly without reservations. The Church, thus, was restricting participation not of a poor or uneducated black, but of a family whose education, prestige, administrative ability, and financial standing was higher than most other members of the Church in Brazil. The family had in turn reacted to the restrictions with a level of faith and devotion few members could claim.[28]

Martins's devotion to the church moved Kimball. The priesthood ban concerned the church president when the two of them attended the Brazil temple cornerstone-laying ceremony in 1977. On that occasion, Martins later recalled, Kimball "put his arm around me, looked me straight in the eye, and said, 'Brother Martins, what is necessary for you is fidelity. Remain faithful and you will enjoy all the blessings of the gospel.'" At the end of the ceremony he repeated what he had said earlier: "Don't forget, Brother Martins, don't forget." These words had special meaning for Martins, even if he did not comprehend them at the time—that blacks would soon receive the Mormon priesthood.[29]

The Brazil temple was indeed a transformative event. It "brought the [priesthood ban] to the forefront with considerable urgency," apostle David B. Haight observed.[30] This urgency resulted from the racially mixed population of Brazil, a country that had a long history of interracial marriage between whites and blacks. With a biracial population of nearly 85 percent, the new temple created a dilemma for church leaders: It would be difficult to determine temple eligibility for dark-skinned Brazilians. William Grant Bangerter, an influential mission president in Brazil, and later general authority with administrative oversight in that country, recalled the difficulty of determining ethnic origin. "I learned that it's impossible to tell by observation, or even by trying to establish facts, who had or had not [a black] lineage. The ultimate recourse," he explained, "would be to consider the case carefully and then, if there was no assurance that they had Black lineage, to present the case to the Lord with a request that he would inspire or prompt the conferral of the priesthood. We knew unless He inspired us we [would] inevitably make mistakes."[31]

Determining eligibility in Brazil was painstakingly difficult, often impossible. Bloodlines could not be scientifically evaluated, nor could ancestry be proven with any degree of certainty. Consequently, when LDS officials first sent missionaries to Brazil in the late 1920s, they cautioned missionaries to avoid teaching blacks. For years, leaders had avoided opening a mission there because of the "mixed blood" that dominated much of the population.[32] Initially the missionaries were told only to proselytize among German-speaking peoples in Brazil whose ethnic origin seemed certain. That policy was difficult to maintain, however, when an increasing number of Portuguese-speaking Brazilians became interested in Mormonism. In the 1940s and 1950s the missionaries began teaching and baptizing them, and soon church leaders discovered that missionaries were unwittingly baptizing and conferring priesthood ordination on persons of African lineage. Alarmed at this development, mission president Rulon S. Howells, an early pioneer in establishing LDS racial policy in Brazil, developed a "lineage lesson" to determine ethnicity.[33]

Mormons followed the one-drop rule when determining lineage. Codified into legal doctrine in the United States in the late nineteenth century, both federal and state courts asserted that if someone had one-quarter "negro blood," they were considered of African descent.[34] Howells facilitated the process by developing a mission-wide genealogy lesson instructing missionaries to discreetly evaluate blacks they might teach. In essence, the approach asked missionaries, one scholar has carefully explained, "to scrutinize the color of the skin, eyes, and hair, the shape of the nose and face, color lines on the hands and feet, and the texture of the hair. If the person did not have negroid physical features, the missionaries would try to interest him or her in the Church." If the missionaries were uncertain, they could visit the investigator's "relatives to check the physical appearance of other family members." Above all, if the missionaries detected African ancestry when tracting door-to-door, Howells instructed them to "ask a question where someone else lived so that they wouldn't offend them and try to avoid teaching the gospel to them."[35]

For black Brazilians who insisted on baptism, the missionaries marked their baptismal certificates with a special designation to denote lineage: "B" for black,

"C" for Cain, "N" for negro, or simply "Cain," "blood of Cain," or "seed of Cain."[36] Church policy until the 1950s stipulated that prospective converts had to "trace their genealogy out of the country," but skin color or other characteristics were not disqualifying factors for priesthood office—only lineage through African bloodlines.[37]

Determining lineage became slightly less complicated in the 1950s when the First Presidency amended the policy by stipulating that dark-skinned persons did not have to prove their lineage to hold the priesthood. They could be denied the priesthood only if it was accepted that they were of African descent.[38] When ethnicity could not be resolved by the mission president, the First Presidency intervened, and its judgments were final. This policy came to an end in early 1978 prior to the lifting of the priesthood ban when the First Presidency and the genealogical department of the church became overwhelmed with the sheer number of requests on the subject. That year leaders decided to push the decision making back to the local leaders, where they would determine the racial origins of prospective converts and therefore priesthood and temple eligibility.[39]

The lineage lesson included here became the standard practice in Brazil until LDS leaders granted priesthood privileges to black men in 1978. The announcement of the temple in São Paulo, and the corresponding difficulty of determining racial origins, constituted powerful factors in Spencer W. Kimball's decision to end the ban.

DOCUMENT

From "Lineage Lesson," Brazil North Mission, 1970, LDS Church History Library, Salt Lake City, Utah (excerpts).

... And still today, Brother Nunes,[40] why do all men have to be called by revelation to receive the priesthood?

-Response-

4. A man must be called by God through revelation to receive the priesthood. As you already know, worthy men in the Church after 12 years of age are called to receive the priesthood. And by what principle are they called?

-Response-

If a man was called by inspiration to receive the priesthood, should he accept this call?

-Response-

If you are called by a servant of God to receive the priesthood, will you accept this responsibility and blessing?

-Response-

5. If I am called I will accept the priesthood. Anciently, it was revealed who could receive the priesthood. We already read about Barnabas, Paul, and Aaron. It was also revealed who could not receive the priesthood. Would you like to read in the

book of Abraham 1:26–27? [Mormon scripture - not in the Bible] What does verse 27 say about Pharaoh and the priesthood.

-Response-

Exactly, Brother Nunes. Pharaoh was a descendant of people who could not receive the priesthood. Let's examine this lineage to learn its origin. Are you acquainted with the story of Abel and Cain?

-Response-

Let's read this story in the Bible. Read Genesis 4:8–15. Cain and his descendants received a mark that distinguished them from all other peoples. This people, the descendants of Cain, for reasons not completely known to men, do not have the right to the priesthood. For example, it was revealed to Abraham that Pharaoh, being from this so called lineage of Cain, could not receive the priesthood. Brother Nunes, we have seen that Aaron, Barnabas, Paul, and others receive the priesthood because they were called by God by revelation. In the same manner, why have the prophets not given the priesthood to the lineage of Cain?

-Response-

In order to understand the mark put on Cain and to understand how the prophets distinguish this lineage, lets read Moses 7:22. "Moses 7:22 And Enoch also beheld the residue of the people which were the sons of Adam; and they were a mixture of all the seed of Adam save it was the seed of Cain, for the seed of Cain were black, and had not place among them." How was this lineage distinguished from the others?

-Response-

And concerning the priesthood, why was this group or this lineage different?
-Response-

6. God revealed anciently that the lineage of Cain could not receive the priesthood. In order to understand what God revealed about this people today, we need to go to the modern prophets. Do you want to read the underlined part of this pamphlet? Read the following part from the letter of the First Presidency published in the Priesthood Bulletin. Vol6. No. 1 - February 1970. Since the beginning of this dispensation, Joseph Smith and all of the successive presidents of the Church have taught that the Negroes, while spiritual children of a common Father, and descendants of our earthly parents Adam and Eve, still cannot receive the Priesthood, for reasons that we believe are known to God, but which He has not made completely known to men. What does this say there about the Negroes and the priesthood?

-Response-

Exactly. Negroes that honestly seek the truth and desire to join the church can be baptized. However, why does the Church not confer the Priesthood on them?
-Response-

7. God revealed that Negroes still cannot receive the priesthood. For this reason the [gospel] is not actively preached to the lineage of Cain. The prophets have told

us to preach the gospel to those that have the right to the priesthood. But let's read what God said about the Negroes in the future. Read the following paragraph from the letter of the First Presidency: President McKay also said that One day in the eternal plan of God, the Negro will be given the right to possess the Priesthood. What did the prophet say about the Negroes and the priesthood?

-Response I know that this is true. And when that time comes, how will we know?

-Response-

8. In the future when it is revealed by God, Negroes will receive the priesthood. Do you accept the teaching that God revealed his will concerning his priesthood to his prophets, Mr. Nunes?

-Response-

Good, I know that this is the truth and that God really guides and directs the Church through modern revelation. Now, Mr. Nunes, do you know if any of your ancestors were Negro or descendants of Negroes?

-Response-

If in the future you discover that one of your ancestors was Negro will you tell your Branch President?

-Response-

If this happened do you think you would remain firm and faithful to the church and your covenants with God?

-Response-

end of lesson

3. LDS FIRST PRESIDENCY "OFFICIAL DECLARATION 2," EXTENDING PRIESTHOOD BLESSINGS TO BLACK MALE MEMBERS OF THE CHURCH, 1978.

DOCUMENT INTRODUCTION

One of the most important events in LDS history occurred in June of 1978 when Spencer W. Kimball announced that black men could hold the Mormon priesthood. This announcement issued in response to the purported revelation constituted a profound policy change. It ended a 126-year-old ban that had restricted persons of African descent from full activity in the Mormon church. Black men could now serve in leadership positions, perform temple rituals, and otherwise serve without restriction in the church. Moreover, LDS officials believed that lifting the ban would accelerate the church's missionary program, especially in cities and nations with significant black populations.[41]

Several events prompted this momentous change.[42] The seminal historical studies of Stephen G. Taggart and Lester E. Bush impressed general authorities with the undeniable fact that priesthood denial was based on a tradition and *not* essential doctrine—thus by implication could be changed. Moreover, the announcement of the Brazil temple in 1975 demonstrated to church leaders the complication of maintaining a racially exclusive policy in a country with a significant biracial population. Thus the Brazil temple created a perplexing dilemma for leaders attempting to determine temple eligibility among dark-skinned Brazilian Mormons.[43] Other factors contributed to the revelation. The First Presidency, besieged with requests from local leaders about how to determine the ethnic origins of prospective converts, became overwhelmed with the sheer volume of such queries. The requests became so intense by the spring of 1978 that the First Presidency transferred the responsibility to stake and ward mission leaders to determine eligibility.[44] Church leaders, moreover, instructed mission presidents, bishops, and stake presidents not to deny men the priesthood based on appearance. "If there is no evidence to indicate that a man has Negro blood," the First Presidency explained in a letter, "you would not be justified in withholding the priesthood and temple blessings from him." This policy change constituted an enormous step toward ending the ban.[45]

In the mid-1970s, potential lawsuits created another problem for LDS officials. In 1974 the NAACP challenged Mormon racial teachings in a lawsuit against the Boy Scouts of America.[46] While the church was not a direct party to the suit, LDS officials feared that the case could have far-reaching implications for the church's racial policy. The church denied an African American boy in an LDS troop the opportunity to serve as a senior patrol leader—a position reserved for the deacon's quorum president, an Aaronic priesthood holder. When the boy's family threatened a lawsuit with the NAACP claiming discrimination, Spencer Kimball, as church president, was subpoenaed. Kimball's longtime secretary, Francis Gibbons, recalled that the subpoena instructed Kimball "to bring to the deposition every document relating to the Church's policy withholding the priesthood to blacks."[47] The court dismissed the case when LDS officials changed the policy, no longer requiring a deacon's quorum president to serve as the patrol leader. This resolution brought closure to a potentially damaging lawsuit and ended an affair that had "dominated" Kimball's "thoughts" for months.[48]

The Internal Revenue Service also played a role in the timing of the revelation, as did a potential threat from the American Bar Association to not accredit BYU's fledgling law school. Specifically, the Mormon hierarchy became concerned about potential lawsuits over their tax exemption status, particularly in light of the student protests against BYU in the late 1960s and early 1970s. They had watched very closely the Bob Jones University case, in which the IRS revoked its tax exemption status in an important 1975 ruling.[49] The IRS determined that Bob Jones's discrimination against African Americans, particularly the school's prohibition against interracial marriage, had violated Title VII of the Civil Rights Act of 1964.[50] In addition, state policies worried Mormon officials. "Various states," LDS church historian Leonard Arrington observed in 1978, refused "to exempt Church property, including temples and chapels and stake houses, from taxation on the grounds that the church discriminates against blacks. This has already been done by Wisconsin, was being considered in Hawaii, and plans were being made to take the case to other states." He extrapolated that the threat of removing the church's tax exemption status constituted one of the reasons "why the Lord might have permitted the announcement at this particular moment."[51]

Similarly, the J. Reuben Clark Law School at BYU came under assault in 1975 when law school officials received a troubling letter from the American Bar Association indicating that its accreditation was in jeopardy owing to the church's "discriminatory" racial policies. Though the ABA eventually granted accreditation, then BYU president and later LDS apostle Dallin H. Oaks remarked that it was a miracle. "I marvel at our overcoming authorities' reservations about approving a new law school . . . whose sponsoring Church did not yet extend the blessings of holding its priesthood to all worthy male Church members."[52]

Furthermore, LDS racial policy affected the church abroad. Internationally, the church faced the threat of expulsion from governments that disagreed with the church's racial policies. In 1976, a lawsuit in Costa Rica concerned church leaders when a black lawyer tried to disenfranchise the church there, stating that LDS officials had violated laws by racially profiling potential converts. Edward Kimball, Spencer Kimball's son, remarked "the man was offended by the missionaries' use of a 'genealogical survey' as a technique for ascertaining whether contacts had Negroid ancestry." The church promptly sent attorney F. Burton Howard to assure government officials that the church did not discriminate against people of African descent.[53]

Finally, two high-profile protests affected church officials and laid a foundation for the end of the priesthood ban. Douglass Wallace, a Mormon lawyer from Vancouver, Washington, became so disillusioned with Mormon racial policy in 1976 that in protest he baptized, then subsequently ordained, a black man to the Mormon priesthood—a move church officials promptly invalidated. Wallace hoped "to force a revision in Mormon doctrine about the Negro race."[54] Undeterred, in the wake of his excommunication, Wallace further protested at general conference in 1976 by storming down the aisle with two associates chanting "Make way for the Lord!" "Don't touch the Lord!" When security guards ushered them out of the Tabernacle, he and his associates told reporters that they wanted to put Kimball "on trial" for "imposing" an unjust racial policy on the church. The church banned Wallace from Temple Square and subsequent general conferences. President Kimball had had a restraining order placed on Wallace to prevent further harassment.[55]

A second Mormon dissident, Byron Marchant, further antagonized LDS officials by opposing the Mormon leader in the 1977 general conference as the church's "prophet, seer, and revelator"—angry over Kimball's perceived racist tendencies.

LDS officials promptly fired Marchant from his job as a church janitor, then excommunicated him. When Marchant tried to distribute literature at Temple Square during the April 1978 general conference, security arrested him for trespassing. In protest, he filed a civil suit against Kimball for failing to appear before a church-sanctioned court to discuss race issues. Marchant dropped the charge when Kimball, weeks later, lifted the priesthood ban.[56]

Combined, these events affected Kimball's decision to lift the ban. All such events, moreover, created a legal and social environment where the Mormon leader could begin asking questions about the propriety of the ban. Of course, Kimball was not the first LDS president to "worry about the priesthood question," one supporter opined, "but he had the compassion to pursue it and a boldness that allowed him to act, to get the revelation."[57]

On June 1, 1978, Kimball reversed the priesthood restriction when he and his two counselors, along with members of the Quorum of the Twelve Apostles, experienced what they believed was a divine epiphany during a special prayer session in the Salt Lake temple. On that historic occasion, the Mormon leadership removed all barriers to priesthood eligibility for black men, allowing "every faithful, worthy man in the Church" to "receive the holy priesthood." The revelation further stipulated that black men and women could experience "the blessings of the temple." The First Presidency announced the doctrinal change through a letter, disseminated to news outlets and various wire services a week after the revelation.[58]

The letter appended below was ratified at the October 1978 general conference by the general body of the church. It became canonized in LDS scripture as "Official Declaration 2" in the 1981 edition of the *Doctrine and Covenants*.

DOCUMENT

From "Official Declaration 2," *Doctrine and Covenants* (Salt Lake City: Church of Jesus Christ of Latter-day Saints, 1981), 293–294.

June 8, 1978

To all general and local priesthood officers of The Church of Jesus Christ of Latter-day Saints throughout the world:

Dear Brethren:

As we have witnessed the expansion of the work of the Lord over the earth, we have been grateful that people of many nations have responded to the message of the restored gospel, and have joined the Church in ever-increasing numbers. This, in turn, has inspired us with a desire to extend to every worthy member of the Church all of the privileges and blessings which the gospel affords.

Aware of the promises made by the prophets and presidents of the Church who have preceded us that at some time, in God's eternal plan, all of our brethren who are worthy may receive the priesthood, and witnessing the faithfulness of those from whom the priesthood has been withheld, we have pleaded long and earnestly in behalf of these, our faithful brethren, spending many hours in the Upper Room of the Temple supplicating the Lord for divine guidance.

He has heard our prayers, and by revelation has confirmed that the long-promised day has come when every faithful, worthy man in the Church may receive the holy priesthood, with power to exercise its divine authority, and enjoy with his loved ones every blessing that flows therefrom, including the blessings of the temple. Accordingly, all worthy male members of the Church may be ordained to the priesthood without regard for race or color. Priesthood leaders are instructed to follow the policy of carefully interviewing all candidates for ordination to either the Aaronic or the Melchizedek Priesthood to insure that they meet the established standards for worthiness.

We declare with soberness that the Lord has now made known his will for the blessing of all his children throughout the earth who will hearken to the voice of his authorized servants, and prepare themselves to receive every blessing of the gospel.

Sincerely yours,
Spencer W. Kimball
N. Eldon Tanner
Marion G. Romney
The First Presidency

Recognizing Spencer W. Kimball as the prophet, seer, and revelator, and president of The Church of Jesus Christ of Latter-day Saints, it is proposed that we as a constituent assembly accept this revelation as the word and will of the Lord. All in favor please signify by raising your right hand. Any opposed by the same sign.

The vote to sustain the foregoing motion was unanimous in the affirmative.
Salt Lake City, Utah, September 30, 1978.

4. LDS CHURCH STATEMENT DISCOURAGING INTERRACIAL MARRIAGE, ISSUED CONCURRENTLY WITH OFFICIAL DECLARATION 2, 1978.

One of the underlying forces behind the church's support of segregation policies in Utah and the United States in the 1950s and 1960s was interracial marriage. The Mormon hierarchy feared that if segregation laws ended whites and blacks would mix and thereby marry. Adhering to a theology of racial superiority that emphasized "chosen" lineages over "cursed" ones, LDS leaders therefore supported national and state laws that supported separating the races.[59] The church's position on miscegenation became somewhat fuzzy after the civil rights era ended in the early 1970s. Even today, the church's position remains ambiguous. On the one hand, general authorities claim they do not oppose interracial marriages; on the other hand, they still reprint old talks in their current manuals discouraging the practice.[60]

The lines became blurred in 1978 when the church lifted its restriction barring blacks from the priesthood. This now meant that worthy black men could receive the priesthood and enjoy the highest rituals of the Mormon church. They could serve in leadership positions, perform baptismal rites, and marry in the temple, the highest expression of Mormon piety. But when the church lifted the priesthood ban in 1978, Mormon officials also reaffirmed their opposition to interracial marriage—primarily at the insistence of apostle Mark Petersen,[61] author of the controversial talk on segregation discussed in chapter 5.

The LDS *Church News* announced the new revelation on the priesthood in its June 17, 1978, edition. It stated that "all worthy men," including those of African descent, could now receive the Priesthood. But it also included an accompanying section that said "Interracial Marriage Discouraged."[62] For most of the twentieth century, church leaders opposed interracial marriage. First Presidency counselor J. Reuben Clark published an address in the church's *Improvement Era* in 1946 calling interracial marriage a "wicked virus," admonishing members not to "mix races."[63] A year later the First Presidency, consisting of George Albert Smith, J. Reuben Clark, and David O. McKay, declared that "intermarriage of the Negro and White races" has been "repugnant to most normal-minded people," and they warned that "social intercourse between the Whites and Negroes should . . . not be encouraged because of leading to intermarriage, which the Lord has forbidden."[64] In 1961, David O. McKay, then church president, stated "that we do not welcome negroes into our social affairs because if we did it would lead to inter-marriage, and we do not favor inter-marriage. We recommend negroes marry negroes, and that whites marry whites, and we cannot modify the statement. We object to negroes marrying whites for their own happiness. We cannot change our attitude until we receive a revelation from the Lord directing otherwise."[65]

Interracial marriage had been strongly condemned by church spokesmen since the days of Brigham Young. In 1852, the Mormon prophet had denounced the "evils" of interracial relationships, calling them a "curse."[66] Young's influence led the Utah territorial legislature to outlaw interracial sex in 1852 and interracial marriage in 1888. The legislature repealed such laws in 1963, when at least a dozen other states abolished their antimiscegenation laws because of pressure from civil rights leaders.[67] In 1967, the Supreme Court struck the final blow to antimiscegenation laws when it declared them unconstitutional in *Loving v. Virginia*.[68] Though church officials remained silent on the Court's decision, the Mormon hierarchy continued discouraging the practice, albeit with a modified tone. By the 1960s, at the height of the civil rights movement, church authorities no longer taught that interracial marriage was "forbidden," as they had in earlier years. Still, they continued to preach against it in their writings and teachings.

The church's *General Handbook of Instructions*, published in 1968, urged religious educators to counsel students to "marry within their own faith and within their own race."⁶⁹ Apostle Spencer W. Kimball gave a series of talks to BYU students imploring them to not "cross racial lines in dating and marrying." In 1976, Kimball, now the church president, averred that "people [should] marry those who are of the same racial background" and "above all the same religious background."⁷⁰ A year later, in a speech to BYU students, apostle Boyd K. Packer reiterated Kimball's remarks. The counsel put black Mormons in a precarious position because there were few blacks in the church.⁷¹

Consequently, when the *Church News* published the proviso discouraging interracial marriage it touched a raw nerve with some black Mormons. Many became confused at the mixed message—that they could now worship with whites in the temple but could not marry them. Furthermore, even though church spokesman Don LeFevre emphatically stated in 1978 that there was "no ban on interracial marriage," some church leaders still objected to the practice.⁷² That same year apostle Packer told a black man that he "could accomplish [his] mission in life and be more effective without being married to a white woman." In 1979, apostle Bruce R. McConkie revised *Mormon Doctrine* and included a passage that was not in previous editions. "Interracial marriages," he explained, "are discouraged by the brethren."⁷³ At the same time church president Spencer W. Kimball met with black members and told them that while church leaders "counsel against" mixed marriages, they do so "because of the problems the *children* could face." He added: "As far as its being incompatible with the Lord's gospel or with your Father in Heaven it is not."⁷⁴

What follows below are excerpts from Spencer W. Kimball's speeches and writings the *Church News* published in 1978 under the headline "Interracial Marriage Discouraged."

DOCUMENT

From "Interracial Marriage Discouraged," *Church News* supplement to *Deseret News*, June 17, 1978, p. 4 (excerpts).

Speaking to Indian Students at Brigham Young University on January 5, 1965, President Kimball, as a member of the Council of the Twelve, said:

"Now, the brethren feel that it is not the wisest thing to cross racial lines in dating and marrying. . . . Marriage is a very difficult thing under any circumstances and the difficulty increases in interrace marriages."

Addressing a Brigham Young University devotional on September 7, 1976, President Kimball counseled students:

"We are grateful that this one survey reveals that about 90 percent of the temple marriages hold fast. Because of this, we recommend that people marry those who are of the same racial background generally, and of somewhat the same economic and social educational background (some of those are not an absolute necessity, but preferred), and above all, the same religious background, without question."[75]

5. APOSTLES LEGRAND RICHARDS AND BRUCE R. MCCONKIE RECOUNT THE CIRCUMSTANCES SURROUNDING THE REVELATION ENDING THE PRIESTHOOD BAN, 1978.

DOCUMENT INTRODUCTION

Announcement of the priesthood revelation was a joyous occasion for most Mormons. Dozens of people wrote President Kimball expressing gratitude for ending the ban. Mormon intellectuals and journalists congratulated him for creating new doctrine. Even then president Jimmy Carter sent him a warm telegram extolling the church leader's courage and compassion.[76] A few hardline Mormons were angry, though, and in fact left the church in protest. A fundamentalist Mormon group published a full-page ad in the *Salt Lake Tribune* with the headline "LDS Soon to Repudiate a Portion of Their Pearl of Great Price."[77] For them, Kimball's revelation seemed to contradict past practice and doctrine as revealed in Mormon scripture. On the other hand, some black Utahns were less than impressed with the lifting of the ban. When asked about it one African American promptly responded, "I'll thank Spencer Kimball when he announces he has had a revelation that Mormons will not practice racial hiring. Then I will be elated."[78]

Despite these differing reactions, most Latter-day Saints welcomed the change. "The announcement was generally well received among Mormons," one newspaper stated.[79] Invariably, some Latter-day Saints had a difficult time understanding the implications of the policy change, wondering if the "curse" had been removed and if the racist language manifested in Mormon scripture still applied. The revelation was silent on these points. So too were the apostles' explanations of the events of June 1. Even so, they produced several testimonials explaining what happened. The most popular accounts were those of apostles LeGrand Richards and Bruce R. McConkie, both of whom asserted that the revelation constituted the most transcendent epiphany they had ever experienced.[80]

The LDS hierarchy never affirmed the validity of Richards's account, although it had received wide circulation among the LDS rank-and-file. For Richards, who was born in 1886 in Farmington, Utah, and served as an apostle from 1952 until his death in 1983,[81] the account appeared in the form of an interview with Chris Vlachos, a Christian missionary in Utah, and Wesley Walters, a Christian minister who lived in Arizona. On August 16, 1978, just two months after the revelation, the pair met with Richards in his office at LDS church headquarters to get his version of the "Negro revelation," as Vlachos put it.[82]

The voluble Mormon apostle, who was in his nineties at the time, explained why the revelation occurred and how it came about. "Down there in Brazil," he affirmed, "there is so much Negro blood in the population there that it's hard to get leaders that don't have Negro blood in them. We just built a temple down there. It's going to be dedicated in October." When Walters asked him if the revelation "brought any new insights or new ways of looking at the *Book of Abraham*," Richards sidestepped the question, positing that if black Mormons lived pious lives they would be entitled to "their blessings." On the linkage to blacks in a pre-earth life, Richard explained that "the Brethren decided that we should never say that. We just don't know what the reason was" for the priesthood ban.[83]

The interview lasted about thirty minutes. When it concluded, Richards agreed to let Vlachos and Walters share his insights with friends. A few weeks later, the pair sent a copy of the transcript to Richards so that he could validate it, to secure his approval for distribution among the other general authorities. They wanted to "confront them with Richards' version of events" and check for discrepancies, they explained to a friend.[84] In a follow-up letter Richards validated the transcript, but it was evident he was not happy with the fact that Vlachos and Walters had recorded the interview with neither Richards's knowledge nor consent. When Vlachos responded that the transcript would just be made for private use, the suspicious apostle wrote back and agreed as long as it would not be for "public purposes." The men ignored his wishes and published a version of the interview in an Arizona publication, much to Richards's dismay.[85]

A more authoritative statement on the priesthood revelation came from apostle Bruce R. McConkie, whose address to seminary and institute teachers on August 18, 1978, came just two days after the Richards interview and some two and a half months after the priesthood revelation. McConkie's talk "All Are Alike unto God" became a classic in Mormon circles. In 1981, the church's publishing house, Deseret Book, republished it as "The New Revelation on the Priesthood" in a volume entitled *Priesthood*.[86] Mormons accorded it a quasi-canonical status, citing it in church meetings, media interviews, and in LDS manuals and symposiums where leaders discussed the revelation of 1978.[87]

"I was present when the Lord revealed to President Spencer W. Kimball that the time had come . . . to offer the fullness of the gospel and the blessings of the holy priesthood to all men," McConkie explained. "I was present, with my brethren of the Twelve and the counselors in the First Presidency, when all of us heard the same voice and received the same message from on high."[88] For McConkie, the revelation marked something of a "day of Pentecost" akin to the dedication of the Kirkland Temple, when angels and heavenly visitors were reported to have the temple with blessings. The apostle noted that all of those present in the Salt Lake Temple experienced something similar. "We heard the same voice" and knew that it was indeed a divine manifestation from God. "The ancient curse is no more," McConkie opined. "The seed of Cain and Ham and Canaan and Egyptus and Pharoah—all these now have the power to rise up and bless Abraham as their father."[89]

In an oft-quoted passage, McConkie cautioned inquirers that they should forget "everything that I have said, or what President Brigham Young or President George Q. Cannon or whosoever has said in days past that is contrary to the present revelation. We spoke with a limited understanding and without the light and knowledge that now has come into the world."[90] McConkie's mea culpa appeared a retraction of past practice and doctrine. However, as LDS sociologist and scholar of Mormon race relations Armand Mauss avers, "any but the most superficial reading of this speech [indicates] that it is in no way intended as a repudiation of all previous doctrine and policy relating to black members. Rather, it is primarily an argument that God bestows rights and blessings differentially on different peoples and that those of African lineage simply got their 'turn' at the priesthood sooner than expected. McConkie's later writings," Mauss concluded, "including even later editions of his *Mormon Doctrine*, continued to perpetuate all the other racial doctrines common in the Mormon heritage."[91]

What follows below are excerpts from apostles Richards and McConkie detailing the circumstances of the 1978 revelation on the priesthood. Even today, nearly four decades after the event, these accounts still constitute the richest, fullest, and most authoritative statements concerning the circumstances relative to lifting the ban.

DOCUMENTS

From LeGrand Richards's interview with Wesley P. Walters and Chris Vlachos, August 16, 1978, transcript in LDS Church History Library, Salt Lake City, Utah; Bruce R. McConkie, "The New Revelation on Priesthood," in (unknown editor) *Priesthood* (Salt Lake City: Deseret Book, 1981), 126, 128, 131–132, 133–134.

a. LeGrand Richards interview with Wesley P. Walters and Chris Vlachos, 1978 (excerpts)

WALTERS: On this revelation, of the priesthood to the Negro, I've heard all kinds of stories: I've heard that Joseph Smith appeared; and then I heard another story that Spencer Kimball had had a concern about this for some time, and simply shared it with the apostles, and they decided that this was the right time to move in that direction. Are any of those stories true, or are they all?

RICHARDS: Well, the last one is pretty true, and I might tell you what provoked it in a way. Down in Brazil, there is so much Negro blood in the population there that it's hard to get leaders that don't have Negro blood in them. We just built a temple down there. It's going to be dedicated in October. All those people with Negro blood in them have been raising the money to build that temple. If we don't change, then they can't even use it. Well, Brother Kimball worried about it, and he prayed a lot about it.

He asked each one of us of the Twelve if we would pray - and we did - that the Lord would give him the inspiration to know what the will of the Lord was. Then he invited each one of us in his office - individually, because you know when you are in a group, you can't always express everything that's in your heart. You're part of the group, you see - so he interviewed each one of us, personally, to see how we felt about it, and he asked us to pray about it. Then he asked each one of us to hand in all the references we had, for, or against that proposal. See, he was thinking favorably toward giving the colored people the priesthood.

Then we had a meeting where we meet every week in the temple, and we discussed it as a group together, and then we prayed about it in our prayer circle, and then we held another prayer circle after the close of that meeting, and he (President Kimball) led in the prayer; praying that the Lord would give us the inspiration that we needed to do the thing that would be pleasing to Him and for the blessing of His children. And then the next Thursday - we meet every Thursday - the Presidency came with this little document written out to make the announcement - to see how we'd feel about it - and present it in written form....

WALTERS: Will this [revelation] affect your theological thinking about the Negro as being less valiant in the previous existence? How does this relate? Have you thought that through?

RICHARDS: Some time ago, the Brethren decided that we should never say that. We don't know just what the reason was.... [God] knows why they were born with black skin or white and so on.... We'll just have to wait and find out.

WALTERS: Is there still a tendency to feel that people are born with black skin because of some previous situation, or do we consider that black skin is no sign anymore of anything inferior in any sense of the word?

RICHARDS: Well, we don't want to get that as a doctrine. Think of it as you will. You know, Paul said "Now we see in part and we know in part; we see through a glass darkly. When that which is perfect is come, then that which is in part shall be done away, then we will see as we are seen, and know as we are known." Now the Church's attitude today is to prefer to leave it until we know. The Lord has never indicated that black skin came because of being less faithful. Now, the Indian; we know why he was changed, don't we? The Book of Mormon tells us that; and he has a dark skin, but he has a promise there that through faithfulness, that they all again become a white and delightsome people. So we haven't anything like that on the colored thing.

WALTERS: Now, with this new revelation - has it brought any new insights or new ways of looking at the Book of Abraham? Because I think traditionally it is thought of the curse of Cain, coming through Canaanites and on the black-skinned people, and therefore denying the priesthood?

RICHARDS: We considered that with all the "for's" and the "against's" and decided that with all of that, if they lived their lives, and did the work, that they were entitled to their blessings.

WALTERS: But you haven't come up with any new understanding of the Book of Abraham? I just wondered whether there would be a shift in that direction. Is the recent revelation in harmony with what the past prophets have taught, of when the Negro would receive the priesthood?

RICHARDS: Well, they have held out the thought that they would ultimately get the priesthood, but they never determined the time for it. And so when this situation that we faced down there in Brazil - Brother Kimball worried a lot about it - how the people are so faithful and devoted. The president of the Relief Society of the stake is a colored woman down there in one of the stakes. If they do the work, why it seems like that the justice of the Lord would approve of giving them the blessing. Now it's all conditional upon the life that they live, isn't it?

WALTERS: Well, I thank you for clarifying that for me, because you know, out in the streets out there, there must be at least five, ten different stories about the way this happened.

RICHARDS: Well, I've told you exactly what happened.

WALTERS: Right. Well, thank you so much. I appreciate it.

RICHARDS: If you quote me you will be telling the truth.

WALTERS: Ok, well fine. You don't mind if we quote you then?

RICHARDS: No.

WALTERS: Ok, that's great!

b. Bruce R. McConkie's address to Seminary and Institute personnel, 1978 (excerpts)

I was present when the Lord revealed to President Spencer W. Kimball that the time had come . . . to offer the fullness of the gospel and the blessings of the holy priesthood to all men.

I was present, with my brethren of the Twelve and the counselors in the First Presidency, when all of us heard the same voice and received the same message from on high.

It was on a glorious June day in 1978. All of us were together in the upper room in the Salt Lake Temple. We were engaged in fervent prayer, pleading with the Lord to manifest his mind and will concerning those who are entitled to receive his holy priesthood. President Kimball himself was mouth, offering the desires of his heart and of our hearts to that God whose servants we are. . . .

It was during this prayer that the revelation came. The Spirit of the Lord rested mightily upon us all; we felt something akin to what happened on the day of Pentecost and at the dedication of the Kirkland Temple. From the midst of eternity, the voice of God, conveyed by the power of the Spirit, spoke to his prophet. The message was that the time had now come to offer the fullness of the everlasting gospel, including celestial marriage, and the priesthood, and the blessings of the temple, to all men, without reference to race or color, solely on the basis of personal worthiness. And we all heard the same voice, received the same message, and became personal witnesses that the word received was the mind and will and voice of the Lord.

President Kimball's prayer was answered and our prayers were answered. He heard the voice and we heard the same voice. All doubt and uncertainty fled. He knew the answer and we knew the answer. . . .

The ancient curse is no more. The seed of Cain and Ham and Canaan and Egyptus and Pharaoh—all these now have the power to rise up and bless Abraham as their father. All these, gentile in lineage, may now come and inherit by adoption all the blessings of Abraham, Isaac, and Jacob. . . .

There are statements in our literature by the early brethren which we have interpreted to mean that the Negroes would not receive the priesthood in mortality. I have said the same things, and people write me letters and say, "You said such and such, and how is it now that we do such and such?" And all I can say to that is that it is time disbelieving people repented and got in line and believed in a living, modern prophet. Forget everything that I have said, or what President Brigham Young or President George Q. Cannon or whomsoever has said in days past that is contrary to the present revelation. We spoke with a limited understanding and without the light and knowledge that now has come into the world. . . .

It doesn't make a particle of difference what anybody ever said about the Negro matter before the first day of June of this year, 1978. It is a new day and a new arrangement, and the Lord has now given the revelation that sheds light out into the world on this subject. As to any slivers of light or any particles of darkness of the past, we forget about them. . . .

On this occasion, because of the importuning and the faith, and because the hour and the time had arrived, the Lord in his providences poured out the Holy Ghost upon the First Presidency and the Twelve in a miraculous and marvelous manner, beyond anything that any then present had ever experienced. The revelation came to the president of the Church; it also came to each individual present. There were ten members of the Council of the Twelve and three of the First Presidency there assembled. The result was that President Kimball knew, and each one of us knew, independent of any other person, by direct and personal revelation to us, that the time had now come to extend the gospel and all its blessings and all its obligations, including the priesthood and the blessings of the house of the Lord, to those of every nation, culture, and race, including the black race. There was no question whatsoever as to what happened or as to the word and message that came. . . .

7

Confronting the Church's Problematic Racial Past after 1978

General Introduction

The Mormon hierarchy lifted the priesthood ban in 1978, but persistent questions remained about the racist teachings related to the now abandoned practice: Did blacks derive from the lineage of Cain? Was there still a connection between skin color and past deeds in a premortal life? How could the perceived racial teachings in the *Book of Mormon* and *Pearl of Great Price* be interpreted relative to the end of the priesthood ban? These and other related questions were not initially addressed by the First Presidency, let alone by the revelation itself.[1]

Equally perplexing was that Deseret Book—the LDS-owned and -operated bookstore—continued to print and sell books that contained antiblack teachings by Joseph Fielding Smith and Bruce R. McConkie.[2] Moreover, the church had failed to officially denounce such antiblack teachings in church-sponsored venues, specifically general conference, the *Ensign* magazine, or the *Church News*. Such inaction caused considerable angst among some Latter-day Saints, particularly African American converts, deeply troubled by the church's erstwhile racist doctrines. Certain LDS religious educators expressed concern, indeed confusion, most vividly reflected in the case of BYU religion professor Randy Bott, that the church's racial teachings had changed. Church officials, in fact, sternly rebuked Professor Bott when he reaffirmed racist theories asserting black priesthood denial to a *Washington Post* reporter during Mitt Romney's 2012 campaign for the presidency.

In sum, the church's position today with respect to the provenance of the priesthood ban is much different than it was in the 1950s and 1960s. It is no longer acceptable to teach that blacks were cursed by God or that they were "fence sitters" in a previous life. These prior assertions have been replaced by a new position. The church now teaches that the ban was rooted in racism, not divine revelation.

1. **LDS CHURCH ACKNOWLEDGES BLACKS ORDAINED TO THE MORMON PRIESTHOOD DURING THE LIFETIME OF JOSEPH SMITH, AS REPORTED IN THE *ENCYCLOPEDIA OF MORMONISM* (1992), A FOUR-VOLUME WORK PUBLISHED WITH APPROVAL FROM THE LDS FIRST PRESIDENCY.**

   DOCUMENT INTRODUCTION

   The *Encyclopedia of Mormonism*, published in 1992, is the fullest, richest, and most expansive coverage of Mormonism ever produced.[3] Totaling some one million words, with nearly fifteen hundred articles and 738 authors, this four-volume work is the first encyclopedia devoted exclusively to Mormons. Although the encyclopedia's editors explained that the work did not "have the force and authority of scripture," nor did it represent the official position of the church, the First Presidency authorized it to be distributed to research and public libraries throughout the United States.[4]

   Most of the writers are practicing members of the LDS faith.[5] Their mission, as the editors note, is to "assist readers" with a "greater understanding and appreciation of the history, scriptures, doctrines, practices, and procedures" of the church.[6] All told, this ambitious work included 250 articles devoted to church doctrine, over 150 articles on church history, and more than 100 articles related to Mormon culture, families, art and literature. To ensure a balance between accuracy and tone, each of the entries went through a rigorous editorial process. Some of the more controversial topics, such as the Mountain Meadows Massacre, went through several iterations.[7]

   What follows below is an entry titled "Blacks," coauthored by Jesse Embry, associate director at the Charles Redd Center at BYU, and Alan Cherry, a black convert to the LDS church.[8] The entry is instructive because it acknowledged for the first time, with the First Presidency's imprimatur, that the church ordained blacks to the priesthood during Joseph Smith's tenure as Mormon leader.[9]

   DOCUMENT

   From Alan Cherry and Jessie L. Embry, entry titled "Blacks," in Daniel H. Ludlow, ed., *Encyclopedia of Mormonism*, 4 vols. (New York: Macmillan, 1992), 1:125–127. Used by permission of Brigham Young University.

   BLACKS

   The history of black membership in The Church of Jesus Christ of Latter-day Saints can be divided between the era from 1830 to June 1978 and the period since then.

HISTORY. Though few in number, blacks have been attracted to the Church since its organization. Early converts (such as Elijah Abel) joined during the 1830s; others (such as Jane Manning James) joined after the Saints moved to Illinois. Among those who came to Utah as pioneers were Green Flake, who drove Brigham Young's wagon into the Salt Lake Valley, and Samuel Chambers, who joined in Virginia as a slave and went west after being freed. Throughout the twentieth century, small numbers of blacks continued to join the Church, such as the Sargent family of Carolina County, Virginia, who joined in 1906; Len and Mary Hope, who joined in Alabama during the 1920s; Ruffin Bridgeforth, a railroad worker in Utah, converted in 1953; and Helvecio Martins, a black Brazilian businessman, baptized in 1972 (he became a general authority in 1990). These members remained committed to their testimonies and Church activities even though during this period prior to 1978 black members could not hold the priesthood or participate in temple ordinances.

The reasons for these restrictions have not been revealed. Church leaders and members have explained them in different ways over time. Although several blacks were ordained to the priesthood in the 1830s, there is no evidence that Joseph Smith authorized new ordinations in the 1840s, and between 1847 and 1852 Church leaders maintained that blacks should be denied the priesthood because of their lineage. According to the book of Abraham (now part of the Pearl of Great Price), the descendants of Cain were to be denied the priesthood of God (Abr. 1:23–26). Some Latter-day Saints theorized that blacks would be restricted throughout mortality. As early as 1852, however, Brigham Young said that the "time will come when they will have the privilege of all we have the privilege of and more" (Brigham Young Papers, Church Archives, February 5, 1852), and increasingly in the 1960s, Presidents of the Church taught that denial of entry to the priesthood was a current commandment of God, but would not prevent blacks from eventually possessing all eternal blessings.

Missionaries avoided proselytizing blacks, and General Authorities decided not to send missionaries to Africa, much of the Caribbean, or other regions inhabited by large populations of blacks. Before World War II, only German-speaking missionaries were sent to Brazil, where they sought out German immigrants. When government war regulations curtailed proselytizing among Germans, missionary work was expanded to include Portuguese-speaking Brazilians. Determining genealogically who was to be granted and who denied the priesthood became increasingly a sensitive and complex issue.

During the civil rights era in the United States, denial of the priesthood to blacks drew increasing criticism, culminating in athletic boycotts of Brigham Young University, threatened lawsuits, and public condemnation of the Church in the late 1960s. When questioned about the Church and blacks, Church officials stated that removal of the priesthood restriction would require revelation from God—not policy changes by men.

RECENT DEVELOPMENTS. On June 9, 1978, President Spencer W. Kimball announced the revelation that all worthy males could hold the priesthood (see Doctrine and Covenants: Official Declaration 2). Following the 1978 priesthood revelation, proselytizing was expanded worldwide to include people of African descent. Between 1977 and 1987, Church membership grew from 3,969,000 to 6,440,000, an increase of 62 percent. Because LDS membership records do not identify race, it is impossible to measure accurately the growth of black membership, except in areas where people are largely or exclusively of African descent. In the Caribbean, excepting Puerto Rico, membership grew from 836 to 18,614 and in Brazil from 51,000 to 250,000 during that decade.

In other areas of Latin America, such as Colombia and Venezuela, increasing numbers of blacks also joined the Church. In Europe, blacks, including African immigrants to Portugal, joined the Church. Moreover, in Ghana, Nigeria, and throughout west and central Africa, missionary work expanded at a phenomenal rate. Excluding South Africa, where the membership was predominantly white, membership grew from 136 in 1977 to 14,347 in 1988, almost all in west Africa (see Africa, the Church in).

The LDS Afro-American Oral History Project, conducted by the Charles Redd Center for Western Studies at Brigham Young University, demonstrated the increasing number of black members in the United States. Through interviews with black Latter-day Saints throughout the country, a symposium on LDS Afro-Americans held at Brigham Young University, and responses to a mailed survey, a more reliable flow of data was generated about the thoughts, feelings, convictions, and experiences of LDS Afro-Americans. The study found that within the Church Afro-Americans experience both high acceptance and, paradoxically, cultural miscommunications. For example, in response to the survey, 81 percent felt their future as blacks in the Church was hopeful. They explained that they experienced more social interactions and more meaningful relationships with Church members of all races, especially whites. At the same time, however, 46 percent said white members were not aware of the "needs and problems of black members." Some felt a lack of fellowship as well as economic and racial prejudice from white members.

Black Latter-day Saints are a nonhomogeneous mix of various "kindreds, tongues, and peoples" emerging from thousands of years of unprecedented religious and cultural exclusions. As with LDS Afro-Americans, many black members outside the United States encounter contrasting circumstances of full ecclesiastical involvement, on the one hand, and general Church ignorance of their respective cultures, on the other hand. Local leaders and members (primarily white Latter-day Saints) often lack a good working knowledge of black members' needs, concerns, and circumstances. Despite the 1978 priesthood revelation and expanded missionary work among blacks, unexplored challenges to their growth and retention remain in counterpoint to their happiness with priesthood inclusion.

Despite the cultural miscommunications that remain, black Latter-day Saints enjoy opportunities in all phases of Church activity, including missionary work, quorum leadership, bishoprics, and stake presidencies, along with other members. The first entirely black African stake was organized in 1988. Indeed, black Latter-day Saints may be an LDS historical enigma that has emerged as a prime example of success in LDS brotherhood and sisterhood.

2. LDS CHURCH CONSIDERS RENOUNCING ITS PAST RACIAL STATEMENTS, 1998.

DOCUMENT INTRODUCTION

David Jackson, an African American Mormon and former Baptist, undertook an effort in the 1990s for the Mormon church to repudiate its past doctrines and policies that identified blacks as the lineage of Cain and to those affirming a correlation between skin color and moral purity. Jackson, a convert to the church from Rancho Santa Margarita, California, was asked by his church leader, Lee Adams, to give a talk on "blacks and the church" in one of the regional Mormon meetings. Jackson knew very little about the subject and was unsettled by what he discovered researching the talk. While examining apostle Bruce R. McConkie's *Mormon Doctrine*, he manifested deep concerns about the theological rationale McConkie gave restricting blacks from the priesthood and temple, namely, that blacks were cursed through the lineage of Cain and that somehow they failed in a premortal life.[10]

Troubled by his findings, Jackson shared his concerns with his church home teacher, Dennis Gladwell. In 1995, Jackson wrote a twelve-page appeal to church president Gordon Hinckley urging him to remove *Mormon Doctrine* from church-owned bookstores and libraries. Accompanying the letter were scriptural references from the "Book of Moses," statements by Brigham Young, and a First Presidency proclamation (1949) in which then church leaders George Albert Smith, J. Reuben Clark, and David O. McKay affirmed the priesthood ban articulated by Brigham Young. The letter also asked Hinckley to include an addendum to "Official Declaration 2" in the *Doctrine and Covenants*, "repudiating any interpretation of doctrine that ties racial characteristics of any kind to spiritual conditions or spiritual worthiness in this life or in the pre-existence."[11]

Hinckley did not respond directly to Jackson, but in a letter to Jackson's bishop, a letter which Jackson himself was not allowed to read. Jackson was offended.[12] The bishop, Sterling Brennan, asked Jackson if he could read Hinckley's letter to him, but Jackson refused. His position "was not to let anyone read something to me that I could not receive a copy of." Nevertheless, Jackson's bishop later summarized the contents of the letter, in which Hinckley insisted that the church's doctrines were devoid of racism.[13] The matter did not end there. Gladwell, with Jackson's encouragement, contacted an acquaintance from law school, Marlin Jensen of the

First Quorum of Seventy who also oversaw the public affairs department of the church.

With Jackson's encouragement, Gladwell sent Jensen a thirty-four-page survey of LDS racial teachings, expressing his frustration that "none of these theories or views have ever been disavowed or qualified officially."[14] Jensen, at Gladwell's prompting, convened a committee to examine the issue. Comprising David and Betty Jackson, Dennis Gladwell, and Armand Mauss, an LDS scholar of race at Washington State University, they had a "long lunch meeting" in Jensen's office in 1997 with Jensen and Bill Evans, a staff member at the church's public affairs department. As Mauss later recalled, he agreed to write a summary of concerns that the committee discussed at the meeting, which Jensen would use "as a basis for a formal proposal to be sent through channels to the First Presidency."[15]

In July of 1997 Mauss sent Jensen a five-page document titled "Racial Ideas as a Continuing Problem in the Church." It provides examples "from extant publications of demeaning references to blacks in LDS literature," underscoring "potential harm." The report surveys Mormon racial teachings and concludes by recommending that either the First Presidency or Quorum of the Twelve Apostles produce "an official declaration or proclamation explicitly repudiating the doctrines in question and any implication that some lineages are spiritually superior or inferior to others." It further calls for church authorities to write an authoritative article in the church's magazine, the *Ensign*, or *Church News*, "or both, reiterating this repudiation and explaining the potential harm such doctrines can cause to any people of color who join the church, and to the public image of the church more generally."[16]

The committee's work was abruptly compromised in May 1998 when someone informed *Los Angeles Times* reporter Larry Stammer about the "Gladwell-Jensen" project. Stammer's article, "Mormons May Disavow Old View on Blacks,"[17] provoked a firestorm at LDS church headquarters. The day the story broke, a church spokesman told a reporter at the news station KSL Channel 5—owned and operated by the LDS church—that the story was "totally erroneous." A church press release on the same day noted that church leaders had "read the story" and were "surprised at its contents. The matter it speaks of has not been discussed by the First Presidency and the Quorum of the Twelve." The press release then went on to explain that "the 1978 official declaration continues to speak for itself."[18]

The affair caused considerable embarrassment and quashed any prospect that LDS leaders would repudiate past racial statements affirming priesthood denial.[19] Armand Mauss, whom Stammer had interviewed for the story, observed that the church "would be seen as bowing to public pressure if they made such a disavowal in the wake of the news stories about secret deliberations on the issue."[20] Mauss was part of a growing chorus of Mormon scholars who believed that the church was best served if it retracted its past positions advancing offensive racial rhetoric.[21]

The documents included below illustrate this crucial episode in Mormon racial history. They also provide context to another article published by the *Los Angeles Times*, in which Larry Stammer interviewed church president Gordon Hinckley just after he returned from Africa in the summer of 1998. Hinckley maintained that he did not intend "to make further changes in reinterpreting historic Mormon teachings" and that he had no intention of recalling troubling church publications still in print." For Hinckley, "the reception he received in Africa convinced him that the church is on the right track."[22]

DOCUMENTS

From David Jackson, letter to President Gordon B. Hinckley, October 9, 1995 (used with permission from David Jackson); Armand Mauss report to Elder Marlin Jensen, "Racial Ideas as a Continuing Problem in the Church," July 1997 (used with permission from Armand Mauss); Larry Stammer, "Mormons May Disavow Old View on Blacks," *Los Angeles Times*, May 18, 1998; *Los Angeles Times* story on "Blacks and Priesthood: First Presidency Statement" (press release from LDS Public Affairs Department), May 24, 1998.

a. David Jackson letter to President Gordon B. Hinckley, 1995 (excerpts)

October 9, 1995

President Gordon B. Hinckley
50 East North Temple Street
Salt Lake City, Utah 84150

Dear President Hinckley:

I am writing you because I am concerned about the negative portrayal of people of African descent in Mormon scriptures, reference books, and statements by the First Presidency of the Church.

The Mormon Church has taught that people of African descent are spiritually and morally inferior to Whites. People of African descent are degraded by an assignment of their heritage to the lineage of Cain. Anyone of the lineage of Cain, according to *Mormon Doctrine*, is associated with iniquities, and have been cursed with black skin, the mark of Cain. This mark of Cain identifies people of African descent as a caste apart, a people with whom the other descendants of Adam should not intermarry. Interracial marriage is not my concern but the reasons given against it is less than kind [*sic*].

I was taught in the Church that if there is anything virtuous, lovely, or of good report or praiseworthy we should seek after these things. I hardly find associating innocent people of African descent with the lineage of Cain and using this along with events in the pre-existence to withhold the blessings of the priesthood for over 130 years to be in good report. People of African descent should not be held accountable for the deeds of others in the past.

In June 1978 the priesthood was granted all worthy males. However, the assignment of the lineage of Cain is still associated with the heritage of the people of African descent. As long as this assignment of lineage is there the people of African descent will continue to be negatively viewed by White saints and they will have the scriptures and reference books to prove it. This assigned lineage to the people of African descent is racism at its best and the account of this doctrine and policy is well documented and interpreted in many reference books and spoken by many Mormon leaders in the Church.

Cain's lineage would be of no consequence to me if it was not being used to degrade people of African descent. This lineage has spawned the connection of innocent people of African descent to Lucifer, Perdition, Satan lovers, liars, murderers, and Master Mahan. Our skin of blackness has been referred to as a curse and other statements and scripture interpretations have proven to follow this same line of thinking. . . .

In my efforts to understand the interpretation of the Church's racist doctrine, I have spoken to many of my friends who are members of the Church. These conversations yielded several reactions which I have attempted to outline as follows.

* Some were totally upset, ashamed and embarrassed as if they knew exactly what I was talking about. They would totally deny the existence of this doctrine and comment that they thought the revelation of 1978 removed all of that.
* Some defended this doctrine by saying there is no proof that you are a descendant of Cain and refer to Bruce McConkie's counsel stating "forget everything I have said that is contrary to the present revelation" adding that "it doesn't make a particle of difference what anybody ever said about the Negro matter before the first day of June 1978." Both of these statements are very misleading.
* Some answered yes I have been taught that and I understand your concerns. We don't believe it to be true and what can I do to help you clear this matter?
* Some said yes I agree that the scriptures and prophet's statements are racist and they could promote racism if a member wished to use them for that purpose. However, no one I know is practicing this. The problem, as I see it, is that nothing can be done because these statements are scripture and the words of the prophet and the Church cannot admit that these statements are wrong. To admit that this is wrong means the membership might question other scriptures and statements by the prophet. So if the Church has a choice between admitting they were wrong or letting racist doctrine stand they will choose to let the racist doctrine stand.
* Some have said if I were Black it would be difficult for me to be a member of this Church knowing about these remarks.

I have gathered from these reactions that a good many of the white membership is indeed aware of these racist statements and do not want to be associated with them, however they are hoping that the church will disassociate themselves [*sic*.] with this doctrine and therefore allow the membership to disassociate themselves as well. If the Church does not want to make a change because they believe that in some way it would be an admission that the prophet or scripture is wrong, I do not think this is the case. As I understand it the Church believes in continuous revelation and a revelation or declaration is a change in policy and not an admission of error, misrepresentation or guilt.

Brother Dennis Gladwell, Brother Armand L. Mauss and Brother Jeff Hiltbrand should be commended for their understanding of my concerns and their candor. To be confused or lied to makes me angry, to be told the truth hurts my feelings. Feelings can be repaired much sooner than confusion, denial and lies. These brothers and others like them are the architects to draft solutions to complex problems through prayer and divine guidance should it be their calling. . . .

I believe the answer to this problem is for the Church to issue a declaration to be included in the Doctrine and Covenants repudiating any interpretation of doctrine that ties racial characteristics of any kind to spiritual conditions or spiritual worthiness in this life or in the pre-existence. I am asking you to remove the book *Mormon Doctrine* from Church owned stores, Church libraries and to ask the membership of the Church not to use this book as a reference in preparing lessons and talks for Church meetings.

"Every spirit of man was innocent in the beginning; and God having redeemed man from the fall, men became again, in their infant state, innocent before God." Doctrine and Covenants 93:38, page 182. "We believe that men will be punished for their own sins, and not for Adam's transgressions." Pearl of Great Price article 2, Articles of Faith, page 60. If these statements are true then nothing done in the preexistence or by Cain could cause the withholding of the priesthood from people of African descent. I cannot find it anywhere where God said withhold the priesthood from anyone who is worthy. Statements which have been made that this is the will of God also include other derogatory inconsistent information. These statements can be found in first presidents statements issued August 17, 1949 and December 15, 1969. . . .

The record should be set straight for the benefit of the church and people of African descent. I am asking you to please do so by issuing declaration 3. Imagine yourself and your children as being of African descent and having to put up with this kind of behavior in the house of the Lord. No prophet of God would want that for himself or anyone else.

Following one of the first presidents of the Church of Jesus Christ of Latter-day Saints' example in the Doctrine and Covenants 1 on how to handle this kind of problem, I have drafted the following:

OFFICAL DECLARATION—3

(To be added to the next printing of the Doctrine and Covenants)

To Whom It May Concern:
   I therefore, as president of the Church of Jesus Christ of Latter-day Saints, do hereby, in the most solemn manner, declare that these charges of practicing or teaching racism are false. We are not teaching racism through our scriptures nor permitting any person to enter into this practice. Some cases have been reported in which the parties alleged that racism was taught or scriptures were interpreted negative to people of African descent. There is nothing in my teaching to the Church that employs racism which can be reasonably construed to inculcate or encourage racism and when the elders of the Church have used language which appears to convey any such teachings he has been properly reproved. And I publicly declare that my advice to the Latter-day Saints is to refrain from any teachings that may show racism to any people of color based on racial characteristics of any kind to spiritual conditions or spiritual worthiness either in this life or in the preexistence.
   I believe this letter contains the work of the Lord in these latter days, please set the members of the Church free from this racist stigma so we can work together in God's great kingdom for the salvation of all. An inquiry has been made of the Lord concerning this issue and he has answered: "Be equal unto all and let them come spotless other than of their own making." I trust you will receive this letter and let all come as they are free from the transgressions of others.
   I will wait for your answer and I am looking forward to the changes that we all know are here, we are just waiting for your announcement.

Sincerely,
A. David Jackson
Santa Margarita Ward
Santa Margarita Stake
Orange County, California

cc: Stake President James B. Whitesides

Bishop Sterling Brennan
Dennis A. Gladwell
Jeff Hildtbrand
Armand L. Mauss

b. Armand Mauss report to Elder Marlin Jensen, "Racial Ideas as a Continuing Problem in the Church," July 1997 (excerpts)

INTRODUCTION

In 1978, the priesthood was made available to all worthy males by direct revelation from the Lord. Although black members were not mentioned by name, the revelation obviously was intended to apply directly to them, as a racial group, because they were the only category then being excluded from the priesthood. ... [T]he implications of this revelation are still unfolding. Of particular concern to the African American church membership is the status of the quasi-doctrinal scaffolding which supported the pre-1978 policy. Although these doctrinal views have a speculative origin, and no revelation has ever applied them to contemporary people of black African ancestry, they were once widely circulated in authoritative LDS literature, providing the principal theological rationale for the policy of priesthood denial. The policy which these doctrines purported to explain has been gone for nearly two decades, but ironically the doctrines themselves continue to circulate, not only in conversations and classes among the Saints at the grassroots, but indeed in authoritative books still published and distributed through the Deseret Book Company, among other outlets.

THE PROBLEM

For most Caucasian Mormons, the 1978 revelation seems to have resolved all the issues about race. Thus today the vast majority of church members, including most priesthood authorities, would almost certainly accept the following statements as accurate:

1) There was once a curse on Africans (and African Americans) but it has been lifted.
2) The curse applied only to Africans, not to other dark-skinned peoples. That is, though the original "curse" was understood to include a dark skin, in the end only one dark-skinned people was affected, namely the so-called Negro.
3) The Negro is a descendant of Cain and Ham, but that does not matter now.
4) The Negro presumably failed somehow in the pre-existence (perhaps was not valiant enough), but that does not matter now.
5) The pre-1978 policy of withholding the priesthood, though now changed, was itself nevertheless based on a specific revelation from the Lord.

Because such views can also be found, explicitly or implicitly, in a 1949 letter from the First Presidency, it is difficult simply to ignore them without some official explanation as to their original efficacy and current status. In the absence of any official repudiation of such ideas, black LDS members tend to be viewed by most other members today as simply having been released from a period of penalty during which they paid for their wrongdoings under the curse, rather than being viewed as a racial group once denied the priesthood through error or misunderstanding of scripture. While the distinction between these two views might not be noticed by our white membership, it continues to be highly salient to our black members, who find the doctrinal views outlined above difficult to reconcile with principles like equality and eternal worth in the Lord's eyes.

As these doctrines come to the attention of black people, especially black Church members, they are a source at least of confusion and usually of pain, as well. Some black members deal with the predicament more easily than do others, perhaps dismissing the traditional doctrines as unofficial, inoperative, or quaint notions from the past resembling those once found in other Christian denominations. Many other black members, however, find these doctrines not only unnecessary and obsolete, but demeaning and particularly difficult to explain to their children, who sometimes even encounter them during discussions in seminary classes. Investigators and potential investigators learning of these doctrines are put off by them. Black converts are sometimes ridiculed by their friends and family members for joining a church in which such doctrines still circulate. These doctrines, therefore, retain a potential for undermining the mission of the Church as it strives to strengthen the Saints and proclaim the Gospel. They also constitute a potentially serious public relations problem, and an entirely unnecessary one. . . .

THE PATH FORWARD

[I]n the current LDS culture, many of the Saints have adopted the posture that almost any statement by a general authority is quasi-scriptural and inspired, especially if expressed as a doctrine or principle. . . . However, the doctrinal framework once used to justify the earlier priesthood restriction is still with us. That framework always had a dubious relationship to the scriptures and to modern revelation, even though it was widely taught even in authoritative books and documents. More recently, there has appeared a disposition on the part of Church presidencies to recognize the doctrines as dubious, obsolete, and unnecessary. Nevertheless, the doctrinal legacy remains not only in common LDS conversation but even in authoritative books distributed to this day by Deseret Book and other outlets, where it is encountered by black Church members to their potential discouragement and demoralization.

Presumably little can be done about ideas from the past that continue to appear in books that are published and republished. Much can be done, however, to neutralize the continuing spread of these doctrines through explicit initiatives on the part of the First Presidency and/or the Quorum of the Twelve. Two examples of such initiatives would be (1) an official declaration or proclamation explicitly repudiating the doctrines in question and any implication that some lineages are spiritually superior or inferior to others, no matter what racial characteristics are involved; and (2) an article, perhaps by one of the presiding brethren, in the *Ensign* or *Church News*, or both, reiterating this repudiation and explaining the potential harm such doctrines can cause to any people of color who join the Church, and to the public image of the Church more generally.

c. Larry B. Stammer, "Mormons May Disavow Old View on Blacks," Los Angeles Times, May 18, 1998 (excerpts)

Twenty years after the Mormon church dropped its ban against African Americans in the priesthood, key leaders are debating a proposal to repudiate historic church doctrines that were used to bolster claims of black inferiority.

The proposal to disavow the teachings, which purport to link African American skin color to curses from God recounted in Hebrew and Mormon Scriptures, is under review by the church's Committee on Public Affairs, made up of members of the church's highest governing circles, known as general authorities.

Sources close to the sensitive and still secret deliberations hope that a statement will be issued as early as next month, the 20th anniversary of the landmark 1978 decision by the Church of Jesus Christ of Latter-day Saints to admit all worthy men to the priesthood, regardless of their race or color.

Although the church's leaders now proclaim racial equality as a "fundamental teaching," the process of repudiating old doctrines remains difficult. Those involved in the internal discussions say church leaders are searching for a formula that will allow them to retract earlier statements without undermining the faith of believers or the credibility of previous church figures whom the Mormons revere as prophets whose pronouncements were inspired by God. . . .

The call for change comes at a time when the 10-million-member church is enjoying unprecedented growth in Africa and other developing countries. . . .

But black members of the church in the United States as well as some Mormon scholars warn that the "racist legacy" contained in various Mormon documents and authoritative statements risks undermining its mission unless they are disavowed. . . .

For most white members, the place of blacks in the church was resolved once and for all by the church's landmark 1978 decision on the priesthood.

For many blacks, however, the decision did not go far enough. "What [the 1978 revelation] doesn't say is we're no longer of the lineage of Cain, that we no longer did these things in preexistence. It does not say we are not cursed with black skin," [David] Jackson said.

Irvine attorney Dennis Gladwell . . . made a similar point in a paper presented in October 1996 to Elder Marlin K. Jensen, a high-ranking official of the church and a public affairs committee member.

"It is the linkage to Cain that so distresses Mormon African Americans today," Gladwell wrote. "It places their spiritual lineage in shambles, since they are alleged descendants of a man who has come to symbolize evil on the same level as Lucifer himself."

Although church officials would not comment directly on what the First Presidency, composed of [Gordon B.] Hinckley and his two counselors, or the Quorum of the Twelve Apostles, may have considered, they confirmed that discussion of the issue is moving forward. The First Presidency and the Twelve Apostles are the principal policymaking and administrative officers of the church. The Quorum of the Seventy, of which Jensen is a member, ranks just below and carries out their policies.

"There appears to be general enthusiasm for moving ahead to clarify anything that would have previously hurt African Americans," one source close to developments in the public affairs committee said.

William S. Evans, a public affairs committee staffer, confirmed that the committee members have discussed the matter. But he cautioned that only the church's highest authorities—not the committee—could make such a statement. . . .

Jackson and Gladwell, who describe themselves as devoted to the church, said they take heart in what they see as the church's forward movement. Now, they said, the time has come to take the next step.

"The doctrinal framework once used to justify the earlier priesthood restriction is still with us," Mauss wrote in a paper presented last July to Jensen. "Presumably little can be done about ideas from the past that continue to appear in books that are published and republished. Much can be done, however, to neutralize the continuing spread of these doctrines through explicit initiatives on the part of the First Presidency and/or the Quorum of the Twelve."

d. First Presidency statement on *Los Angeles Times* story (press release from LDS Public Affairs Department, May 24, 1998)

We have read the story which appeared in the May 18, 1998, *Los Angeles Times*, and are surprised at its contents. The matter it speaks of has not been discussed by the First Presidency and the Quorum of the Twelve.

Since the 1978 revelation granting the priesthood to all worthy males, millions of people of all races have embraced the restored gospel of Jesus Christ and are enjoying the full blessings of membership in the Church.

The 1978 official declaration continues to speak for itself.

3. CHURCH PRESIDENT GORDON B. HINCKLEY DENOUNCES RACISM, 2006.

DOCUMENT INTRODUCTION

Immediately after the priesthood ban ended in 1978, the church systematically expanded its missionary efforts in predominantly black areas in Brazil and sub-Saharan Africa. In addition, the church established missions in Puerto Rico (1979), the Dominican Republic and Santo Domingo (1981), the West Indies (1983), Haiti at Port-au-Prince (1984), and Jamaica (1985). By 2000, one church leader observed, "Church members now live[d] in nearly every country of the world," totaling some 500,000 members of African ancestry.[23] In 1997, about 300,000 black Mormons resided in Africa, 150,000 in Brazil (mostly biracial), and 20,000 in North America.[24] The growth rate in the Democratic Republic of Congo and Nigeria has been brisk, but in Mozambique, Ghana, South Africa, Zimbabwe, and the Ivory Coast the rate has been modest, except in areas of the world traditionally neglected by LDS missionaries, where the church has found greater success.[25]

In the United States, the convert rate among African Americans has been much slower. Black Americans constitute less than 3 percent of the LDS church membership in the United States, with whites totaling about 90 percent of the membership.[26] Still, black Mormon congregations exist in many U.S. cities, including Atlanta, New York City, and Los Angeles. Similarly, by the twenty-first century the black student population at church-owned schools continued to increase, albeit at a slow pace. In 2002, BYU elected its first African American president of the BYU student association, though only a small number of students at BYU were black at the time.[27] More significantly, black Mormons hold a number of important church positions, including bishop, stake president, mission president, and various positions in the women's and youth organizations of the church. In April 1990, Helvécio Martins, a Brazilian, became the first black general authority in LDS history when he was named to the Second Quorum of the Seventy.[28]

Some white members responded to these new converts with prejudice and bigotry.[29] Although Mormon scholars have argued that LDS racial attitudes in the United States mirror national trends,[30] the Mormon hierarchy became concerned about ongoing racism in the church. An LDS bishop asked a black woman to run the young woman's basketball program in her ward; the woman believed it was because of her race. A black athlete at Ricks College (now BYU-Idaho) spoke of the tremendous pressure to perform on the football field.[31] A black instructor of sociology detailed his frustrations teaching white students at BYU and Utah Valley State College, citing racial stereotypes they expressed in class.[32] An English professor at BYU complained that his students still harbored demeaning racial views, taught to them by their "parents or Seminary or Sunday School teachers."[33] An unnamed woman in the Relief Society told a black Mormon actress that she would be white in the resurrection and difficult to recognize in the next life.[34] Some ward members proposed holding a "slave auction" to raise money in which black members would be the "slaves" and whites would do the bidding.[35] Some members made insensitive jokes: "Now [with blacks joining the church], we can have the best basketball team in the country."[36]

As late as 2006, racial prejudice remained a continuing problem. Church president Gordon B. Hinckley addressed racial prejudice in general conference. Called into church leadership, first as an apostle in 1961, then as a First Presidency counselor during the 1980s and 1990s, and then as church president in 1995, where he served until his death in 2008, Hinckley became one of the most articulate church spokesmen in the twentieth century. His interviews with the national news media became well known throughout the church, and Hinckley is generally credited for bridging a divide between the media and the church, part of which reflects his training as a journalist at the University of Utah.[37]

In his sermon "A Need for Greater Kindness," given at the April 2006 priesthood session of the conference, the aging president urged the men to take care of their families, spiritually and temporally, and to demonstrate greater piety in their lives. He also spoke against racism, warning that anyone who uses "racial slurs" cannot be considered a disciple of Christ. The context for Hinckley's sermon derives from several conversations he had with Darius Gray, an African American Mormon and president of Genesis, a support group for black Latter-day Saints. Gray expressed to Hinckley his concerns about racism in the church. As one account explains, Gray had received "countless calls from men and women all over the United States who were still dealing with the ripples of racist folklore—people whose children were told that they were cursed, or that all blacks had been 'neutral' in the pre-existence; white members who pulled their children from Sunday school because they didn't want them in the same class as a black child; investigators or new converts who were addressed with racial epithets." Gray then recounted these experiences to Hinckley, who found them very disturbing.[38]

Hinckley's remarks, parts of which are included below, remind Mormons that the church is becoming more diverse, and that "we must make an effort to accommodate that diversity."[39]

DOCUMENT

From Gordon B. Hinckley, "The Need for Greater Kindness," *Ensign* 36 (May 2006): 58–61 (excerpts).

. . . Racial strife still lifts its ugly head. I am advised that even right here among us there is some of this. I cannot understand how it can be. It seemed to me that we all rejoiced in the 1978 revelation given President Kimball. I was there in the temple at the time that that happened. There was no doubt in my mind or in the minds of my associates that what was revealed was the mind and the will of the Lord.

Now I am told that racial slurs and denigrating remarks are sometimes heard among us. I remind you that no man who makes disparaging remarks concerning those of another race can consider himself a true disciple of Christ. Nor can he consider himself to be in harmony with the teachings of the Church of Christ. How can any man holding the Melchizedek Priesthood arrogantly assume that he is eligible for the priesthood whereas another who lives a righteous life but whose skin is of a different color is ineligible?

Throughout my service as a member of the First Presidency, I have recognized and spoken a number of times on the diversity we see in our society. It is all about us, and we must make an effort to accommodate that diversity.

Let us all recognize that each of us is a son or daughter of our Father in Heaven, who loves all of His children.

Brethren, there is no basis for racial hatred among the priesthood of this Church. If any within the sound of my voice is inclined to indulge in this, then let him go before the Lord and ask for forgiveness and be no more involved in such. . . .

4. APOSTLE JEFFREY HOLLAND REPUDIATES THE DOCTRINAL FRAMEWORK USED TO JUSTIFY THE CHURCH'S RACIAL POLICY, 2006.

DOCUMENT INTRODUCTION

At the turn of the twenty-first century the church shifted its position on the doctrinal framework used to justify the priesthood ban. The "seed of Cain" explanations that originated with Brigham Young were deemed outdated and offensive to modern racial sensibilities. Likewise, the church no longer teaches that blacks were "less valiant" in a premortal life. As for the priesthood ban itself, church leaders at the highest levels reaffirmed the 1969 First Presidency statement asserting that "we don't know why" it started. President Kimball, in an August 1978 interview with *Time* magazine reporter Richard Ostling noted "flatly that Mormonism no longer holds to . . . a theory" that blacks "failed God during their pre-existence."[40] At the same time, apostle LeGrand Richards explained that "the Brethren decided that we should never say" that "the Negro" was denied for being "less valiant in the previous existence," or that they were cursed with a "dark skin." "We just don't know what the reason was" for the recently lifted ban.[41]

In 1988, celebrating the ten-year anniversary of the priesthood revelation, apostle Dallin H. Oaks explained: "it's not the pattern of the Lord to give reasons. We can put reasons to commandments. When we do we're on our own. Some people put reasons to [the ban] and they turned out to be spectacularly wrong. There is a lesson in that."[42] Nine years later, on the eve of the twenty-year commemoration of the priesthood revelation, church president Gordon B. Hinckley echoed Oaks's views. When asked by a reporter what the reason was for "not ordaining blacks," Hinckley said he did not "know what the reason was" but whatever it was, he did not "think it was wrong."[43] In 1998 Alexander B. Morrison, a member of the First Quorum of the Seventy, gave an interview to a Salt Lake news station in which he reaffirmed Hinckley's remarks.[44] Deseret Book, the church's publishing house, supported the new focus in several of its publications.[45] Church symposiums also affirmed the shifting position, as did apostle M. Russell Ballard, who explained, "we don't know all the reasons why the Lord does what he does," referring to the ban.[46]

The clearest, sharpest, and most forceful statement, however, came from apostle Jeffrey R. Holland, who attributed the ban to racial folklore that he went on to refute. In 2006, award-winning producer and director Helen Whitney interviewed Holland for her PBS documentary *The Mormons*.[47] She interviewed several scholars, laypersons, and church leaders, striving to create a production of inquiry, tolerance, and mutual understanding about Mormon theology, history, and practice. Holland was one of several high-ranking church officials who participated.[48] A PhD-trained scholar in American Studies from Yale University, former dean of the College of Religious Education at BYU, commissioner of church education, president of BYU, and ordained an apostle in 1994, he was well equipped to answer questions about Mormon racial policies.[49]

Holland explained that his predecessors were wrong for promoting a racial "folklore" that had neither substance nor doctrinal support. "The folklore must never be perpetuated," he intoned. Even though his predecessors "were doing the best they knew to give shape to [the policy], to give context to it, to give even history to it," their explanations, however "well intended," were "almost all . . . inadequate and/or wrong." He was particularly concerned that the folklore not be reproduced in church books and manuals. He wanted to make sure that "earlier writings and teachings" were "not perpetuated in the present." In Holland's view, "we simply do not know why" blacks could not hold the priesthood. For this apostle, all earlier explanations were wrong, however well intentioned.[50]

Holland's interview, excerpts of which are included below, marks a turning point in Mormon racial discourse. It is the first time a high-ranking church official has openly repudiated the doctrinal framework sustaining the priesthood ban. Leaders now teach that the "folklore [for the priesthood ban] is not part of and never was taught as doctrine by the Church."[51]

DOCUMENT

From Jeffrey R. Holland interview with Helen Whitney, March 4, 2006, for the PBS documentary *The Mormons* (2007), http://www.pbs.org/mormons/interviews/holland.html (excerpts).

HW: I've talked to many blacks and many whites as well about the lingering folklore [about why blacks couldn't have the priesthood]. These are faithful Mormons who are delighted about this revelation, and yet who feel something more should be said about the folklore and even possibly about the mysterious reasons for the ban itself, which was not a revelation; it was a practice. So if you could, briefly address the concerns Mormons have about this folklore and what should be done.

JH: One clear-cut position is that the folklore must never be perpetuated....
I have to concede to my earlier colleagues. They, I'm sure, in their own way, were doing the best they knew to give shape to [the policy], to give context for it, to give even history to it. All I can say is however well intended the explanations were, I think almost all of them were inadequate and/or wrong.

It probably would have been advantageous to say nothing, to say we just don't know, and, [as] with many religious matters, whatever was being done was done on the basis of faith at that time. But some explanations were given and had been given for a lot of years.... At the very least, there should be no effort to perpetuate those efforts to explain why that doctrine existed. I think, to the extent that I know anything about it, as one of the newer and younger ones to come along, we simply do not know why that practice, that policy, that doctrine was in place.

HW: What is the folklore, quite specifically?

JH: Well, some of the folklore that you must be referring to are suggestions that there were decisions made in the pre-mortal councils where someone had not been as decisive in their loyalty to a Gospel plan or the procedures on earth or what was to unfold in mortality, and that therefore that opportunity and mortality was compromised. I really don't know a lot of the details of those, because fortunately I've been able to live in the period where we're not expressing or teaching them, but I think that's the one I grew up hearing the most, was that it was something to do with the pre-mortal councils. But I think that's the part that must never be taught until anybody knows a lot more than I know. We just don't know, in the historical context of the time, why it was practiced. . . . That's my principal [concern], is that we don't perpetuate explanations about things we don't know.

We don't pretend that something wasn't taught or practice wasn't pursued for whatever reason. But I think we can be unequivocal and we can be declarative in our current literature, in books that we reproduce, in teachings that go forward, whatever, that from this time forward, from 1978 forward, we can make sure that nothing of that is declared. That may be where we still need to make sure that we're absolutely dutiful, that we put [a] careful eye of scrutiny on anything from earlier writings and teachings, just [to] make sure that that's not perpetuated in the present. That's the least, I think, of our current responsibilities on that topic.

5. BYU RELIGION PROFESSOR RANDY BOTT TEACHES THAT BLACKS ARE CURSED AND THE LDS CHURCH REBUKES HIM, 2012.

DOCUMENT INTRODUCTION

On February 28, 2012, Brigham Young University religion professor Randy Bott gave an interview to *Washington Post* reporter Jason Horowitz that caused great consternation among LDS church leaders. Bott recalled certain Mormon racial teachings that upset the Mormon hierarchy. Linking blacks to Cain, the biblical counterfigure who murdered his brother, Bott explained that blacks were cursed, which made them ineligible for priesthood and temple privileges. "God has always been discriminatory" to those "whom he grants the authority of the priesthood," Bott affirmed, bolstering his claims in Mormon scripture, citing passages from the Bible and the *Pearl of Great Price*. The interview demonstrates that even though the ban ended over three decades ago, the theological rationale was still being advanced by influential Latter-day Saints.[52]

Within hours of the interview, critics denounced Bott for his views. Daniel Peterson, a professor of Islamic Studies and Arabic at BYU and outspoken church apologist, said he "feels[s] sorry for Bott. Our speculations as to the reason[s] for the priesthood ban have been essentially worthless, and sometimes harmful," he blogged. "God has not seen fit to explain why he commanded or at least permitted the denial of priesthood to blacks." Another blogger opined, "Professor Bott . . . should not try to explain or rationalize the blacks and the priesthood issue. All the rationalizations are based on fiction, including the Cain and Abel link. It was never a divine doctrine."[53] Finally, Terry Ball, the dean of BYU religious education and Bott's boss, criticized him, emphatically stating that Bott's position "does not reflect the teachings in the classroom at Brigham Young University."[54]

Bott's critics contend that his theological assertion linking skin color with moral purity is a relic from the past. For many Mormons, when the priesthood ban ended in 1978, the doctrinal framework for the ban ended as well, even though the revelation of 1978 does not mention "the curse" or anything about a pre-mortal life. Furthermore, the church hierarchy had never officially repudiated this racial doctrine in church-sponsored venues or in authoritative publications, despite certain church leaders speaking to the media discounting its significance. Indeed, at that time there was never a First Presidency statement, an *Ensign* article, or a general conference address "casting off the curse of Cain," to borrow one scholar's words.[55] What is more, the church still published books perpetuating the divine-curse doctrine, which made it all the more confusing for Professor Bott and African American converts like David Jackson, whose story is recounted elsewhere in this chapter.[56]

The Bott interview, then, was troubling not only for its outdated theological assertions, but because it threatened to undermine the goodwill the church had enjoyed in recent years working with people of color in community outreach programs. The interview also upset many among the church's black population—totaling some 500,000 members throughout the world.[57] Finally, it cast unwelcome attention on Mitt Romney's presidential campaign, which was then underway when the story exploded across the news media.[58] The story was particularly vexing for Romney, because he had already been dogged about the race issue in a number of newspaper articles prior to Bott's interview, and also by national news programs like NBC's *Meet the Press*, in which the moderator, Tim Russert, had asked Romney what he was doing in a church that many view "as a racist organization."[59]

Given the potential harm of the story, the church denounced Bott's statement swiftly and vigorously. A day after the story broke, the church issued two press releases excoriating Professor Bott's views, making it clear that "BYU faculty members do not speak for the Church." This came from a "Church Statement Regarding 'Washington Post' Article on Race and the Church,"[60] marking the first time the church had ever singled out an individual for rebuke in a national press release. The second statement, titled "The Church and Race: All Are Alike unto God," reaffirmed the church's commitment to racial equality, then offered a line that has become the official church position: "The origins of priesthood availability are not entirely clear. Some explanations with respect to this matter were made in the absence of direct revelation and references to these explanations are sometimes cited in publications. These previous personal statements do not represent Church doctrine."[61]

Understandably, Bott was dismayed by the whole incident, as were his colleagues in the BYU religion department. "We all taught what Randy taught," one of Bott's colleagues lamented. This could have happened to any one of us. We had no idea that the church's position had changed."[62] For Bott, the incident marked a tragic end to a long and distinguished career in religious education, both as a professor of religion at BYU and in the LDS Church Education system, where he taught for nearly forty years. Though he retired at the end of the spring term 2012, just months after the story broke, his faculty webpage remained intact for a period, claiming he is an expert on the "Doctrines of the Gospel."[63] On this particular doctrine, he was behind the curve. He did not understand that the church's position had changed.

DOCUMENTS

From Jason Horowitz, "The Genesis of a Church's Stand on Race," *Washington Post*, February 28, 2012; "Church Statement Regarding 'Washington Post' Article on Race and the Church" (press release from LDS Public Affairs Department, February 29, 2012); "The Church and Race: All Are Alike unto God" (press release from LDS Public Affairs Department, February 29, 2012).

a. BYU Professor Randy Bott interview with the *Washington Post*, 2012 (excerpts)

... The origins of the policy

The ground floor of the Joseph Smith building, which houses BYU's religion department, showcases a likeness of the golden tablets from which Joseph Smith is said to have translated the Book of Mormon. Paintings upstairs depict the Lamanites, the tribe in Mormon scripture that bears dark skin as a sign of God's curse.

In his office, religion professor Randy Bott explains a possible theological underpinning of the ban. According to Mormon scriptures, the descendants of Cain, who killed his brother, Abel, "were black." One of Cain's descendants was Egyptus, a woman Mormons believe was the namesake of Egypt. She married Ham, whose descendants were themselves cursed and, in the view of many Mormons, barred from the priesthood by his father, Noah. Bott points to the Mormon holy text the Book of Abraham as suggesting that all of the descendants of Ham and Egyptus were thus black and barred from the priesthood.

It's not clear whether Joseph Smith, the religion's founder, who ordained at least one black priest, supported the ban. But his successor, Brigham Young, enforced it enthusiastically as the word of God, supporting slavery in Utah and decreeing that the "mark" on Cain was "the flat nose and black skin." Young subsequently urged immediate death to any participant in mixing of the races. As recently as 1949, church leaders suggested that the ban on blacks resulted from the consequences of the "conduct of spirits in the pre-mortal existence." As a result, many Mormons believed that blacks were less valiant in the pre-Earth life, or fence sitters in the war between God and Satan. That view has fallen out of favor in recent decades.

"God has always been discriminatory" when it comes to whom he grants the authority of the priesthood, says Bott, the BYU theologian. He quotes Mormon scripture that states that the Lord gives to people "all that he seeth fit." Bott compares blacks with a young child prematurely asking for the keys to her father's car, and explains that similarly until 1978, the Lord determined that blacks were not yet ready for the priesthood.

"What is discrimination?" Bott asks. "I think that is keeping something from somebody that would be a benefit for them, right? But what if it wouldn't have been a benefit to them?" Bott says that the denial of the priesthood to blacks on Earth—although not in the afterlife—protected them from the lowest rungs of hell reserved for people who abuse their priesthood powers. "You couldn't fall off the top of the ladder, because you weren't on the top of the ladder. So, in reality the blacks not having the priesthood was the greatest blessing God could give them. . . ."

b. "Church Statement Regarding '*Washington Post*' Article on Race and the Church," 2012

Salt Lake City—The Church issued the following statement today in response to news media requests:

The positions attributed to BYU professor Randy Bott in a recent *Washington Post* article absolutely do not represent the teachings and doctrines of The Church of Jesus Christ of Latter-day Saints. BYU faculty members do not speak for the Church. It is unfortunate that the Church was not given a chance to respond to what others said.

The Church's position is clear—we believe all people are God's children and are equal in His eyes and in the Church. We do not tolerate racism in any form.

For a time in the Church there was a restriction on the priesthood for male members of African descent. It is not known precisely why, how, or when this restriction began in the Church but what is clear is that it ended decades ago. Some have attempted to explain the reason for this restriction but these attempts should be viewed as speculation and opinion, not doctrine. The Church is not bound by speculation or opinions given with limited understanding.

We condemn racism, including any and all past racism by individuals both inside and outside the Church.

c. "The Church and Race: All Are Alike unto God," 2012

The gospel of Jesus Christ is for everyone. The Book of Mormon states, "black and white, bond and free, male and female; . . . all are alike unto God" (2 Nephi 26:33). This is the Church's official teaching.

People of all races have always been welcomed and baptized into the Church since its beginning. In fact, by the end of his life in 1844 Joseph Smith, the founding prophet of The Church of Jesus Christ of Latter-day Saints, opposed slavery. During this time some black males were ordained to the priesthood. At some point the Church stopped ordaining male members of African descent, although there were a few exceptions. It is not known precisely why, how or when this restriction began in the Church, but it has ended. Church leaders sought divine guidance regarding the issue and more than three decades ago extended the priesthood to all worthy male members. The Church immediately began ordaining members to priesthood offices wherever they attended throughout the world.

The Church unequivocally condemns racism, including any and all past racism by individuals both inside and outside the Church. In 2006, then Church president Gordon B. Hinckley declared that "no man who makes disparaging remarks concerning those of another race can consider himself a true disciple of Christ. Nor can he consider himself to be in harmony with the teachings of the Church. Let us all recognize that each of us is a son or daughter of our Father in Heaven, who loves all of His children."

Recently, the Church has also made the following statement on this subject:

"The origins of priesthood availability are not entirely clear. Some explanations with respect to this matter were made in the absence of direct revelation and references to these explanations are sometimes cited in publications. These previous personal statements do not represent Church doctrine."

6. LDS CHURCH ISSUES OFFICIAL STATEMENT ENTITLED "RACE AND THE PRIESTHOOD," 2013.

DOCUMENT INTRODUCTION

On December 6, 2013, the Mormon church posted on its website a two-thousand-word document entitled "Race and the Priesthood," which the LDS church–owned *Deseret News* modestly described as an "enhanced page" on this admittedly "hot topic." *Deseret News* reporter Tad Walch described the contents of this document in extremely brief, almost cryptic terms, noting in passing that church founder Joseph Smith "openly opposed slavery and allowed the ordination of a few black men" and then stating, almost as an afterthought, that his successor Brigham Young "publically announced that men of black African descent could no longer be ordained to the priesthood." Walsh added that Young "also said that in the future black church members would 'have (all) the privileges and more' enjoyed by other members."[64]

The independently owned *Salt Lake Tribune*, by contrast, was more explicit in discussing the meaning of this noteworthy document in its own front-page article entitled "Mormon church traces black priesthood ban back to Brigham Young." *Tribune* reporter Peggy Fletcher Stack explained that "[i]n the past the LDS church has said that history isn't clear why blacks were banned from its all-male priesthood for more than a century," adding, "apparently, it now has." Stack further noted that the statement "disavows the theories advanced in the past . . . [and that] church leaders today unequivocally condemn all racism, past and present, in any form." She characterized the essay in general terms as "part of an ongoing series of 'gospel topics pages' published by the LDS church to give Mormons resources for understanding complex topics."[65]

The news coverage of this seminal document illustrates how controversial it is, both for what it says and what it omits. Significantly, it ascribes the ban to racism rather than divine revelation. It attributes it to Brigham Young, theorizing that he was a product of the "racial distinctions and prejudice" of his day. Further, it breaks with the long-held belief that Joseph Smith instituted the ban under divine decree, and moves still further from the position that "church records offer no clear insights into the origins" of the ban.[66] In another candid admission, the document unequivocally repudiates the church's decades-old teachings—specifically on interracial marriages, the divine curse, and racial superiority. It claims, finally, that the church's racial teachings were theories, accepted uncritically for nearly 126 years by church presidents Brigham Young to Spencer W. Kimball, the man who lifted the ban.

These stark admissions came after a wave of unflattering news stories affirming that Mormons, particularly of a younger generation, had become disillusioned when they encountered websites critical of the faith's history and doctrine, prodding them to leave the faith.[67] Mormonism's more controversial teachings affected them, specifically the *Book of Abraham*, DNA and the *Book of Mormon*, polyandry and polygamy, and race and the priesthood. LDS church historian Steven E. Snow candidly acknowledged this problem, explaining that the church needs "to provide a series of answers that will help our members better understand these chapters in our history." The "Race and Priesthood" document emerged in this context, along with other essays, in an effort to provide Latter-day Saints with answers to difficult "gospel" questions. These new resources, general authority Paul B. Pieper explained, were geared to "strengthen their testimony and deepen their conversion."[68]

Reaction to the document was on the whole positive, particularly from spokesmen from the church's small but noteworthy black community. In particular, Darius Gray, a black member of some fifty years' standing and a founding member of the church's Genesis Group, called it "'an absolutely marvelous document' of great clarity and sensitivity," adding that "it should be viewed as an official comment" from the top Mormon leaders, specifically the First Presidency and the Quorum of the Twelve Apostles. Gray, in fact, "played a role in creating the essay."[69] Another longtime black Latter-day Saint, Catherine Stokes, was equally effusive, stating "Hallelujah" in proclaiming the document "a Christmas gift to each and every member of the church—black, white, or whatever ethnicity."[70] Yet another black Mormon, Don Harwell, current head of the Genesis Group, colorfully stated that the document "renounced the silliness that blacks were fence-sitters and less valiant (in the premortal existence), all the things that some [church] members used to justify the racism."[71]

Younger Latter-day Saints are more circumspect. Alexis Henson, a BYU student, stated that she was "super excited" when the statement was first issued but some six months later expressed her frustration at its limited exposure to the rank-and-file church membership, lamenting, "nobody even knows about it." Likewise, Devan Mitchell, a twenty-eight-year-old member in Seattle, claimed that certain church members who "had seen the essay haven't accepted it," further stating that "We might still need something a little more if we still have people defending" past racial theories used to justify the priesthood restriction, which he termed "folklore."[72] And finally, Darron Smith, a professor at the University of Tennessee and author of three books dealing with blacks within Mormonism, feels that the church needs to go further in renouncing its past practices relative to blacks, specifically calling for a formal apology.[73]

Also providing insights were an array of LDS scholars, a number of whom had written on the subject of blacks within the church. Washington State University sociology professor emeritus Armand L. Mauss, who had been consulted during the process of crafting the document, stated, "Naturally I was delighted to see it," going on to praise the church for its "new and greater level of candor and transparency" and frankly adding that "In this age of instant access through the web to any and all kinds of information, the church can no longer ignore such issues." Mauss further noted, "It's nice to feel vindicated after fifty years and various encounters with stake presidents for promulgating" misinformation justifying the priesthood ban.[74]

University of Utah history professor Paul Reeve, who offered significant input in the drafting of the document, optimistically predicted that the information contained within would have a "direct impact . . . in the pews of Mormon congregations," adding: "You continue to hear stories of people citing or clinging to old racist teachings, and so the hurt and harm of those teachings can hopefully start to fade and diminish." And Patrick Mason, Howard W. Hunter Chair of Mormon Studies at Claremont Graduate University, who also offered advice in the preliminary drafting of the document, declared it a "statement . . . welcomed by [church] members concerned about outside charges of racism," showing that "the church has repudiated that past" and with "a kind of collective sigh of relief . . . we can move on from that troubled part of our legacy."[75]

Distinguished Mormon scholar Richard L. Bushman, author of *Rough Stone Rolling*, a highly acclaimed biography of Joseph Smith, also weighed in on the implications of the document, characterizing it as "written as a historian might tell the story [and] not as a theological piece, trying to justify the practice." By depicting the priesthood ban "as fitting the common practices of the day," Bushman commented that it was "something that just grew up and, in time, had to be eliminated." But "accepting that," Bushman added, "requires a deep reorientation of Mormon thinking," specifically noting that "Mormons believe that their leaders are in regular communication with God, so if you say [Brigham] Young could make a serious error, it brings into question all of the prophet's inspiration." Black Mormon writer Marvin Perkins, coauthor of the DVD series *Blacks and the Scriptures*, echoed similar concerns: "The disavowal says to the church and the world, 'Everything we taught you justifying the restriction is wrong.' But what would be ideal would be for every member to be as well-versed regarding the truths of the priesthood ban and scriptural truths regarding skin color and curses as they are with the Joseph Smith story and the First Vision. We need it repeated over and over in church curriculum in manuals and over the pulpit. That's the way this will be resolved."[76]

Excerpts of this seminal document are included below.

DOCUMENT

From "Race and the Priesthood," posted December 6, 2013, http://www.lds.org/study/topic/print/race-and-the-priesthood (excerpts).

In 1852, President Brigham Young publicly announced that men of black African descent could no longer be ordained to the priesthood.... The justifications for this restriction echoed the widespread ideas about racial inferiority that had been used to argue for the legalization of black "servitude" in the Territory of Utah. According to one view... blacks descended from the same lineage as the biblical Cain, who slew his brother Abel. Those who accepted this view believed that God's "curse" on Cain was the mark of a dark skin....

Around the turn of the century, another explanation gained currency: blacks were said to have been less than fully valiant in the premortal battle against Lucifer and, as a consequence, were restricted from priesthood and temple blessings.

Today, the Church disavows the theories advanced in the past that black skin is a sign of divine disfavor or curse, or that it reflects actions in a premortal life; that mixed-race marriages are a sin; or that blacks or people of any other race or ethnicity are inferior in any way to anyone else. Church leaders today unequivocally condemn all racism, past and present, in any form....

Notes

Introduction

1. On the Mormon succession crisis, see D. Michael Quinn, "The Mormon Succession Crisis of 1844," *BYU Studies* 16 (1976): 187–233; and Newell G. Bringhurst and John C. Hamer, eds., *Scattering of the Saints: Schism within Mormonism* (Independence, MO: John Whitmer Books, 2007).

2. The standard accounts of this complicated subject are Newell G. Bringhurst, *Saints, Slaves, and Blacks: The Changing Place of Black People within Mormonism* (Westport, CT: Greenwood Press, 1981), and Lester E. Bush Jr., "Mormonism's Negro Doctrine: An Historical Overview," *Dialogue: A Journal of Mormon Thought* 8 (Spring 1973): 11–68.

3. Richard L. Bushman, *Joseph Smith: Rough Stone Rolling* (New York: Alfred A. Knopf, 2005), and Fawn McKay Brodie, *No Man's Knows My History: The Life of Joseph Smith the Mormon Prophet*, 2nd ed. (orig. pub., 1945; New York: Alfred A. Knopf, 1977), mark the best expressions of Smith's evolving views on race. Also useful are the essays in *The Prophet Puzzle: Interpretive Essays on Joseph Smith*, ed. Bryan Waterman (Salt Lake City: Signature Books, 1999).

4. John G. Turner, *Brigham Young: Pioneer Prophet* (Cambridge, MA: Harvard University Press, 2012); Newell G. Bringhurst, *Brigham Young and the Expanding Mormon Frontier* (Boston: Little, Brown, 1986); and Leonard J. Arrington, *Brigham Young: An American Moses* (New York: Alfred A. Knopf, 1985) also explain the legalization of slavery in the Utah territory and Young's role in instituting the ban. A more recent and useful article is Christopher B. Rich Jr., "The True Policy for Utah: Servitude, Slavery, and 'An Act in Relation to Service,'" *Utah Historical Quarterly* 80 (2012): 54–74.

5. For the emergence of Mormonism in relation to other Great Awakening religions, see especially Paul K. Conkin, *American Originals: Homemade Varieties of Christianity* (Chapel Hill: University of North Carolina Press, 1997); Nathan O. Hatch, *The Democratization of American Christianity* (New Haven, CT: Yale University Press, 1989); and Daniel

Walker Howe, *What Hath God Wrought: The Transformation of America, 1815–1848* (New York: Oxford University Press, 2009).

6. Indeed, Harold Bloom, the eminent literary scholar, applied the term "religious genius" to Smith. See *The American Religion: The Emergence of the Post-Christian Nation* (New York: Simon and Schuster, 1992), 80. Noted historian Robert V. Remini extolled Smith as "unquestionably the most important reformer and innovator in American religious history." See his biography *Joseph Smith* (New York: Viking Penguin, 2002), ix. Smith's role as a purveyor of scripture is the subject of many scholarly appraisals. For sympathetic views, see Terryl L. Givens, *By the Hand of Mormon: The American Scripture that Launched a New World Religion* (New York: Oxford University Press, 2003); Grant Hardy, *Understanding the Book of Mormon: A Reader's Guide* (New York: Oxford University Press, 2010); Paul C. Gutjahr, *The Book of Mormon: A Biography* (Princeton, NJ: Princeton University Press, 2012); Hugh Nibley, John Gee, and Michael D. Rhoades, *Message of the Joseph Smith Papyri: An Egyptian Endowment*, 2nd ed. (Salt Lake City: Deseret Book, 2005). For critical views, consult Dan Vogel and Brent Lee Metcalf, eds., *American Apocrypha: Essays on the Book of Mormon* (Salt Lake City: Signature Books, 2002); Brent Lee Metcalf, ed., *New Approaches to the Book of Mormon: Explorations in Critical Methodology* (Salt Lake City: Signature Books, 1993); H. Michael Marquardt, *The Joseph Smith Revelations: Texts and Commentary* (Salt Lake City: Signature Books, 1999); and Robert K. Ritner, *The Joseph Smith Egyptian Papyri: A Complete Edition* (Salt Lake City: Signature Books, 2013). For Smith's translation of the Bible, see Robert J. Matthews, *Joseph Smith's Translation of the Bible: A History and Commentary* (Provo: Brigham Young University Press, 1985).

7. On the development of the Mormon priesthood, see Gregory A. Prince, *Power from On High: The Development of Mormon Priesthood* (Salt Lake City: Signature Books, 1995); D. Michael Quinn, *The Mormon Hierarchy: Origins of Power* (Salt Lake City: Signature Books, 1994); and the various entries under "priesthood" in Daniel H. Ludlow, ed., *The Encyclopedia of Mormonism*, 4 vols. (New York: Macmillan, 1992), 3: 1133–1146. A succinct explication of priesthood functions and offices can be found in general authority essays in a volume titled (no author or editor) *Priesthood* (Salt Lake City: Deseret Book, 1981). For various general authority titles, see Matthew Bowman, *The Mormon People: The Making of An American Faith* (New York: Random House, 2012), 255–256. D. Michael Quinn, *The Mormon Hierarchy: Extensions of Power* (Salt Lake City: Signature Books, 1997), 631–745, captures the demographics and family relationships of general authorities in some detail. For the comparison of Mormon stakes and wards to Catholic dioceses and parishes, see Bowman, *Mormon People*, xix.

8. Prince, *Power from On High*, explains the organization of the Mormon priesthood. For black ordination to the priesthood during Joseph Smith's era, see Newell G. Bringhurst, "Elijah Abel and the Changing Status of Blacks within Mormonism," *Dialogue: A Journal of Mormon Thought* 12 (Summer 1979): 22–36; Connell O'Donovan, "The Mormon Priesthood Ban and Elder Q. Walker Lewis: An Example for His More Whiter Brethren to Follow," *John Whitmer Historical Association Journal* 26 (2006): 47–99; Russell W. Stevenson, "'A Negro Preacher': The Worlds of Elijah Abels," *Journal of Mormon History* 39 (Spring 2013): 165–254; Stevenson, *Black Mormon: The Story of Elijah Abels* (Salt Lake

City: Self-published, 2013); W. Kesler Jackson, *Elijah Abel: The Life and Times of a Black Priesthood Holder* (Springville, UT: Cedar Fort, 2013).

9. The fullest expression of Mormon race and lineage can be found in Armand L. Mauss, *All Abraham's Children: Changing Perceptions of Race and Lineage* (Urbana: University of Illinois Press, 2003); and "In Search of Ephraim: Traditional Mormon Conception of Lineage and Race," *Journal of Mormon History* 25 (1999): 131–173. Mauss is the first scholar to treat Mormon lineage in a systematic fashion.

10. See, in particular, David M. Goldenberg, *The Curse of Ham: Race and Slavery in Early Judaism, Christianity, and Islam* (Princeton, NJ: Princeton University Press, 2003); David Brion Davis, *The Problem of Slavery in Western Culture* (Ithaca, NY: Cornell University Press, 1966); and Stephen R. Haynes, *Noah's Curse: The Biblical Justification of American Slavery* (New York: Oxford University Press, 2002).

11. Christians did not articulate the rationale for African enslavement in a systematic fashion. Rather, it emerged somewhat haphazardly over a period of several years from various writers and thinkers. For this point, consult Colin Kidd, *The Forging of Races: Race and Scripture in the Protestant Atlantic World, 1600–2000* (New York: Cambridge University Press, 2006); Winthrop Jordan, *White over Black: American Attitudes toward the Negro, 1550–1812* (Chapel Hill: University of North Carolina Press, 1968); and David Brion Davis, *Inhuman Bondage: The Rise and Fall of Slavery in the New World* (New York: Oxford University Press, 2006).

12. Abolitionist Protestant ministers did not accept the divine curse, but conservative-minded Protestants did. For biblical justifications of slavery and the curse among Protestant ministers, see Molly Oshatz, *Slavery and Sin: The Fight against Slavery and the Rise of Liberal Protestantism* (New York: Oxford University Press, 2012); Paul Finkelman, ed., *Defending Slavery: Proslavery Thought in the Old South* (Boston: Bedford/St. Martin's, 2003); Sylvester A. Johnson, *The Myth of Ham in Nineteenth-Century American Christianity: Race, Heathens, and the People of God* (New York: Palgrave Macmillan, 2004); and Mark A. Noll, *America's God: From Jonathan Edwards to Abraham Lincoln* (New York: Oxford University Press, 2002), chapter 19. For Brigham Young on race and lineage, see Turner, *Brigham Young*; Bringhurst, *Brigham Young and the Expanding Mormon Frontier*; and Arrington, *Brigham Young: An American Moses*.

13. LDS racial policy only applied to persons of African ancestry. Skin color or other characteristics were not disqualifying factors—only lineage through African bloodlines. On this point, see Matthew L. Harris, "Mormonism's Problematic Racial Past and the Evolution of the Divine Curse Doctrine," *John Whitmer Historical Association Journal* 33 (Spring–Summer 2013): 93–94n10. See also the discussion in chapter 6.

14. For the one-drop rule, consult Ariela J. Gross, *What Blood Won't Tell: A History of Race on Trial in America* (Cambridge, MA: Harvard University Press, 2008); Matthew Pratt Guterl, *The Color of Race in America, 1900–1940* (Cambridge, MA: Harvard University Press, 2002); Walter Johnson, "The Slave Trader, the White Slave, and the Politics of Racial Determination in the 1850s," *Journal of American History* 87 (June 2000): 13–38. For the emergence of Jim Crow legislation in the United States, see C. Vann Woodward, *The Strange Career of Jim Crow*, 3rd ed. rev. (1955; Oxford University Press, 1974); Michael J. Klarman, *From Jim Crow to Civil Rights: The Supreme Court and the Struggle for Racial*

Equality (New York: Oxford University Press, 2004); Williamjames Hull Hoffer, *Plessy v. Ferguson: Race and Inequality in Jim Crow America* (Lawrence: University Press of Kansas, 2012). The best treatment of miscegenation laws, passed in the two decades after the Civil War, include Peggy Pascoe, *What Comes Naturally: Miscegenation Law and the Making of Race in America* (New York: Oxford University Press, 2009); Fay Botham, *Almighty God Created the Races: Christianity, Interracial Marriage, and American Law* (Chapel Hill: University of North Carolina Press, 2009); Peter Wallenstein, *Tell the Court I Love My Wife: Race, Marriage, and Law—An American History* (New York: Palgrave Macmillan, 2002); Werner Sollors, *Interracialism: Black-White Intermarriage in American History, Literature, and Law* (New York: Oxford University Press, 2000). The disenfranchisement of blacks in the aftermath of the Civil War is best explained in Eric Foner, *Reconstruction: America's Unfinished Revolution, 1863–1877* (New York: Harper Perennial, 1988); and Alexander Keyssar, *The Right to Vote: The Contested History of Democracy in the United States* (New York: Basic Books, 2000). Jill Lepore, *The Mansion of Happiness: A History of Life and Death* (New York: Alfred A. Knopf, 2012), provides a succinct overview of the eugenics movement in the first half of the twentieth century.

15. Joseph Fielding Smith was the church's foremost doctrinal authority in the twentieth century. His many volumes constitute a landmark in the construction and exposition of Mormon doctrine. His most prominent works include *The Way to Perfection: Short Discourses on Gospel Themes* (Salt Lake City: Deseret Book, 1931); *Doctrines of Salvation: Sermons and Writings of Joseph Fielding Smith*, comp. by Bruce R. McConkie, 3 vols. (Salt Lake City: Bookcraft, 1954–1956); and *Answers to Gospel Questions*, 5 vols. (Salt Lake City: Deseret Book, 1957–1966).

16. This doctrine is most prominently expressed in Joseph Fielding Smith's various works, as well as Bruce R. McConkie, *Mormon Doctrine* (Salt Lake City: Bookcraft, 1958). A nuanced assessment of LDS doctrine on the premortal life is Boyd Jay Petersen, "'One Soul Shall Not Be Lost': The War in Heaven in Mormon Thought," *Journal of Mormon History* 38 (Winter 2012): 1–50.

17. On this point, see Mauss, *All of Abraham's Children*, 30–31.

18. On this point, see Harris, "Mormonism's Problematic Racial Past and the Evolution of the Divine Curse Doctrine," 107–108. The most dramatic expression of this position can be found in the revised doctrinal commentaries the church published in 2013. Under "Official Declaration 2" it reads: "Church records offer no clear insights into the origins of this practice [priesthood ban]. See http://www.lds.org/scriptures/dc-testament/od?lang=eng. See also chapter 7 of this volume.

19. See Jason Horwitz, "The Genesis of a Church's Stand on Race," *Washington Post*, February 28, 2012; Harris, "Mormonism's Problematic Racial Past," 90–91; Mauss, *All Abraham's Children*, 31–32, 248–249; Eugene England, "Are All Alike unto God?: Prejudice against Blacks and Women in Popular Mormon Theology," *Sunstone* 15, no. 2 (April 1990): 21–31; Keith E. Norman, "The Mark of the Curse: Lingering Racism in Mormon Doctrine?" *Dialogue* 32 (Spring 1999): 119–136; Darron T. Smith, "Unpacking Whiteness in Zion: Some Personal Reflections and General Observations," in Newell G. Bringhurst and Darron T. Smith, eds., *Black and Mormon* (Urbana: University of Illinois Press, 2004), 148–166.

20. This is a point made most prominently by Bruce R. McConkie. See his "New Revelation on Priesthood," in *Priesthood*, 126–137. Church educators have also advanced this point. See E. Dale Lebaron, "Official Declaration 2: Revelation on the Priesthood," in *The Heavens Are Open* (Salt Lake City: Deseret Book, 1993), 194–207; Juan Henderson, "A Time for Healing: Official Declaration 2," in *Out of Obscurity: The LDS Church in the Twentieth Century* (Salt Lake City: Deseret Book, 2000), 151–160; Joseph Fielding McConkie, *Answers: Straightforward Answers to Tough Gospel Questions* (Salt Lake City: Deseret Book, 1998), 29–30; Mary Jane Woodger, "Revelation Attitudes: The Coming Forth of Official Declaration 2," *Religious Educator* 3, no. 2 (2002): 185–200; Richard E. Bennet, "'That Every Man Might Speak in the Name of God the Lord': A Study of Official Declaration 2," *Religious Educator* 4, no. 2 (2003): 41–56; Rachel Cope, "Teaching Official Declaration 2" (2012), *Juvenile Instructor*, http://www.juvenileinstructor.org/teaching-official-declaration-2/. See also Armand L. Mauss, *Shifting Borders and a Tattered Passport* (Salt Lake City: University of Utah Press, 2012), 232–232n32, who critiques the notion that the 1978 priesthood revelation mitigated past teachings on race; and chapter 7 of this volume.

21. See General Authority Sheldon Child in Carrie A. Moore, "LDS Marking 30-Year Milestone," *Deseret News*, June 7, 2008; church spokesmen Mark Tuttle in Peggy Fletcher Stack, "Mormon and Black," *Salt Lake Tribune*, June 6, 2008; and a 2012 LDS church press release, "Race and the Church: All Are Alike unto God," February 29, 2012, http://www.mormonnewsroom.org/article/race-church.

22. General Authority Alexander B. Morrison explained in the fall 2000 general conference that he was happy that the church "has from its beginnings stood strongly against racism in any of its malignant manifestations." See Morrison, "No More Strangers," *Ensign* 30 (September 2000): 16. In 2006, church president Gordon B. Hinckley counseled priesthood holders not to use racial slurs or make denigrating remarks about blacks. See Hinckley, "The Need for Greater Kindness," *Ensign* 36 (May 2006): 58–61. For context to Hinckley's address, see chapter 7.

23. "Race and the Priesthood" (2013): https://www.lds.org/topics/race-and-the-priesthood. For context and background to this seminal document, see chapter 7.

24. In 2000 there were roughly twelve million Mormons. While the church does not keep membership data based on race or ethnicity, most estimates place the number of blacks in the church at roughly 500,000. See *Deseret News 1999–2000 Church Almanac* (Salt Lake City: Deseret News, 2000), 119. In the United States, scholars estimate that nearly 90 percent of Mormons are white, while less than 3 percent are black. See Pew Forum on Religion and Public Life titled "A Portrait of Mormons in the U.S.," http://pewforum.org/Christian/Mormon/A-Portrait-of-Mormons-in-the-US.aspx.

25. Bowman, *Mormon People*, 220–221, makes the point that black Africans are instructed to shed their culture when they join the LDS church. Helvécio Martins, a Brazilian, was the first black general authority of the LDS church after the revelation of 1978. He served in the Second Quorum of the Seventy from 1990 to 1995 and died in 2005. See *The Autobiography of Elder Helvécio Martins*, Helvécio Martins with Mark Grover (Salt Lake City: Aspen Books, 1994); and Mark L. Grover, "Helvécio Martins: First Black General Authority," *Journal of Mormon History* 36 (Summer 2010): 27–54. Joseph Sitati of Kenya became the second black general authority and first from Africa following the end of the

ban. He was ordained in 2009 to the First Quorum of Seventy, where he continues to serve today. See Peggy Fletcher Stack, "Africa's 'Mormon Superstar' Is First Black African LDS General Authority," *Salt Lake Tribune*, April 20, 2009; and Sitati's biography on the church website: http://www.lds.org/church/leader/joseph-w-sitati?lang=eng. The third black general authority called is Edward Dube of Zimbabwe. He was ordained to the First Quorum of Seventy in 2013 and continues in that position today. For Dube's biography, see the church website: http://www.lds.org/church/leader/edward-dube?lang=eng.

26. For Mormon outreach to blacks, see Newell G. Bringhurst, "The Image of Blacks within Mormonism as Presented in the Church News (1978–1988)," *American Periodicals: A Journal of History, Criticism, and Bibliography* 2 (Fall 1992): 113–123; Mauss, *All Abraham's Children*, 245–247; and Claudia L. Bushman, *Contemporary Mormonism: Latter-day Saints in Modern America* (Westport, CT: Praeger, 2006), 71–72.

27. For Knight's conversion to Mormonism, see Mark Albright, "The Gladys Knight Conversion Story," *Meridian Magazine*, January 21, 2013, http://www.ldsmag.com/article/12092. On Bailey's conversion, see Doug Robinson, "Thurl Bailey's Wonderful Life," *Deseret News*, February 26, 2003. Jesse L. Embry, *Black Saints in a White Church: Contemporary African American Mormons* (Salt Lake City: Signature Books, 1994), xiii, perceptively observes that "most African Americans are still more comfortable in traditional black churches."

28. Mormon scholars David E. Campbell, John C. Green, and J. Quin Monson conducted the survey. See "Survey Clarifies Mormons' Beliefs about Race," *Deseret News*, March 30, 2012. Compare this survey with "white LDS attitudes about race" in LDS sociologist Cardell K. Jacobson's study "African American Latter-day Saints: A Sociological Perspective," in Bringhurst and Smith, eds., *Black and Mormon*, 118–130.

29. This is one of two documentary histories of LDS racial teachings and only the fourth book ever published extensively examining Mormons and blacks. See Bringhurst, *Saints, Slaves, and Blacks*; Bringhurst and Smith, eds., *Black and Mormon*; Lester E. Bush Jr. and Armand L. Mauss, eds., *Neither Black nor White: Mormon Scholars Confront the Race Issue in a Universal Church* (Midvale, UT: Signature Books, 1984); and Russell W. Stevenson, ed., *For the Cause of Righteousness: A Global History of Blacks and Mormonism, 1830–2013* (Salt Lake City: Greg Kofford Books, 2014). Although Mauss's *All Abraham's Children* and W. Paul Reeve's *Religion of a Different Color: Race and the Mormon Struggle for Whiteness* (New York: Oxford University Press, 2015) discuss race and Mormonism, only part of their work deals with blacks.

30. These publications include church magazines like the *Improvement Era* and *Ensign*, to authoritative books published by the church-owned and -operated Deseret Book, to the private bookstore Bookcraft, a prolific publisher of LDS books and music.

31. It is the prerogative of the First Presidency to declare doctrine for the church. On this point, see Harris, "Mormonism's Problematic Racial Past," 101–102. The First Presidency statements referred here can be found in chapters 5–7 of this volume.

Chapter 1. Three Mormon Scriptural Works

1. For many Latter-day Saints, the standard version of the *Book of Mormon* is the 1981 edition. We use the 1902 version to avoid conflict with copyright laws.

2. Two works articulately defending this orthodox Mormon view are Richard Lyman Bushman, *Joseph Smith: Rough Stone Rolling* (New York: Alfred A. Knopf, 2005), 57–108, and Terryl L. Givens, *By the Hand of Mormon: The American Scripture that Launched a New World Religion* (New York: Oxford University Press, 2002). For two contrasting secular views concerning the origins of the *Book of Mormon*, see Fawn M. Brodie, *No Man Knows My History: The Life of Joseph Smith* (New York: Alfred A. Knopf, 1945), and Dan Vogel, *Joseph Smith: The Making of a Prophet* (Salt Lake City: Signature Books, 2004). A good overview discussing complex aspects of the *Book of Mormon* is a collection of essays by various scholars contained in Dan Vogel and Brent Lee Metcalfe, eds., *American Apocrypha: Essays on the Book of Mormon* (Salt Lake City: Signature Books, 2002).

3. The introduction to the 1981 edition of the *Book of Mormon* states that the Lamanites "are the principal ancestors of the American Indians" (*Book of Mormon* [Salt Lake City: Church of Jesus Christ of Latter-day Saints, 1981], intro.). In 2007, church officials changed the language to read that the Lamanites "are among the ancestors of the American Indians." This slight change was published in a revised edition of the *Book of Mormon* for a commercial press (New York: Doubleday, 2007), with LDS officials announcing that the change would appear in the next official version published by the church. See Carrie A. Moore, "Debate Renewed with Change in Book of Mormon Introduction," *Deseret News*, Nov. 8, 2007. For more on the vexed topic of Native Americans and the *Book of Mormon*, consult the LDS church's recently released document "Book of Mormon and DNA Studies" (2014): https://www.lds.org/topics/book-of-mormon-and-dna-studies?lang=eng.

4. Compare *Book of Mormon*, 2 Nephi 5:21, with Alma 3:13. In describing these same people, the book also uses the terms *dark* and *darkness* on four occasions: 1 Nephi 12:23; Jacob 3:9; Alma 3:6; Mormon 5:15; and the term *filthiness* three times: Jacob 3:5–9. LDS officials considered the *Book of Abraham* to be the main "proof text" justifying priesthood denial (see the discussion below), but they sometimes associated the *Book of Mormon* with their racial teachings. See, for example, Mark E. Petersen, "Race Problems—As They Affect the Church," speech to LDS religious educators, August 27, 1954, typescript in LDS Church History Library; Bruce R. McConkie, *Mormon Doctrine* (Salt Lake City: Bookcraft, 1958), 108; Melvin R. Brooks, *L.D.S. Reference Encyclopedia* (Salt Lake City: Bookcraft, 1960), 328; Alvin R. Dyer, "For What Purpose?" speech to LDS missionaries, March 18, 1961, Oslo Norway, LDS Church History Library. For a discussion explaining how the *Book of Mormon* text has changed over time, see Royal Skousen, *The Book of Mormon: The Earliest Text* (New Haven, CT: Yale University Press, 2009); John S. Dinger, *Significant Textual Changes in the Book of Mormon: The First Printed Edition Compared to the Manuscripts and to the Subsequent Major LDS English Printed Editions* (Salt Lake City: Signature Books, 2013).

5. *Book of Mormon*, Helaman 6:27; Ether 8:15.

6. Ibid., Ether 1–5.

7. Parley P. Pratt to John Van Cott, May 7, 1843, Parley P. Pratt Papers, LDS Church History Library. In making this observation, Pratt expressed his reaction to discovering the so-called Kinderhook Plates in 1843. For additional commentary on the Jaredites, see Sidney B. Sperry, *Book of Mormon Compendium* (Salt Lake City: Bookcraft, 1968), 461; Brooks, *L.D.S. Reference Encyclopedia*, 209; and Hugh Nibley, *Lehi in the Desert, the World of the Jaredites, There Were Jaredites* (Salt Lake City: Deseret Book, 1988).

8. *Book of Mormon*, Ether 1:3, 5, 33, 2:1.

9. Ibid., Jacob 3:8; Alma 3:16. Discussion of the Jaredites was a digression from the main text of the *Book of Mormon*, which was primarily concerned with discussion of the Nephites and Lamanites.

10. Such concepts are discussed in Marvin Harris, *Rise of Anthropological Theory: A History of Theories of Culture* (New York: Thomas Y. Crowell, 1968), 25–26, 58, 86; William Stanton, *The Leopard's Spots: Scientific Attitudes toward Race in America, 1815–59* (Chicago: University of Chicago Press, 1960), 9–11. According to Harris, some Americans believed that such racial change could take place within a single lifetime. For a more complete discussion of such theories as articulated in the *Book of Mormon*, see Newell G. Bringhurst, *Saints, Slaves, and Blacks: The Changing Place of Black People within Mormonism* (Westport, CT: Greenwood Press, 1981), 3–14. Also see Armand L. Mauss, *All Abraham's Children: Changing Mormon Conceptions of Race and Lineage* (Urbana: University of Illinois Press, 2003), 49–52.

11. Harris, *Rise of Anthropological Theory*, 54; and Klaus J. Hansen, "The Millennium, the West, and Race," *Western History Quarterly* 3 (October 1972): 381.

12. *Book of Mormon*, Alma 24:17–18; 3 Nephi 3:15–16.

13. Ibid., 2 Nephi 30:6. In 1981, LDS officials changed the term "white and delightsome" to "pure and delightsome." According to BYU scholar Royal Skousen, Joseph Smith changed this phrase, but the original stayed in the standard printings of the *Book of Mormon* until 1981. For more on this point, see Skousen, *Book of Mormon*; Dinger, *Significant Textual Changes in the Book of Mormon*. The *Book of Mormon* teachings on "whiteness" appears to have influenced LDS leadership well into the twentieth century. In 1954, apostle Joseph Fielding Smith candidly admitted that "we know of cases" where the "dark skin . . . really has disappeared" (Joseph Fielding Smith and Mark E. Petersen, "Discussion after Talk on Racial Prejudice," October 7, 1954, p. 22, in box 4, folder 7, William E. Berrett Papers, L. Tom Perry Special Collections, Harold B. Lee Library, BYU). Similarly, apostle Spencer W. Kimball appealed to 2 Nephi 30:6, claiming that the Lamanites' skin color grew lighter when they converted to the LDS faith (Kimball, *Conference Report* [October 1960]: 32–37). The LDS church no longer accepts this version of "whiteness." See "Race and the Priesthood" (2013): https://www.lds.org/topics/race-and-the-priesthood.

14. As noted by Marvin Harris, *Rise of Anthropological Theory*, 84.

15. *Book of Mormon*, 2 Nephi 9:5–22, 25:16; 26:13.

16. Ibid., Alma 5:1:30.

17. Ibid., Alma 5:49, 29:2, 17:8, 23:4–13; Helaman 5:18–19, 48–52; 3 Nephi 2:2:12–16; 2 Nephi 26:28.

18. Ibid., Alma 27:9.

19. Ibid., Alma 44:2. See also Alma 27:9. It is worth noting the comparisons between such *Book of Mormon* prohibitions with those Old Testament verses condoning the holding of slaves by God's chosen peoples along with the rules to be followed in such slaveholding. Specifically see: Genesis 14:14, 24:34, 30:43; Exodus 20:17, 21:2–32; Leviticus 25:39–55; 2 Samuel 8:2, 614; 1 Chronicles 18:2, 6, 13; Proverbs 29–30.

20. *Book of Mormon*, Mosiah 7:15; Alma 43:29.

21. Ibid., Alma 50:22.

22. Ibid., Alma 43:45–49, 48:10–11, 53:17.

23. Ibid., Jacob 5:15–75; Mosiah 7:15, 20, 22; 11:21, 23, 29:18; Alma 50:22, 61:12.

24. Thomas F. Gossett, *Race: The History of an Idea in America* (New York: Oxford University Press, 1963), 243; George M. Fredrickson, *The Black Image in the White Mind* (New York: Harper and Row, 1971), 43.

25. Ernest Lee Tuveson, *Redeemer Nation: The Idea of America's Role* (Chicago: University of Chicago, 1968), 53, 78.

26. For most Latter-day Saints, the standard edition of the *Pearl of Great Price* is the 1981 version. We use the 1907 version to avoid conflict with copyright laws.

27. In addition to the *Book of Moses* and *Book of Abraham*, the *Pearl of Great Price* also contains two sets of additional writings of Joseph Smith, specifically "An extract from his Translation of the New Testament," Matthew Chapter 23:39 and Chapter 24; Extracts from Joseph Smith's History; and the Thirteen Articles of Faith of the Church of Jesus Christ of Latter-day Saints. For Smith's translation of the Bible, see Robert J. Matthews, *Joseph Smith's Translation of the Bible: A History and Commentary* (Provo: Brigham Young University Press, 1985).

28. "The Prophecy of Enoch," *Evening and Morning Star*, August 1832 and "Book of Moses," March and April 1833. Joseph Smith's revision of the Bible was essentially complete by 1833, but the entire biblical manuscript was not published until 1867, some twenty-three years after Joseph Smith's death. Such publication under the title *Holy Scriptures* was done by the Missouri-based Reorganized Church of Jesus Christ of Latter Day Saints under the direction of Joseph Smith III, leader of that denomination and the eldest son of Joseph Smith Jr. The Utah-based Church of Jesus Christ of Latter-day Saints never published the complete revision of Joseph Smith's Old and New Testaments, proclaiming it "incomplete." The Utah Mormon church ultimately included the "Book of Moses" as part of the *Pearl of Great Price*, initially published in 1851. It was canonized as Mormon scripture in 1880.

29. *Pearl of Great Price*, Moses 5:49–50.

30. Ibid., Moses 5:49–50. For a more extensive discussion, see Armand L. Mauss, "Mormonism and the Negro: Faith, Folklore and Civil Rights," *Dialogue: The Journal of Mormon Thought* 4 (1967): 19–39.

31. Ibid., Moses 6:52, 54.

32. There is controversy concerning the origins of the Egyptian papyri as it relates to the *Book of Abraham*. Generally, non-Mormon Egyptologists have maintained that Joseph Smith could not have translated this work from the papyri in his position as Mormon prophet during the 1830s and early 1840s. On the other hand, Latter-day Saint scholars have retorted that Smith could have translated the *Book of Abraham* from papyri other than those examined by Egyptologists. Other Mormon defenders have suggested that the examined papyri have a double meaning. They acknowledge the findings of non-Mormon Egyptologists, which indicate a meaning different from the *Book of Abraham*, but they maintain that Joseph Smith in his translation came up with a second, subtle meaning representing the writings of Abraham. This debate has waxed strong particularly since the late 1960s and past the turn of the century. See, for example, John A. Wilson, Richard

A. Parker, Richard P. Howard et al., "The Joseph Smith Egyptian Papyri: Translations and Interpretations," *Dialogue: A Journal of Mormon Thought* 3 (Autumn 1968): 109–34; Klaus Baer, "The Breathing Permit of Hor: A Translation of the Apparent Source of the Book of Abraham," *Dialogue: A Journal of Mormon Thought* 3 (Autumn 1968): 109–34; H. Donl Peterson, *The Story of the Book of Abraham: Mummies, Manuscripts, and Mormonism* (Salt Lake City: Deseret Book, 1995); Hugh Nibley, *The Message of the Joseph Smith Papyri: An Egyptian Endowment* (Salt Lake City: Deseret Book, 1975); Hugh Nibley, John Gee, and Michael D. Rhoades, *Message of the Joseph Smith Papyri: An Egyptian Endowment*, 2nd ed. (Salt Lake City: Deseret Book, 2005). For a critical account of the *Book of Abraham*, see Robert K. Ritner, *The Joseph Smith Egyptian Papyri: A Complete Edition* (Salt Lake City: Signature Books, 2013). For the LDS church's latest expression on the *Book of Abraham*, see "Translation and Historicity of the *Book of Abraham*" (2014): https://www.lds.org/topics/translation-and-historicity-of-the-book-of-abraham?lang=eng.

33. *Times and Seasons* (Nauvoo, Illinois), March 1 and 15, 1842.

34. For three different perspectives on Joseph Smith's acquisition and translation of the Egyptian papyrus leading to the *Book of Abraham*, see Richard Lyman Bushman, *Joseph Smith: Rough Stone Rolling*, 131–32, 285–93, 452–58; Donna Hill, *Joseph Smith: The First Mormon* (New York: Doubleday, 1977), 192–94; Fawn M. Brodie, *No Man Knows My History*, 170–71.

35. Richard Bushman, *Rough Stone Rolling*, 288–289.

36. For a nuanced view of the "war in heaven," see Boyd Jay Petersen, "'One Soul Shall Not Be Lost': The War in Heaven in Mormon Thought," *Journal of Mormon History* 38 (Winter 2012): 1–50.

37. Orson Hyde, *Speech Given Before the High Priests Quorum in Nauvoo*, April 25, 1845 (Liverpool, England, 1845), 30. It should be noted that Brigham Young himself rejected Hyde's argument that preexistent behavior contributed to the unfavorable status of blacks. When asked "if the spirits of negroes were neutral in Heaven," Young replied: "The posterity of Cane are Black because he commit murder." In Wilford Woodruff journal, December 25, 1869, Scott G. Kenney, ed., *Wilford Woodruff's Journal, 1833–1898, Typescript*, 9 vols. (Midvale: Signature Books, 1983–1985), 6:511.

38. See, in particular, Brigham H. Roberts, writing in *The Contributor*, an official LDS publication, who stated that the black race "is the one through which is ordained those spirits that were not valiant in the great rebellion in heaven should come; who through their indifference or lack of integrity to righteousness, rendered themselves unworthy of the Priesthood and its powers, and hence it is withheld from them to this day." See *The Contributor* (1885): 6:296–97. Further developing this so-called "preexistence hypothesis" was influential Mormon leader and future LDS church president Joseph Fielding Smith, most evident in his *The Way to Perfection*, published in 1931. In that seminal work, he referred to the black race as derived from those "who did not stand valiantly," who "were almost persuaded, were indifferent, and who sympathized with Lucifer, but did not follow him" in the War in Heaven. See Joseph Fielding Smith, *The Way to Perfection* (Salt Lake City: Deseret Book, 1931), 43–44, 105–6. And Lester E. Bush Jr. asserts that from 1931 on "the 'pre-existence hypothesis' was presented with increasing frequency and confidence

until 1949 when it formed a major portion of the first public statement of church policy towards blacks to be issued by the First Presidency." See Lester E. Bush Jr., "Mormonism's Negro Doctrine: An Historical Overview," 56, in Lester E. Bush Jr. and Armand L. Mauss, *Neither White nor Black: Mormon Scholars Confront the Race Issue in a Universal Church* (Midvale, UT: Signature Books, 1984), 88.

39. For most Latter-day Saints, the standard edition of the *Doctrine and Covenants* is the 1981 version. We use the 1876 version to avoid conflict with copyright laws.

40. As described by Bushman, *Rough Stone Rolling*, 182, 184. The bulk of Smith's published revelations are included in Robin Scott Jensen et al., eds., *Joseph Smith Papers: Revelations and Translations*, Vol. 2: Published Revelations (Salt Lake City: Church Historian's Press, 2011).

41. The precise rationale for its omission is unclear. Writing years later, Brigham Young suggested that "it was not wisdom to publish [the revelation] to the world." Brigham Young, *Journal of Discourses* (May 29, 1860): 8:58. A twentieth-century scholar has theorized that Joseph Smith chose not to include the revelation in the *Doctrine and Covenants* because by 1835 "the nullification crisis had subsided." Dan Erickson, *As a Thief in the Night: The Mormon Quest for Millennial Deliverance* (Salt Lake City: Signature Books, 1998), 78. LDS spokesmen, in fact, chose not to make the revelation public until 1851, some seven years after Smith's death, when it was included in the first edition of the *Pearl of Great Price*. Ultimately it was moved from the *Pearl of Great Price* into the *Doctrine and Covenants* as Section 87, commencing with the 1876 edition of the latter work. An early copy of Smith's "Revelation and Prophecy on War" can be found in Robin Scott Jensen et al., eds., *The Joseph Smith Papers, Revelations and Translations: Manuscript Revelation Books* (Salt Lake City: Church Historian's Press, 2009), 291.

42. Two older accounts of this revolt are Herbert Aptheker, *Nat Turner's Slave Rebellion* (New York: Humanities Press, 1966), and Stephen B. Oats, *The Fires of Jubilee: Nat Turner's Fierce Rebellion* (New York: Harper and Row, 1975). For a recent analysis of the rebellion, consult the essays in Kenneth S. Greenburg, ed., *Nat Turner: A Slave Rebellion in History and Memory* (New York: Oxford University Press, 2003). Turner's own recollection of the uprising is recorded in Kenneth S. Greenberg, ed., *The Confessions of Nat Turner and Related Documents* (Boston: St. Martin's Press, 1996).

43. The two major book-length studies discussing this event are Richard R. Ellis, *The Union at Risk: Jacksonian Democracy, States' Rights, and the Nullification Crisis* (New York: Oxford University Press, 1987), and William W. Freeling, *Prelude to Civil War: The Nullification Controversy in South Carolina, 1816–1836* (New York: Harper and Row, 1965). A more full account of the secessionist crisis can be found in William W. Freeling, *The Road to Disunion, vol. 1, Secessionists at Bay, 1776–1854* (New York: Oxford University Press, 1990).

44. Two major studies dealing with Mormon millenarianism, albeit from different perspectives, are Grant Underwood, *The Millenarian World of Early Mormonism* (Urbana: University of Illinois Press, 1993), and Erickson, *As a Thief in the Night*.

45. Erickson, *As a Thief in the Night*, 67. In April 1838 the official name of the church was changed one more time to The Church of Jesus Christ of Latter Day Saints—this latter designation the official designation of the Utah-based Mormon Church.

46. For an overview of various aspects of William Miller and the so-called Millerites, see Ronald Numbers and Jonathan Butler, eds., *The Disappointed: Millerism and Millenarianism* (Bloomington: University of Indiana Press, 1987). For a comparison of the millenarian teachings of the Millerites vis-à-vis the Mormons, see Underwood, *The Millenarian World of Early Mormonism*, in particular his chapter "Apocalyptic Adversaries: Mormonism Meets Millerism," 112–26.

47. For a discussion of the importance of Independence, Missouri, as Mormonism's Zion or central gathering place, see Craig S. Campbell, *Images of the New Jerusalem: Latter Day Saint Interpretations of Independence, Missouri* (Knoxville: University of Tennessee Press, 2004).

48. *Evening and Morning Star* (Independence, Missouri), October 1832, December 1832, May 1833, June 1833. Although on one occasion in June 1832 the *Star* made a passing reference (without comment) to "the insurrection of negroes in the southern states." For a more complete discussion of such behavior, see Bringhurst, *Saints, Slaves, and Blacks*, 16–17.

49. Lester E. Bush Jr., "Mormonism's Negro Doctrine," 56.

50. Lester E. Bush Jr., "A Commentary on Stephen G. Taggart's Mormonism's Negro Policy: Social and Historical Origins," in Bush and Mauss, *Neither White nor Black*, 34. The later revelation is contained in *Doctrine and Covenants* 104, Sections 16–18, 83, 84, given April 23, 1834.

51. This declaration was initially printed in the *Latter Day Saint Messenger and Advocate*, August 1835. This publication had replaced the *Evening and Morning Star* as the church's official publication.

52. For a more complete discussion of this Mormon objective, see Bringhurst, *Saints, Slaves, and Blacks*, 15–33. For Smith's nuanced views relative to slavery and abolitionism, see Bushman, *Rough Stone Rolling*, 327–28, and Hill, *Joseph Smith*, chapter 12.

53. Gilbert Hobbs Barnes, *The Anti-Slavery Impulse, 1830–1844* (New York: Peter Smith, 1964); Dwight L. Dumond, *The Antislavery Origins of the Civil War* (Ann Arbor: University of Michigan Press, 1939); and W. G. Burroughs, "Oberlin's Part in the Slavery Conflict," *Ohio Archaeological and Historical Quarterly* 20 (1911): 269–83.

54. Edward Coleman Reilley, "The Early Slavery Controversy in the Western Reserve" (PhD diss., Western Reserve University, 1940), 160. For a comprehensive study of anti-abolitionist violence during this period, see Leonard L. Richards, *"Gentlemen of Property and Standing": Anti-Abolitionist Mobs in Jacksonian America* (New York: Oxford University Press, 1970); and Paul Goodman, *Of One Blood: Abolitionism and the Origins of Racial Equality* (Berkeley: University of California Press, 1988).

Chapter 2. Joseph Smith and Evolving Mormon Attitudes and Practices on Slavery and Race, 1830–1844

1. *Evening and Morning Star*, June 1832; also in Robin Scott Jensen et al., eds., *Joseph Smith Papers: Revelations and Translations, Vol. 2: Published Revelations* (Salt Lake City: Church Historian's Press, 2011), 202–216. For a discussion of William Wines Phelps's editorship of the *Evening and Morning Star*, and his role as an important early Mormon

leader, see Walter D. Bowen, "The Versatile W. W. Phelps—Mormon Writer, Educator, and Pioneer" (MA thesis, Brigham Young University, 1958).

2. For a discussion of such attitudes as reflected in this seminal scriptural work, see chapter 1.

3. Specifically, this statement declared that the Latter-day Saints did "not believe it right to interfere with bond servants, neither preach the gospel to, nor baptize them contrary to the will or wish of their masters, nor to meddle with or influence them in the least to cause them to be dissatisfied with their situations in this life." As noted in chapter 1, this statement was first adopted as a resolution by a "General Assembly" of the church in August 1835 and subsequently published in the *Latter Day Saints' Messenger and Advocate*, which replaced the *Evening and Morning Star* as the church's official newspaper. The statement itself eventually became church law by virtue of its incorporation in the *Doctrine and Covenants* as Section 134.

4. For a reliable discussion of the importance of Zion, see Craig S. Campbell, *Images of the New Jerusalem: Latter Day Saint Faction Interpretations of Independence, Missouri* (Knoxville: University of Tennessee Press, 2004).

5. For two perspectives on this development, see Lester E. Bush Jr., "Mormonism's Negro Doctrine: An Historical Overview," *Dialogue: A Journal of Mormon Thought* 8 (1973): 12–15; and Newell G. Bringhurst, *Saints, Slaves, and Blacks: The Changing Place of Black People within Mormonism* (Westport, CT: Greenwood Press, 1981), 19–24. For a perceptive discussion of northern anti-abolitionist activity during the 1830s, see Leonard L. Richards, *Gentlemen of Property and Standing: Anti-Abolition Mobs in Jacksonian America* (New York: Oxford University Press, 1970); Lewis Perry, *Radical Abolitionism: Anarchy and the Government of God in Antislavery Thought* (Ithaca, NY: Cornell University Press, 1973); John Stauffer, *The Black Hearts of Men: Radical Abolitionists and the Transformation of Race* (Cambridge, MA: Harvard University Press, 2002); and David Brion Davis, *Inhuman Bondage: The Rise and Fall of Slavery in the New World* (New York: Oxford University Press, 2006), chapter 13.

6. *Doctrine and Covenants*, 130:15–17. Also see Joseph Smith Jr., "Discourse," July 19, 1840, Joseph Smith Papers, LDS Church History Library. Smith expressed his belief that the Second Coming was at least fifty years away. For more on this topic, see Richard Bushman, *Rough Stone Rolling: A Cultural Biography of Mormonism's Founder* (New York: Alfred Knopf, 2005); and Grant Underwood, *The Millenarian World of Early Mormonism* (Urbana: University of Illinois Press, 1994).

7. For a detailed discussion of this development, see Bringhurst, *Saints, Slaves and Blacks*, 54–60. For the abolition of slavery in Great Britain, go to Christopher Leslie Brown, *Moral Capital: Foundations of British Abolitionism* (Chapel Hill: University of North Carolina Press, 2006). For abolitionism in the United States, see Davis, *Inhuman Bondage*.

8. For biographical sketches of the above three individuals, see W. Kesler Jackson, *Elijah Abel: The Life and Times of a Black Priesthood Holder* (Springville, UT: Cedar Fort, 2013); Russell W. Stevenson, "'A Negro Preacher': The Worlds of Elijah Abels," *Journal of Mormon History* 39 (Spring 2013): 165–254; Newell G. Bringhurst, "Elijah Abel and the Changing Status of Blacks within Mormonism," *Dialogue: A Journal of Mormon Thought*

12 (Summer 1979): 22–36; Connell O'Donovan, "The Mormon Priesthood Ban and Elder Q. Walker Lewis: An Example for His More Whiter Brethren to Follow," *John Whitmer Historical Association Journal* 26 (2006): 48–100; and Connell O'Donovan, "Brigham Young, African Americans, and Plural Marriage: Schism and the Beginnings of Black Priesthood Denial," in Newell G. Bringhurst and Craig L. Foster, eds., *The Persistence of Polygamy: From Joseph Smith's Martyrdom to the First Manifesto, 1844 to 1890* (Independence, MO: John Whitmer Books, 2013), 48–86.

9. For an insightful discussion of Enoch Lovejoy Lewis, among the first African Americans to embrace Mormonism, see O'Donovan, "Brigham Young, African Americans, and Plural Marriage," 59–60. For Black Pete, see Mark Lyman Staker, *Hearken, O Ye People: The Historical Setting of Joseph Smith's Ohio Revelations* (Salt Lake City: Greg Kofford Books, 2009).

10. Parley P. Pratt, *Late Persecutions of the Church of Latter-day Saints* (New York, 1840), 28.

11. See Bringhurst, *Saints, Slaves and Blacks*, 218. Also see tables 7 and 8 on pages 222 and 223 in this same work. For Smith's association with Elijah Abel and other black people, see Bushman, *Rough Stone Rolling*, 289; and Donna Hill, *Joseph Smith: The First Mormon* (New York: Doubleday, 1977), 381–382, who notes that "Black convert Elijah Abel was ordained an elder under Joseph Smith's direction . . . [and] received his patriarchal blessing from Joseph Smith, Sr." Hill (*Joseph Smith*, 381) contains a brief discussion of missionaries apprising Smith of southern blacks seeking baptism.

12. The total number of Mormons who settled in this region went from 300 in May 1832 to 1,200 by July 1833. These numbers are particularly significant given that the total population of Jackson County was just 5,071 in 1832. These are figures compiled from Fawn M. Brodie's *No Man Knows My History: A Biography of Joseph Smith*, 2nd ed. (New York: Alfred A. Knopf, 1977). See also Stephen C. LeSueur, *The 1838 Mormon War in Missouri* (Columbia: University of Missouri Press, 1987), 35–36.

13. *Evening and Morning Star*, July 1833, 111.

14. "The Manifesto of the Mob," as reprinted in Joseph Smith Jr., *History of the Church of Jesus Christ of Latter-day Saints*, B. H. Roberts, ed., 7 vols. (Salt Lake City: Deseret News, 1902–12), 1:378.

15. *Evening and Morning Star*, "Extra," July 16, 1833, reprinted in Smith's *History of the Church*, 1:378. For more on Phelps's article, see John Whitmer, "History, 1831–Circa 1847," in Karen Lynn Davidson et al., eds., *The Joseph Smith Papers: Histories, Vol. 2: Assigned Histories, 1831–1847* (Salt Lake City: Historians Press, 2012), 53.

16. At least two authors have argued that issues other than slavery and race were more crucial in causing non-Mormon violence in Jackson County, culminating in the Mormons' ultimate expulsion. See Richard L. Bushman, "Mormon Persecutions in Missouri, 1833," *Brigham Young University Studies* 3 (Autumn 1960): 11–20; Warren A. Jennings, "Factors in the Destruction of the Mormon Press in Missouri, 1833," *Utah Historical Quarterly* 35 (Winter 1967): 56–76.

17. The definitive work on this development is LeSueur, *1838 Mormon War in Missouri*.

18. For a detailed discussion of this development, see Bringhurst, *Saints, Slaves, and Blacks*, 15–16.

19. Joseph Smith to Oliver Cowdery, April 1836, in *Latter Day Saints' Messenger and Advocate* (Kirtland, Ohio), 2: 289.

20. As outlined by Bush, "Mormonism's Negro Doctrine," 14.

21. Smith to Cowdery, April 1836, in *Latter Day Saints Messenger and Advocate* 2: 289-90.

22. Ibid., 290-291.

23. Ibid., 291.

24. *Latter Day Saints' Messenger and Advocate* (Kirtland, Ohio), April and May 1836.

25. For three perspectives concerning the life and career of Elijah Abel, see Bringhurst, "Elijah Abel and the Changing Status of Blacks within Mormonism"; Jackson, *Elijah Abel*; Stevenson, "'A Negro Preacher.'"

26. *Latter Day Saints' Messenger and Advocate* (Kirtland, Ohio), June 1836; Bringhurst, *Saints, Slaves, and Blacks*, 38. See also Stevenson, "'A Negro Preacher,'" 191-96.

27. Jackson, *Elijah Abel*, 56-59; Stevenson, "'A Negro Preacher,'" 194, 199.

28. Jackson, *Elijah Abel*, 56-59.

29. Bush, "Mormonism's Negro Doctrine," 32.

30. Jackson, *Elijah Abel*, 57.

31. Three book-length studies discuss Joseph Smith's 1844 presidential campaign, albeit from differing perspectives: Arnold K. Garr, *Joseph Smith: Presidential Candidate* (Orem, UT: Millennial Press, 2007); Robert S. Wicks and Fred R. Foister, *Junius & Joseph: Presidential Politics and the Assassination of the First Mormon Prophet* (Logan: Utah State University Press, 2005); and LeGrand Baker, *Murder of the Mormon Prophet: Prelude to the Death of Joseph Smith* (Salt Lake City: Eborn Books, 2006). For a chapter-length analytical overview, see Newell G. Bringhurst and Craig L. Foster, *The Mormon Quest for the Presidency: From Joseph Smith to Mitt Romney and Jon Huntsman* (Independence, MO: John Whitmer Books, 2011), 7-49.

32. See, for example, Eric Burin, *Slavery and the Peculiar Solution: A History of the American Colonization Society* (Gainesville: University Press of Florida, 2005); and David Brion Davis, *Inhuman Bondage: The Rise and Fall of Slavery in the New World* (New York: Oxford University Press, 2006), chapter 13.

33. The feasibility of Smith's proposal to liberate the black slaves through the payment of a "reasonable price" to southern slaveholders with funds obtained from the sale of public lands has been questioned by at least one writer, who explained, "There were almost 3,000,000 slaves in 1844, with the average value in excess of $500. Total public land sales in the 1840s averaged approximately $2,000,000 yearly, and the proposed cutbacks in congressional membership and pay (which Smith suggested as an additional source of revenue) would have produced perhaps $500,000." According to these figures, at 1840 rates it would have taken about seven hundred years, rather than the five to six estimated by Smith to carry out his program. See Martin B. Hickman, "Editorial Footnotes to General Smith's Views . . .," *Dialogue: A Journal of Mormon Thought* 3 (Autumn 1968): 28.

34. It should be noted that Smith's call for gradual, compensated emancipation was far from unique. In fact, a number of prominent Americans, including Thomas Jefferson and Henry Clay, had made similar proposals. See Davis, *Inhuman Bondage*, 256, and P. J. Staudenraus, *The African Colonization Movement, 1816-1865* (New York: Columbia University Press, 1961).

35. Fredrick Merk, *Manifest Destiny and Mission in American History* (New York: Alfred Knopf, 1963), 24–88; Louis Filler, *The Crusade against Slavery, 1830–1860* (New York: Harper and Row, 1960), 176–77. See also Joel H. Silbey, *Storm over Texas: The Annexation Controversy and the Road to Civil War* (New York: Oxford University Press, 2005); Michael F. Holt, *The Rise and Fall of the American Whig Party: Jacksonian Politics and the Onset of the Civil War* (New York: Oxford University Press, 1999); and Steven E. Woodworth, *Manifest Destinies: America's Westward Expansion and the Road to the Civil War* (New York: Alfred Knopf, 2010).

36. As quoted in Joseph Smith Jr., *History of the Church*, 2nd ed., 7 vols. (Salt Lake City: Deseret Book, 1978), 6:244.

37. Joseph Smith, "Views of the Powers and Policy of the Government," *Times and Seasons* (May 15, 1844), 5:531.

38. William W. Phelps and John M. Bernhisel, Smith's political advisors, helped craft his presidential platform. For this point, see Bushman, *Rough Stone Rolling*, 515; and Bringhurst and Foster, *Mormon Quest for the Presidency*, 28.

Chapter 3. Brigham Young, the Beginning of Black Priesthood Denial, and Legalization of Slavery in Utah, 1844–1877

1. For five differing perspectives on this seminal development, see Lester E. Bush Jr., "Mormonism's Negro Doctrine: An Historical Overview," *Dialogue: A Journal of Mormon Thought* 8 (Spring 1973): 22–31; Newell G. Bringhurst, *Saints, Slaves, and Blacks*, 62–143; Armand L. Mauss, *All Abraham's Children: Changing Mormon Conceptions of Race and Lineage* (Urbana: University of Illinois Press, 2003), 212–217; John G. Turner, *Brigham Young: Pioneer Prophet* (Cambridge, MA: Harvard University Press, 2012), 218–229; and Connell O'Donovan, "Brigham Young, African Americans, and Plural Marriage: Schism, Race, and the Beginnings of Black Priesthood Denial," in Newell G. Bringhurst and Craig L. Foster, eds., *The Persistence of Polygamy: From Joseph Smith's Martyrdom to the First Manifesto, 1844 to 1890* (Independence, MO: John Whitmer Books, 2013), 48–86.

2. Lester Bush asserts that the ban may have begun in 1849, but recent scholarship by W. Paul Reeve affirms that it began in 1852. See Bush, "Mormonism's Negro Doctrine," 25, and Reeve, *Religion of a Different Color: Race and the Mormon Struggle for Whiteness* (New York: Oxford University Press, 2015), 148–155. Church leaders applied the ban unevenly. The evidence suggests that several Mormons of African American ancestry received the priesthood after Joseph Smith's death. These include, among others, Samuel Chambers, Eduard Legroan, Enoch Abel, and Elijah Abel. For this point, see Lester Bush, "A Commentary on Stephen G. Taggart's Mormonism's Negro Policy: Social and Historical Origins," in Bush and Armand L. Mauss, eds., *Neither White Nor Black: Mormon Scholars Confront the Race Issue in a Universalist Church* (Midvale, UT: Signature Books, 1984), 44–45n30.

3. For a detailed discussion of Joseph T. Ball and his Mormon involvement, see O'Donovan, "Brigham Young, African Americans, and Plural Marriage," 49–56.

4. "General Minutes," April 15, 1847, LDS Church History Library. For a full discussion of McCary's activities, see O'Connell, "Brigham Young, African Americans, and Plural Marriage," 60–76, and Bringhurst, *Saints, Slaves, and Blacks*, 84–86.

5. William I. Appleby to Brigham Young, May 19, 1847, LDS Church History Library.

6. For Lewis's ordination, see Connell O'Donovan, "The Mormon Priesthood Ban and Elder Q. Walker Lewis: 'An Example for his More Whiter Brethren to Follow,'" *John Whitmer Historical Association Journal* 26 (2006): 66–67.

7. As labeled by Mauss in *All Abraham's Children*, 9.

8. For this discussion, see Bringhurst, *Saints, Slaves, and Blacks*, 95. For an extended discussion of Mormonism and "whiteness," see Reeve, *Religion of a Different Color*. For a general discussion about "whiteness" as it relates to the construction of race, see Matthew Frye Jacobson, *Whiteness of a Different Color: European Immigrants and the Alchemy of Race* (Cambridge, MA: Harvard University Press, 1998); and David Roediger, *The Wages of Whiteness: Race and the Making of the American Working Class*, rev. ed. (New York: Verso, 1998).

9. Mauss, *All Abraham's Children*, 21–22.

10. Ibid., 96–97.

11. Ibid., 91, 97.

12. For a detailed discussion of this development, see O'Donovan, "Brigham Young, African Americans, and Plural Marriage."

13. For a detailed discussion of this development, see Bringhurst, *Saints, Slaves, and Blacks*, 61–63.

14. The literature on the Compromise of 1850 is extensive. For the best works, see Michael F. Holt, *The Fate of Their Country: Politicians, Slavery Extension, and the Coming of the Civil War* (New York: Hill and Wang, 2005); David M. Potter, *The Impending Crisis, 1848–1861* (New York: Harper Perennial, 1977); and Holman Hamilton, *Prologue to Conflict: The Crisis and Compromise of 1850* (New York: W. W. Norton, 1966).

15. As stated by John G. Turner in *Brigham Young: Pioneer Prophet* (Cambridge, MA: Harvard University Press, 2012), 225.

16. Turner, *Brigham Young*, 225.

17. For a listing and description of these various Mormon slaveholders, see "Appendix C: Mormon Slaveholders, Black Slaves, Free Blacks, and Census Information on Utah's Black Population," in Bringhurst, *Saints, Slaves, and Blacks*, 218–228.

18. For two different perspectives on the circumstances surrounding the issue of slavery and Utah statehood, see Christopher B. Rich Jr., "The True Policy for Utah: Servitude, Slavery, and 'An Act in Relation to Service,'" *Utah Historical Quarterly* 80 (2012): 54–74; and Turner, *Brigham Young*, 198–199.

19. "Speech [sic] by Gov. Young in Counsel on a Bill relating to the Affrican [sic] Slavery," January 23, 1852, Brigham Young Papers, LDS Church History Library. For a discussion of this development, see Bringhurst, *Saints, Slaves, and Blacks*, 68.

20. Bush, "Mormonism's Negro Doctrine," 25. Some European Christians and nineteenth-century Protestant ministers also accepted uncritically the Cain-Ham genealogy. For a sampling of this literature, consult Stephen R. Haynes, *Noah's Curse: The Biblical*

Justification of American Slavery (New York: Oxford University Press, 2002); Colin Kidd, *The Forging of Races: Race and Scripture in the Protestant Atlantic World, 1600–2000* (New York: Cambridge University Press, 2006); Molly Oshatz, *Slavery and Sin: The Fight Against Slavery and the Rise of Liberal Protestantism* (New York: Oxford University Press, 2012); Paul Finkelman, ed., *Defending Slavery: Proslavery Thought in the Old South* (Boston: Bedford/St. Martin's, 2003); and Mark A. Noll, *America's God: From Jonathan Edwards to Abraham Lincoln* (New York: Oxford University Press, 2002), chapter 19.

21. Contrary to their title, the county probate courts in Utah, under the direct control of Latter-day Saint officials, had judicial authority over more than just property matters, but more specifically power over original jurisdiction in all types of civil and criminal actions. For an overview of this unique judicial institution, see James B. Allen, "The Unusual Jurisdiction of Country Probate Courts in the Territory of Utah," *Utah Historical Quarterly* 36 (1968): 133–142.

22. In fact, a number of the provisions in the 1852 act were remarkably similar to those in an 1819 Illinois provision regulating indentured servants in that state. See Paul M. Angle, "The Illinois Black Laws," *Chicago History* 8 (Spring 1967): 66–67.

23. Brigham Young, "Message to the Joint Session of Legislature," December 13, 1852, LDS Church History Library. Also reprinted in the *Deseret News*, December 25, 1852.

24. In "General Minutes," April 15, 1847, LDS Church History Library.

25. *Book of Abraham*, 1:21, 27.

26. William I. Appleby to Brigham Young, May 19, 1847, LDS Church History Library.

27. As quoted in Turner, *Brigham Young*, 221. Also see O'Connell, "Brigham Young, African Americans, and Plural Marriage," 82.

28. This according to Turner, *Brigham Young*, 222, and Bush, "Mormonism's Negro Doctrine," 25.

29. As quoted in Turner, *Brigham Young*, 224.

30. According to LaJean Purcell Carruth of the LDS Church History Library, Young first mentioned priesthood denial in a January 23, 1852, speech. See her paper "'To Bind the African Because He is Different From us in Color Enough to Cause the Angels in Heaven to Blush': Orson Pratt's Opposition to Slavery in the 1852 Territorial Legislature." Unpublished paper delivered at the Mormon History Association Conference, June 2014, San Antonio, Texas.

31. From Brigham Young's "Speech in Joint Session of the Legislature," February 5, 1852, box 48, folder 3, Brigham Young Papers, LDS Church History Library.

32. Ibid.

33. Ibid.

34. For the practice of "blood atonement" in early Mormonism, see Turner, *Brigham Young*, 185–188, 258–260; and D. Michael Quinn, *The Mormon Hierarchy: Origins of Power* (Salt Lake City: Signature Books, 1994), 94, 112–113, 151, 182. This early Mormon practice required murders and adulterers to shed their own blood to atone for the sin. Mormon leaders abandoned this practice by the late nineteenth century. For more on this controversial topic, see Lowell M. Snow, "Blood Atonement," in *The Encyclopedia of Mormonism*, ed. Daniel H. Ludlow, 4 vols. (New York: Macmillan, 1992), 1:131.

35. From Brigham Young's "Speech in Joint Session of the Legislature," February 5, 1852, box 48, folder 3, Brigham Young Papers, LDS Church History Library.

36. Brigham Young and other church leaders were not unique in the conviction that slavery was a divinely sanctioned institution. For more on this point, see Haynes, *Noah's Curse*; Finkelman, ed., *Defending Slavery*; and Noll, *America's God*.

37. Horace Greeley, "Two Hours with Brigham Young," *New York Herald*, August 24, 1859.

38. Bringhurst, *Saints, Slaves, and Blacks*, 111–112.

39. Turner, *Brigham Young*, 227–229.

40. Bringhurst, *Saints, Slaves, and Blacks*, 112.

41. Turner, *Brigham Young*, 318.

42. Sarah Barringer Gordon, *The Mormon Question: Polygamy and Constitutional Conflict in Nineteenth-Century America* (Chapel Hill: University of North Carolina Press, 2002), provides a good discussion of the nineteenth-century conflict between the federal government and Latter-day Saints, as do Edwin Brown Firmage and Richard Collin Mangrum in *Zion in the Courts: A Legal History of the Church of Jesus Christ of Latter-day Saints, 1830–1900* (Urbana: University of Illinois Press, 2001).

43. For two perspectives on this conflict, see William P. MacKinnon, *"At Sword's Point": A Documentary History of the Utah War to 1858*, Part I (Norman, OK: The Arthur H. Clark Co., 2008), and Norman F. Furness, *Mormon Conflict, 1850–1859* (New Haven, CT: Yale University Press, 1966). It should be noted that the notorious 1857 Mountain Meadows Massacre occurred in the midst of this conflict, resulting in the cold-blooded murder of 120 California-bound immigrants at the hands of an armed force of Mormon militiamen and their Indian allies, this occurring in southern Utah. For two differing perspectives on this incident, see Ronald W. Walker, Richard E. Turley Jr., and Glen M. Leonard, *Massacre at Mountain Meadows* (New York: Oxford University Press, 2008); and Will Bagley, *Blood of the Prophets: Brigham Young and the Massacre at Mountain Meadows* (Norman, OK: University of Oklahoma Press, 2002).

44. This was because the Morrill Act assumed, in the words of Carmon Hardy, that "the solemnization of such unions by a magistrate or other public officer," whereas "Mormon plural marriages were performed privately by church rather than state officials. And no announcements or public records of these events were made." As a result, "polygamous couples, joined in ecclesiastical ceremonies were, so far as the law was concerned were only irregular partners." See Hardy, *Doing the Works of Abraham, Mormon Polygamy: Its Origin, Practice, and Demise* (Norman, OK: The Arthur H. Clark Co., 2007), 328–329. See also Firmage and Mangrum, *Zion in the Courts*.

45. See Bringhurst, *Saints, Slaves, and Blacks*, 109–122, for a full discussion of these developments. See also Gordon, *Mormon Question*, and Firmage and Mangrum, *Zion in the Courts*.

46. Brigham Young speech, March 8, 1863, in Franklin D. Richards and Stephen W. Richards, eds., *Journal of Discourses*, 26 vols. (Liverpool, Eng., 1855–1887), 10: 110–111.

47. Ibid.

48. Minutes of December 3, 1847, box 1, folder 59, General Church Minutes, LDS Church History Library, as quoted in Turner, *Brigham Young*, 222.

49. For a discussion of this development, see Bringhurst, *Saints, Slaves, and Blacks*, 115–118.

50. Brigham Young speech, March 8, 1863, in Richards and Richards, eds., *Journal of Discourses*, 10: 110–111.

Chapter 4. Justifying and Perpetuating Black Priesthood Denial, 1877–1949

1. One notable exception to temple ordinances concerns proxy baptisms for deceased ancestors, what Mormons call "baptisms for the dead." Church policy allowed faithful Latter-day Saints to perform proxy baptisms for "the people of African descent," but blacks could not receive their endowment or be sealed in the temple to their families. For "Colored Brethren and Sisters" receiving a proxy baptism in the "Endowment House," Salt Lake City, September 3, 1875, see microfilm 255498, LDS Family History Library (our thanks to Mike Quinn and Craig Foster for assisting us with this document). For other evidence allowing blacks to be "baptized" and "confirmed" relative to temple work, see Wilford Woodruff to David H. Cannon, June 27, 1889, and George Reynolds to Levi Savage, December 17, 1895, both in Devery S. Anderson, ed., *The Development of LDS Temple Worship: A Documentary History, 1846–2000* (Salt Lake City: Signature Books, 2011), 82, 101–102. See also "Extract from George F. Richards' Record of Decisions by the Council of the First Presidency and Twelve Apostles," 1907, box 78, folder 7, George Albert Smith Papers, Special Collections, Marriott Library, University of Utah: "The descendants of Ham may receive baptism and confirmation but no one known to have in his veins negro blood (it matters not how remote a degree) can either have the Priesthood in any degree or the blessings of the Temple of God; no matter how otherwise worthy he may be."

2. The literature on Reconstruction is extensive. For a sampling, see C. Vann Woodward, *The Strange Career of Jim Crow*, 3rd ed. rev. (1955; Oxford University Press, 1974); Michael J. Klarman, *From Jim Crow to Civil Rights: The Supreme Court and the Struggle for Racial Equality* (New York: Oxford University Press, 2004); Williamjames Hull Hoffer, *Plessy v. Ferguson: Race and Inequality in Jim Crow America* (Lawrence: University Press of Kansas, 2012). The best treatment of antimiscegenation laws, passed in the two decades after the Civil War, include Peggy Pascoe, *What Comes Naturally: Miscegenation Law and the Making of Race in America* (New York: Oxford University Press, 2009); and Fay Botham, *Almighty God Created the Races: Christianity, Interracial Marriage, and American Law* (Chapel Hill: University of North Carolina Press, 2009). For Ku Klux Klan efforts to disenfranchise blacks, consult Eric Foner, *Reconstruction: America's Unfinished Revolution, 1863–1877* (New York: Harper Perennial, 1988); and Alexander Keyssar, *The Right to Vote: The Contested History of Democracy in the United States* (New York: Basic Books, 2000).

3. For three perspectives on this development, see Newell G. Bringhurst, *Saints, Slaves, and Blacks: The Changing Place of Black People within Mormonism* (Westport, Conn.: Greenwood Press, 1981), 143–167; Lester E. Bush Jr., "Mormonism's Negro Doctrine: An Historical Overview," *Dialogue: A Journal of Mormon Thought* 8 (Spring 1973): 31–39; and Armand L. Mauss, *All Abraham's Children: Changing Perceptions of Race and Lineage* (Ur-

bana: University of Illinois Press, 2003), 215–217. A trenchant overview of the "modernization" of the Mormon church during this period is Thomas G. Alexander, *Mormonism in Transition: A History of the Latter-day Saints, 1890–1930* (Urbana: University of Illinois Press, 1986).

4. Mauss, *All Abraham's Children*, 25–27.

5. Ibid., 216–217.

6. *Latter-day Saints Millennial Star*, February 29, 1868, and November 7, 1868, as reprinted from the *New York Herald* [n.d.]. For Radical Republicans' displeasure with Mormons, see also Sarah Barringer Gordon, *The Mormon Question: Polygamy and Constitutional Conflict in Nineteenth-Century America* (Chapel Hill: University of North Carolina Press, 2002), chapter 2.

7. John Taylor, *Journal of Discourses*, April 23, 9, 1882; Franklin D. Richards, *Journal of Discourses*, April 8, 1882; Franklin D. Richards, *Journal of Discourses*, January 26, 18, 1885. Mormon racial attitudes seemed to converge with larger trends in American society in the late nineteenth century. For this point, see Patrick Q. Mason, *The Mormon Menace: Violence and Anti-Mormonism in the Postbellum South* (New York: Oxford University Press, 2011), 17. For a broader look at American racial attitudes after Reconstruction, see Edward L. Ayers, *The Promise of the New South: Life After Reconstruction* (New York: Oxford University Press, 1992).

8. LDS Church Council Meeting, August 26, 1908, box 78, folder 7, George A. Smith Papers, Special Collections, Marriott Library, University of Utah. Church policy affirmed that missionaries were not to actively proselytize among blacks, but they could be baptized if they requested it. For this point, see the "Council Meeting Minutes," May 27, 1908, Adam S. Bennion Papers, LDS Church History Library.

9. Joseph F. Smith and Anthon H. Lund to Rudger Clawson, November 18, 1910, Adam S. Bennion Papers, LDS Church History Library.

10. Bush, "Mormonism's Negro Doctrine," 39.

11. L. John Nuttal Journal, May 31, 1879, in L. Tom Perry Special Collections, Harold B. Lee Library, Brigham Young University.

12. Ibid.

13. Ibid.

14. LDS Church Council Minutes, June 4, 1879, Adam S. Bennion Papers, LDS Church History Library. Joseph F. Smith's son, Joseph Fielding Smith, took a different view, alleging that it was "not true" that "Joseph Smith ordained a Negro and sent him on a mission. . . ." See Joseph Fielding Smith to Eulis E. Hubbs, March 5, 1958, box 9, folder 7, Joseph Fielding Smith Papers, LDS Church History Library.

15. For three different perspectives on this most important Mormon figure, see Truman G. Madsen, *Defender of the Faith: The Brigham H. Roberts Story* (Salt Lake City: Bookcraft, 1980); Gary James Bergera, ed., *The Autobiography of B. H. Roberts* (Salt Lake City: Signature Books, 1990); and Brigham Madsen, *The Essential B. H. Roberts* (Salt Lake City: Signature Books, 1999).

16. B.H. Roberts, "To the Youth of Israel," *The Contributor* 6 (1885): 297.

17. Roberts, "To the Youth of Israel," 297.

18. Ibid., 297.

19. Much of the material for this biographical sketch of Jane Elizabeth Manning James has been drawn from the following: Henry J. Wolfinger, "A Test of Faith: Jane Elizabeth James and the Origins of the Utah Black Community," in Clark Knowlton, ed., *Social Accommodation in Utah* (American West Center, Occasional Papers, University of Utah, Salt Lake City, 1975), 126–172; and Quincy D. Newell, "The Autobiography and Interview of Jane Elizabeth Manning James," *Journal of Africana Religions* 1:2 (2013): 251–291. Max Perry Mueller, "Playing Jane: Re-presenting Black Mormon Memory through Reenacting the Black Mormon Past," *Journal of Africana Religions* 1:4 (2013): 513–561, is another important work discussing Jane Manning James's life, as is Ronald G. Coleman, "'Is There No Blessing for Me?' Jane Elizabeth James, A Mormon African American Woman," in Quintard Taylor and Shirley Ann Wilson Moore, eds., *African American Women Confront the West, 1600–2000* (Norman: University of Oklahoma Press, 2003), 144–162.

20. Newell, "The Autobiography and Interview of Jane Elizabeth Manning James," 5.

21. Wolfinger, "A Test of Faith," 135.

22. The LDS church magazine, the *Ensign*, downplays Jane's repeated attempts for temple inclusion. See Linda King Newell and Valeen Tippetts Avery, "Jane Manning James Black Saint, 1847 Pioneer," *Ensign* 9 (August 1979): 26–29.

23. Wolfinger, "A Test of Faith," 137.

24. Jane E. James to President John Taylor, December 27, 1884, John Taylor Papers, LDS Church History Library.

25. Angus M. Cannon President of the Salt Lake Stake, to Jane E. James, June 16, 1888, Angus M. Cannon Letterpress Copybooks, LDS Church History Library.

26. Jane E. James to Apostle Joseph F. Smith, February 7, 1890, Joseph F. Smith Papers, LDS Church History Library.

27. As noted in letter from Zina D. H. Young to Apostle Joseph F. Smith, January 15, 1894, Zina D. H. Young Papers, LDS Church History Library.

28. Wilford Woodruff, Journals, October 16, 1894, in Scott G. Kenney, ed., *Wilford Woodruff's Journal, 1833–1898, Typescript*, 9 vols. (Midvale, UT: Signature Books, 1983–1985), 9:322.

29. "Minutes of a Meeting of the Council of the Twelve Apostles," August 22, 1895. As given in "Excerpts from the Weekly Council Minutes of the Quorum of Twelve Apostles, Dealing with the Rights of Negroes in the Church, 1849–1940," box 78, folder 7, George Albert Smith Papers, Special Collections, Marriott Library, University of Utah.

30. "Minutes of a Meeting of the Council of the Twelve Apostles," January 2, 1902. As given in "Excerpts from the Weekly Council Minutes of the Quorum of Twelve Apostles, Dealing with the Rights of Negroes in the Church, 1849–1940," box 78, folder 7, George Albert Smith Papers, Special Collections, Marriott Library, University of Utah. Jane's blessing sealing her as a servant to "the Prophet Joseph Smith . . . and . . . his household" can be found in "Book of Temple Ordinances," May 18, 1894, pp. 33–34, in Anderson, ed., *Development of LDS Temple Worship*, 97–98.

31. Jane E. James to President Joseph F. Smith, August 31, 1903, Joseph F. Smith Papers, LDS Church History Library.

32. Wolfinger, "A Test of Faith," 139.

33. According to Margaret Blair Young and Darius Aidan Gray, *The Last Mile of the Way: A Trilogy of Historical Novels about Black Mormon Pioneers* (Salt Lake City: Bookcraft, 2003), 423, Jane's temple work was done for her in 1979. See also Newell and Avery, "Jane Manning James," 28–29.

34. Arnold K. Garr, "Liahona: The Elder's Journal," in Daniel H. Ludlow, ed., *The Encyclopedia of Mormonism*, 4 vols. (New York: Macmillan, 1992), 2:830.

35. LDS Church Council Meeting, August 26, 1908, box 78, folder 7, George A. Smith Papers, Special Collections, Marriott Library, University of Utah.

36. "The Negro and the Priesthood," *Liahona: The Elder's Journal* 5 no. 2 (April 18, 1908): 1165.

37. Ibid., 1166.

38. Ibid, 1166–1167.

39. Ibid., 1167.

40. Smith frequently received queries about this work. He later noted that some of the themes of the book come "back to me constantly as a plague," underscoring its controversial nature. See Smith to Alfred J. Burdett, January 28, 1957, box 39, folder 9, Joseph Fielding Smith Papers, LDS Church History Library.

41. Two perspectives of Smith's life are provided in Joseph Fielding Smith Jr. and John J. Stewart, *The Life of Joseph Fielding Smith: Tenth President of the Church of Jesus Christ of Latter-day Saints* (Salt Lake City: Deseret Book, 1972); and Francis M. Gibbons, *Joseph Fielding Smith: Gospel Scholar, Prophet of God* (Salt Lake City: Deseret Book, 1992).

42. See D. Michael Quinn, *The Mormon Hierarchy: Extensions of Power* (Salt Lake City: Signature Books, 1997), 173; and Smith and Stewart, *Life of Joseph Fielding Smith*, 174–175.

43. For a succinct discussion of Smith's writings, see Ronald W. Walker, David J. Whittaker, and James B. Allen, *Mormon History* (Urbana: University of Illinois Press, 2001), 35, 217–218; and Matthew Bowman, *The Mormon People: The Making of an American Faith* (New York: Random House, 2012), 200–203. There are numerous letters in the Joseph Fielding Smith Papers (LDS Church History Library) where the First Presidency asked him to provide answers to challenging "gospel questions." See, for example, First Presidency (Stephen L. Richards and J. Reuben Clark Jr.) to Joseph Fielding Smith, May 29, 1951, box 17, folder 13. In this instance, the First Presidency asked Smith to answer a question from a mission president in Australia relating to "the ancestry of Australian blacks," specifically whether they had "the seed of Cain." After extensive research, Smith affirmed he did "not know." See also Smith's *Answers to Gospel Questions*, 5 vols. (Salt Lake City: Deseret Book, 1957–1966), which comprises the bulk of his responses to members who queried him about specific Mormon teachings. These questions, along with Smith's answers, were first published in the *Improvement Era*, the church's official magazine in the 1950s and 1960s.

44. A brief overview of Smith's life is Francis Gibbons, *Joseph Fielding Smith*; and Joseph F. McConkie, *True and Faithful: The Life Story of Joseph Fielding Smith* (Salt Lake City: Bookcraft, 1971).

45. Joseph Fielding Smith. *The Way to Perfection: Short Discourses on Gospel Themes*, 5th ed. (orig. pub., 1931; Independence, MO: Genealogical Society of Utah, Zion's Printing and Publishing Co., 1945), 97–98.

46. Ibid., 101–102.

47. Ibid., 106–107.

48. Ibid., 110–111. See "Race and Priesthood" (2013): https://www.lds.org/topics/race-and-the-priesthood (also in chapter 7 of this work). For Smith's views embraced by church leaders, see the First Presidency statements of 1949 and 1969 in chapter 5 of this volume.

Chapter 5. Church Growth, Confronting Civil Rights, and Official Affirmations of Black Priesthood Denial, 1945–1970

1. The total LDS membership in 1940 was 862,664, whereas by 1970 the total had reached 2,930,810. See *Deseret News 1980 Church Almanac* (Salt Lake City, 1980). See also Rodney Stark, *The Rise of Mormonism*, ed. by Reid L. Neilson (New York: Columbia University Press, 2005), 144–145.

2. For a brief discussion of this development, see "Membership Totals and the Shifting Geographic-Ethnic focus of the Latter-day Saint Movement, 1830–1980," and Appendix A in Bringhurst, *Saints, Slaves and Blacks*, 205–212.

3. A. Hamer Reiser, interviewed by William G. Hartley, October 16, 1974, LDS Church History Library. For population figures in South Africa in 1951, see John Reader, *Africa: A Biography of a Continent* (New York: Alfred Knopf, 1999), 679.

4. David O. McKay to his counselors Stephen L. Richards and J. Reuben Clark Jr., January 19, 1954, in David O. McKay diary, box 32, folder 3, David O. McKay Papers, Special Collections, Marriott Library, University of Utah.

5. Frank S. Loescher, *The Protestant Church and the Negro: A Pattern of Segregation* (Philadelphia: Association Press, 1948), 28–50. See also David L. Chappell, *A Stone of Hope: Prophetic Religion and the Death of Jim Crow* (Chapel Hill: University of North Carolina Press, 2004); Mark Noll, *God and Race in American Politics: A Short History* (Princeton, NJ: Princeton University Press, 2008), chapter 4; and Frank Lambert, *Religion in American Politics: A Short History* (Princeton, NJ: Princeton University Press, 2008), chapter 6.

6. See J. Reuben Clark Jr. to the Young Women's Mutual Improvement Association conference, *Improvement Era* 49 (August 1946): 492. For more on LDS leaders' views on interracial marriage, see chapter 6 of this volume.

7. Nelson's memoir provides a comprehensive account of his life and career. See his *In the Direction of His Dreams: Memoirs* (New York: Philosophical Library, 1985). Also useful is Leonard J. Arrington and David Bitton, *The Mormon Experience: A History of the Latter-day Saints* (New York: Alfred Knopf, 1979), 316–317, which provides a brief biography of Nelson.

8. Meeks to Nelson, June 20, 1947, box 20, folder 1, Lowry Nelson Papers, Marriott Library, University of Utah.

9. Nelson, *In the Direction of His Dreams*, 334; Nelson to Meeks, June 26, 1947, box 20, folder 1, Lowry Nelson Papers, Special Collections, Marriott Library, University of Utah.

10. Nelson to President George Albert Smith, June 26, 1947, box 20, folder 1, Lowry Nelson Papers, Special Collections, Marriott Library, University of Utah.

11. First Presidency to Nelson, July 17, 1947, box 20, folder 1, Lowry Nelson Papers, Special Collections, Marriott Library, University of Utah. For a discussion of interracial marriage in the church, see chapter 6.

12. Nelson, *In the Direction of His Dreams*, 340.

13. Nelson to First Presidency, October 8, 1947, box 20, folder 1, Lowry Nelson Papers, Marriott Library, University of Utah. In 1952, Nelson wrote a scathing article in a national magazine, in which he called the church's racial position "a source of embarrassment and humiliation to thousands of members . . . who find no basis for it in the teachings of Jesus Christ." This was the first time the Mormon racial story had been aired in a national publication, and it brought considerable embarrassment to the church. Nelson's piece, as he later explained, "was simply polemical; an expression of his disgust" with Mormon racial doctrine. See his "Mormonism and the Negro," *The Nation* 174 (May 24, 1952): 488; and his letter to Lester Bush, October 13, 1972, box 3, folder 29, Lester E. Bush Papers, Special Collections, Marriott Library, University of Utah.

14. First Presidency to Lowry Nelson, November 12, 1947, box 20, folder 1, Lowry Nelson Papers, Special Collections, Marriott Library, University of Utah.

15. At least two LDS writers gave the year 1951 as the genesis of the First Presidency statement on Mormon racial doctrine. They had mistakenly assumed that because Joseph Anderson had copied verbatim from the statement of 1949 and sent it to private interlocutors in 1951, the later year marked the date of the letter. See John J. Stewart, *Mormonism and the Negro* (Salt Lake: Bookmark Press, 1960), 16–18, and John L. Lund, *The Church and the Negro* (Salt Lake: Paramount Publishers, 1967). A careful study by Lester Bush, however, reveals that the presidency issued the original letter in 1949. See Lester Bush, "Writing 'Mormonism's Negro Doctrine: An Historical Overview' (1973): Context and Reflections, 1998," *Journal of Mormon History* 25 (Spring 1999): 243–244n25.

16. The First Presidency has the sole authority to declare doctrine in the LDS church. For a discussion of this theme, consult Matthew L. Harris, "Mormonism's Problematic Racial Past and the Evolution of the Divine-Curse Doctrine," *John Whitmer Historical Association Journal* 33 (Spring–Summer 2013): 101–102. See also J. Reuben Clark Jr., "When Are Church Leaders' Words Entitled to Claim of Scripture?" *Church News* (July 31, 1954): 9–10.

17. The First Presidency secretary, Joseph Anderson, referred to the 1949 statement when he received inquiries about the church's racial policy. See Anderson to Herbert Ford, April 10, 1951, box 9, folder 7, Adam S. Bennion Papers, L. Tom Perry Special Collections, Harold B. Lee Library, Brigham Young University; and Anderson to Lowry Nelson, May 23, 1952, and Anderson to Chauncy Harris, May 4, 1952, both in box 20, folder 5, Lowry Nelson Papers, Marriott Library, University of Utah. LDS general authorities appealed to the statement when they instructed LDS missionaries on priesthood restriction. See Alvin R. Dyer's address to missionaries in Oslo, Norway, "For What Purpose" (March 18, 1961), and Henry D. Moyle's address to "French East Missionaries in Geneva, Switzerland" (October 30, 1961), both in the LDS Church History Library. BYU religious educators understood that the document was an authoritative statement as well. See David H. Yarn Jr. to Ernest L. Wilkinson, May 3, 1968, box 556, folder 12, and Daniel L. Ludlow to Ernest L. Wilkinson, February 18, 1969, box 556, folder 17, both in the Ernest L. Wilkinson Papers, L. Tom Perry Special Collections, Harold B. Lee Library, Brigham Young University. See also John J. Stewart, *Mormonism and the Negro* (Orem, UT: Bookmark, 1960), 16–17.

18. By 1965, the church began to move away from the 1949 statement. BYU religious educator James R. Clark was preparing a multivolume account of the *Messages of the First Presidency* and had planned to include the 1949 letter in one of the volumes (see box 2, folder 9, James R. Clark Papers, L. Tom Perry Special Collections, Harold B. Lee Library, Brigham Young University). Church leaders balked. Joseph Fielding Smith, who was then president of the Quorum of the Twelve Apostles, had warned him about including statements issued "during controversial periods in Church history since they would probably be misunderstood today." See Clark's "Memorandum on a trip to see Presidency Joseph Fielding Smith," June 29, 1964, box 7, folder 9, James R. Clark Papers, L. Tom Perry Special Collections, Harold B. Lee Library, Brigham Young University. Clark published the *Messages of the First Presidency* in six volumes (Salt Lake: Bookcraft, 1965–1975). There is nothing on race in any of the volumes.

19. Apostle N. Eldon Tanner made this observation in a meeting with the First Presidency. See the First Presidency minutes, March 20, 1963, in the David O. McKay diary, box 52, folder 6, David O. McKay Papers, Special Collections, Marriott Library, University of Utah.

20. Petersen, "Race Problems—As They Affect the Church," August 27, 1954, typescript in LDS Church History Library. There is also a copy in the L. Tom Perry Special Collections, Harold B. Lee Library, Brigham Young University.

21. The literature of the *Brown* decision is voluminous. The best treatments include James T. Patterson, *Brown v. Board of Education: A Civil Rights Milestone and Its Troubled Legacy* (New York: Oxford University Press, 2001); Robert J. Cottrol, Raymond T. Diamond, and Leland B. Ware, *Brown v. Board of Education: Caste, Culture, and the Constitution* (Lawrence: University of Kansas Press, 2003); Mark V. Tushnett, *Making Civil Rights Law: Thurgood Marshall and the Supreme Court, 1936–1961* (New York: Oxford University Press, 1994); Michael J. Klarman, *From Jim Crow to Civil Rights: The Supreme Court and the Struggle for Racial Equality* (New York: Oxford University Press, 2004); and Martha Minow, *In Brown's Wake: Legacies of America's Educational Landmark* (New York: Oxford University Press, 2010).

22. Wallace R. Bennett, "The Negro in Utah," *Utah Law Review* 3 (Spring 1953): 340–348. See also Margaret Judy Maag's MS thesis, "Discrimination Against the Negro in Utah and Institutional Efforts to Eliminate It" (June 1971), a copy of which is in box 289, folder 2, of the Sterling McMurrin Papers, Special Collections, Marriott Library, University of Utah. See also "Negro Relates Rejection by Café in S.L.," *Deseret News*, July 23, 1963. In an editorial on "Mormons and Civil Rights," a writer opines that there "is no racial segregation in schools, employment or elsewhere in our communities," though there is no evidence to support that claim. See *Deseret News*, April 15, 1959.

23. H. Ross Peterson, "'Blindside': Utah on the Eve of *Brown v. Board of Education*," *Utah Historical Quarterly* 73 (2005): 5. David Ward, "100 Years since Booker T. Washington's Historic Visit to the Mormons," *Deseret News*, March 29, 2013. On the LDS tabernacle, see David O. McKay diary, September 30, 1952, box 30, folder 4, David O. McKay Papers, Special Collections, Marriott Library, University of Utah. J. Reuben Clark ordered apostle Mark Petersen, who edited the *Deseret News* prior to his call as an apostle, to instruct the

Deseret News staff to not shoot pictures with whites and blacks, for "they [blacks] are trying to break down the color line." See Clark's diary entry of May 1, 1950, box 16, folder 1, J. Reuben Clark Papers, L. Tom Perry Special Collections, Harold B. Lee Library, Brigham Young University.

24. See also McKay's diary entry of August 6, 1952, in which he "told the Presiding Bishopric that negroes should not be invited to speak in sacrament meetings and at Firesides." In box 30, folder 3, David O. McKay Papers, Special Collections, Marriott Library, University of Utah.

25. First Presidency to Ezra Taft Benson, June 23, 1942, Adam S. Bennion Papers, L. Tom Perry Special Collections, Harold B. Lee Library, Brigham Young University; Petersen, "Race Problems," 13.

26. J. Reuben Clark to Albin Matson, April 12, 1948, box 378, folder 1, J. Reuben Clark Papers, L. Tom Perry Special Collections, Harold B. Lee Library, Brigham Young University; and Clark diary entry of June 9, 1949, box 15, folder 2, ibid. See also Presiding Bishop Thorpe Isaacson's letter to Clark of November 9, 1959, box 295, "Negro" folder, in ibid. For segregated blood banks in the United States, particularly in the North, see Thomas J. Sugrue, *Sweet Land of Liberty: The Forgotten Struggle for Civil Rights in the North* (New York: Random House, 2008). For the segregation of Utah blood banks, see Susan E. Lederer, *Flesh and Blood: Organ Transplantation and Blood Transfusion in Twentieth-Century America* (New York: Oxford University Press, 2008), 197.

27. See *Shelley v. Kramer* (1948). Klarman, *From Jim Crow to Civil Rights*, 213–217, and Tushnet, *Making Civil Rights Law*, 94–98, provide the best overview of this landmark case.

28. See George Albert Smith diary, June 16, 1945, George A. Smith Family Papers, Special Collections, Marriott Library, University of Utah. In 1944, J. Reuben Clark authorized church leaders in Salt Lake to join a "civic organization whose purpose is to restrict and control negro settlement." See Clark's diary entry of August 30, 1944, box 13, folder 3, J. Reuben Clark Papers, L. Tom Perry Special Collections, Harold B. Lee Library, Brigham Young University. Clark also instructed one church member, Preston Richards, who was chairman of a Home Owner's group in California, "to control the colored situation" by authorizing him to look into purchasing property for the church that would prevent blacks from moving into white areas. See Clark to Richards, September 16, 1947, box 376, folder 17, ibid. See also Lowry Nelson to Armand Mauss, July 21, 1975, box 20, folder 6, Lowry Nelson Papers, Special Collections, Marriott Library, University of Utah, who recounted a conversation he had with a friend about Lowell Bennion. Bennion heard apostle Petersen say after his speech at BYU in 1954 that "if he had his way he would restrict blacks to a limited area in Salt Lake."

29. First Presidency to Virgil H. Sponberg, May 5, 1947, Adam S. Bennion Papers, LDS Church History Library. Sponberg, a stake president in California, said this to the First Presidency: "Here in California we have such a lot of Negroes and are we as Latter-day Saints required to associate with them or talk the Gospel with them?" In ibid. J. Reuben Clark's secretary, Rowena Miller, echoed a similar remark. Speaking on Clark's behalf, she wrote to an interested inquirer noting that "the Church discourages social intercourse with the negro race, because such intercourse leads to marriage." See Miller to Leone

Rose, September 20, 1949, box 380, folder 8, J. Reuben Clark Papers, L. Tom Perry Special Collections, Harold B. Lee Library, Brigham Young University. For more on the church's views on interracial marriage, see chapter 6.

30. On this point, see generally, Gregory A. Prince and Wm. Robert Wright, *David O. McKay and the Rise of Modern Mormonism* (Salt Lake City: University of Utah Press, 2005), chapter 4; and Peterson, "'Blindside,'" 13.

31. Approximately 672 African Americans lived in Utah in 1900, the year Petersen was born. By 1940, that number had increased to 1,235. Most of them lived in Salt Lake, although compared to other western cities, Salt Lake had a small African American population. See Quintard Taylor, *In Search of the Racial Frontier: African Americans in the American West, 1528-1990* (New York: W. W. Norton, 1998), 135, 253.

32. Peggy Petersen Barton, the apostle's daughter, provides a general overview of her father's life in *Mark E. Petersen: A Biography* (Salt Lake City: Deseret Book, 1985).

33. For more on this subject, see Lavina Fielding Anderson, "The LDS Intellectual Community and Church Leadership: A Contemporary Chronology," *Dialogue: A Journal of Mormon Thought* 26 (Spring 1993): 20–22; and Lester Bush, "Writing 'Mormonism's Negro Doctrine: An Historical Overview' (1973): Context and Reflections, 1998," *Journal of Mormon History* 25 (Spring 1999): 267. For Petersen as an influential "doctrinally conservative" leader in the church, see Terryl L. Givens, *People of Paradox: A History of Mormon Culture* (New York: Oxford University Press, 2007), 206. For Petersen as a self-appointed "doctrinal watchdog," see Quinn, *Extensions of Power*, 55.

34. Petersen, "Race Problems," 1, 11–12.

35. Ibid., 3–5, 8–9.

36. For Lee's teachings on lineage, see "Youth of a Noble Birthright," May 6, 1945, typescript in LDS Church History Library, and Lee, *Youth of the Church* (Salt Lake City: Deseret Book, 1955), esp. 170–171. For similar views, see also Joseph Fielding Smith, *The Way to Perfection: Short Discourses on Gospel Themes*, 5th ed. (Salt Lake City: Genealogical Society, 1943), chapter 7, and Bruce R. McConkie, *Mormon Doctrine* (Salt Lake City: Bookcraft, 1958), 107–108. For a trenchant analysis of lineage in Mormon thought and practice, see Mauss, *All Abraham's Children*.

37. Petersen, "Race Problems," 9, 12–13. In arguing that blacks would be servants to whites in a post-mortal life, Petersen probably drew inspiration from Jane Manning James's blessing, in which she was sealed to Joseph Smith as a servant. See chapter 4 for this discussion.

38. O. Kendall White Jr., "Mormonism's Anti-Black Policy and Prospects for Change," *Journal of Religious Thought* 29 (Autumn–Winter 1972): 44. Lowell Bennion was a prominent religious educator at the LDS Institute near the University of Utah. It is not clear how Petersen responded to Bennion's question. See Mary Lythgoe Bradford, *Lowell L. Bennion: Teacher, Counselor, Humanitarian* (Salt Lake City: Dialogue Foundation, 1995), 132. JD Williams, a political science professor at the University of Utah and later an LDS bishop, wrote that Petersen's address was a gross misreading of LDS scriptures. See his "Analysis of 'Race Problems—As They Affect the Church'" [1954], box 24, folder 2, JD Williams Papers, Special Collections, Marriott Library, University of Utah.

39. Mark Petersen to Jerald Tanner, February 13, 1965, letter in Matt Harris's files (thanks to Sandra Tanner for sharing a copy). This story is also recounted in Wallace Turner, *The Mormon Establishment* (Boston: Houghton Mifflin Co., 1966), 253–254. Mormon dissident Jerald Tanner reprinted the Petersen speech in a book he coauthored with his wife, Sandra Tanner, in *Joseph Smith's Curse upon the Negro* (Salt Lake City: Modern Microfilm Co., 1965).

40. Turner, *Mormon Establishment*, 249–254. Turner was a relentless critic of Mormon racial policy. Gene Roberts, one of his colleagues at the *New York Times*, claimed with some exaggeration that Turner "probably did more than any single person to change the Mormon policy on race." See Dennis Hevesi, "Wallace Turner, Prize-Winning Reporter," *New York Times*, September 20, 2010.

41. In a letter to LDS scholar Lowry Nelson, Petersen denied giving the speech. "You referred to a copy of an address that I am supposed to have given at BYU in late 1954," Petersen told him. "I have heard from other people that copies of such an address are being passed around," but "I have never seen the copy and I do not know whether it is authentic or not." See Petersen to Nelson, May 30, 1975, box 20, folder 11, Lowry Nelson Papers, Special Collections, Marriott Library, University of Utah. Petersen's response confirmed what Nelson already believed about the speech. "It appears to be clear that Bro. Petersen is a little embarrassed about his address, and does not want it circulated," Nelson told a friend. See Nelson to John Fitzgerald, May 6, 1975, in ibid.

42. BYU religious educators frequently referred to the talk when discussing the church's racial doctrine. See BYU dean of religious education Daniel Ludlow's memo on "Mormonism and the Negro" to BYU President Ernest Wilkinson, February 18, 1969, box 556, folder 17, Ernest L. Wilkinson Papers, L. Tom Perry Special Collections, Harold B. Lee Library, Brigham Young University; and BYU religious educator David H. Yarn's memo to Wilkinson, May 3, 1968, box 556, folder 12, in ibid. See also BYU religion professor James R. Clark, whose study guide, "Cain and Satan—And Two Modern Problems, (1) Racial Segregation and (2) Subversive Groups," he distributed to students in his "Doctrines of the Pearl of Great Price" class, in which he drew on apostle Petersen's address to bolster his pro-segregation views (in box 49, folder 24, Richard D. Poll Papers, Special Collections, Marriott Library, University of Utah). Dean Jesse, a research historian in the church's historical department, likewise appealed to the talk to advance a pro-segregationist view. See his article, "The Attitude of the Church of Jesus Christ of Latter-day Saints toward Segregation" [1954], box 40, folder 8, Leonard J. Arrington Papers, Merrill-Cazier Library, Utah State University.

43. See McConkie's three volumes on the New Testament: *Doctrinal New Testament Commentary: Volume 1, The Gospels* (Salt Lake: Deseret Book, 1965), *Doctrinal New Testament Commentary: Volume 2, Acts–Philippians* (Salt Lake: Deseret Book, 1970), *Doctrinal New Testament Commentary: Volume 3, Colossians–Revelation* (Salt Lake: Deseret Book, 1972); and his six volumes on the life of Jesus Christ: *The Promised Messiah* (Salt Lake: Deseret Book, 1978), *The Mortal Messiah*, 4 vols. (Salt Lake City: Deseret Book, 1979–1981), and *The Millennial Messiah* (Salt Lake: Deseret Book, 1982).

44. For an insightful overview of McConkie's work, including its popularity in the church, see David John Buerger, "Speaking with Authority: The Theological Influence of

Elder Bruce R. McConkie," *Sunstone* 10, no. 2 (March 1985): 8–13; O. Kendal White, *Mormon Neo-Orthodoxy* (Salt Lake: Signature Books, 1987); Armand L. Mauss, *The Angel and the Beehive: The Mormon Struggle with Assimilation* (Urbana: University of Illinois Press, 1994), 162–163; and Matthew Bowman, *The Mormon People: The Making of an American Faith* (New York: Random House, 2012), 201–206.

45. Joseph Fielding Smith's main works include *The Way to Perfection: Short Discourses on Gospel Themes* (Salt Lake City: Desert Book, 1931); *Doctrines of Salvation: Sermons and Writings of Joseph Fielding Smith*, 3 vols., compiled by Bruce R. McConkie (Salt Lake: Bookcraft, 1954–1956); and *Answers to Gospel Questions*, 4 vols. (Salt Lake: Deseret Book, 1957–1966). McConkie's son, Joseph Fielding McConkie, discusses Smith's influence on his father in *The Bruce R. McConkie Story: Reflections of a Son* (Salt Lake: Deseret Book, 2003); and "Bruce R. McConkie: A Special Witness," *Mormon Historical Studies* 14 (Fall 2013): 191–211. For a brief biography of McConkie, see "In Memoriam: Elder Bruce R. McConkie, Advocate for Truth," June 1985, https://www.lds.org/new-era/1985/06/in-memoriam-elder-bruce-r-mcconkie-advocate-for-truth?lang=eng.

46. Buerger, "Speaking with Authority," 10.

47. In the early 1980s, McConkie had high-profile dustups with two BYU professors: Eugene England and George Pace. England and Pace taught a version of the godhead that McConkie believed could not be reconciled with orthodox Mormon teachings. These episodes are recounted in Lavina Fielding Anderson, "The LDS Intellectual Community and Church Leadership: A Contemporary Chronology," *Dialogue: A Journal of Mormon Thought* 26 (Spring 1993): 15, 19.

48. McConkie, *Mormon Doctrine* (Salt Lake City: Bookcraft, 1958), 5. Unless otherwise indicated, all references from *Mormon Doctrine* derive from the 1958 edition.

49. For McKay's statement as a "source of concern to the Brethren," see his diary entry of January 28, 1960, box 45, folder 1, David O. McKay Papers, Special Collections, Marriott Library, University of Utah. Apostle Marion Romney identified the controversial topics in a letter to church president David O. McKay. See Romney to McKay, January 28, 1959, in McKay diary, box 43, folder 1, David O. McKay Papers, Special Collections, Marriott Library, University of Utah. McConkie's entry on "Catholicism," specifically characterized as the "great and abominable church," elicited considerable commentary among Mormons and non-Mormons alike, as did McConkie's doctrinal characterizations on a range of other topics, including "pre-Adamic peoples," "the virgin birth of Mary," and "Evolution and Evolutionists." For these controversial topics, see McConkie, *Mormon Doctrine*, 129–130, 229–238, 262.

50. David O. McKay diary, January 7, 1960, box 45, folder 1, David O. McKay Papers, Special Collections, Marriott Library, University of Utah.

51. Gregory A. Prince and Wm. Robert Wright, *David O. McKay and the Rise of Modern Mormonism* (Salt Lake: University of Utah, 2005), 50, 52.

52. For McKay's permission to republish the book, see McKay diary entry of July 5, 1966, box 63, folder 2, David O. McKay Papers, Special Collections, Marriott Library, University of Utah; and Prince and Wright, *David O. McKay and the Rise of Modern Mormonism*, 52. For an analysis of the errors, see David O. McKay diary, January 7, 1960, box 45, folder 1, and Marion Romney to McKay, January 28, 1959, box 43, folder 1, both in David O. McKay Papers, Special Collections, Marriott Library, University of Utah. Petersen, in particular,

found the book troubling. He wrote that the "volume presumes to give the final word on many doctrines of the Church, some of which have never been completely explained even in the revelations." See Petersen's unpublished editorial entitled "Seek Ye Out of the Best Books," Box 289, J. Reuben Clark Papers, L. Tom Perry Special Collections, Harold B. Lee Library, Brigham Young University (our thanks to Stirling Adams for calling this document to our attention).

53. One writer observes that "approximately 313 pages contained one or more changes." The most conspicuous revisions in the 1966 edition include changes to "Communism," "conceived in sin," "forgiveness," "good works," in addition to removing the entry titled "church of the devil," which equated Catholicism with the devil. See Dennis B. Horne, *Bruce R. McConkie: Highlights from His Life and Times* (Roy, UT: Eborn Books, 2000), 67. Joseph Fielding McConkie, Bruce McConkie's son, downplays the changes in *Mormon Doctrine* in *The Bruce R. McConkie Story*, chapter 11.

54. See, in particular, chapters 2–4 of this volume.

55. The seventh and final printing of *Mormon Doctrine* occurred in 1997. It still contains the racial entries of the first edition, including the "caste system" (segregation) and the divine curse. See *Mormon Doctrine* (seventh printing), 108–109, 114, 343, 526–528. For *Mormon Doctrine* going out of print, see Peggy Fletcher Stack, "Landmark 'Mormon Doctrine' goes out of print," *Salt Lake Tribune*, May 21, 2010. The LDS church newspaper, *Deseret News*, did not comment on *Mormon Doctrine* going out of print.

56. An admission McKay made to Ernest Wilkinson. See Wilkinson's recollection of the conversation in a letter of Wilkinson to McKay, January 31, 1953, box 9, folder 7, Adam S. Bennion Papers, L. Tom Perry Special Collections, Harold B. Lee Library, Brigham Young University. For a provocative analysis of McKay, see Newell G. Bringhurst, "The Private versus Public David O. McKay: Profile of a Complex Personality," in Stephen C. Taysom, ed., *Dimensions of Faith: A Mormon Studies Reader* (Salt Lake City: Signature Books, 2011), 1–24.

57. In his diary, McKay noted that "the South knows how to handle [blacks] and they do not have any trouble, and the colored people are better off down there." See diary entry of February 25, 1949, box 26, folder 4, David O. McKay Papers, Special Collections, Marriott Library, University of Utah. McKay's diary entries are replete with references to Mormons asking him about the church's segregation policies at the Hotel Utah. His typical response was that the Hotel handled "its reservations in the same manner as other leading hotels throughout the country"—in effect, it was segregated because other hotels were too. See, for one example, the entry on May 19, 1953, in box 31, folder 3, Special Collections, Marriott Library, University of Utah.

58. In addition to apostle Mark Petersen, whose opposition to civil rights is recounted elsewhere in this chapter, First Presidency counselor J. Reuben Clark, church president David O. McKay, and apostles Ezra Taft Benson, Joseph Fielding Smith, Delbert Stapley, Spencer W. Kimball, Henry D. Moyle, Harold B. Lee, and others opposed "negro equality." See F. Ross Peterson, "'Blindside': Utah on the Eve of *Brown v. Board of Education*," *Utah Historical Quarterly* 73 (2005): 13; Prince and Wright, *David O. McKay and the Rise of Modern Mormonism*, chapter 4; Newell G. Bringhurst, *Saints, Slaves, and Blacks: The Changing Place of Black People within Mormonism* (Westport, CT: Greenwood Press,

1981), chapter 9; D. Michael Quinn, "Prelude to the National 'Defense of Marriage' Campaign: Civil Discrimination Against Feared or Despised Minorities," *Dialogue: A Journal of Mormon Thought* 33 (Fall 2000): 28–36.

59. Brown's grandson, Edwin Firmage, who knew his grandfather well, commented that "Grandfather was a considerable slice to his left on ideology, on politics, and on ecclesiastical leadership, a substantial slice." In the early 1950s, he proposed ordaining blacks to the Aaronic priesthood, hoping that it would blaze the way to remove all priesthood restrictions. Apostle Harold Lee and others "torpedoed it," Firmage recalled his grandfather saying. On the priesthood restriction, Brown thought "the Mormon church was dead wrong. He never viewed it as a doctrine," just a "policy." See his oral history interview with Greg Prince, October 10, 1996, box 22, folder 2, Gregory A. Prince Papers, Special Collections, Marriott Library, University of Utah. See also Edwin B. Firmage, ed., *An Abundant Life: The Memoirs of Hugh B. Brown* (Salt Lake City: Signature Books, 1988). For the genesis of Brown's racial views, see chapter 6.

60. On the changing dynamics of church leadership in the early 1960s, see Prince and Wright, *David O. McKay and the Rise of Modern Mormonism*, 67–68; and D. Michael Quinn, *Elder Statesman: A Biography of J. Reuben Clark* (Salt Lake City: Signature Books, 2002).

61. For these points, consult Robert Dallek, *An Unfinished Life: John F. Kennedy, 1917–1963* (Boston: Little, Brown, 2003), and Robert Caro, *The Passage of Power: The Years of Lyndon Johnson* (New York: Alfred A. Knopf, 2012).

62. For two of these articles, see Wallace Turner, "Mormons Weigh Stand on Negro," *New York Times*, June 7, 1963; and Clare Boothe Luce, whose article on George Romney appeared in numerous newspapers in September 1963. She wrote that Romney will have difficulty overcoming his church's demeaning racial views because the Mormon church "hold[s] the human dignity of the Negroes in low esteem." First Presidency counselor Henry D. Moyle responded to the letter noting that the Mormon church has "more to offer the negro than any other church. . . . We . . . believe that our position on the priesthood is rather one of selection than of discrimination." In private, he fumed that Luce's understanding of Mormon racial doctrine was an "erroneous understanding of the position of the church upon the Negro question." See his letter to Luce, September 13, 1963, box 509, folder 3, Ernest L. Wilkinson Papers, L. Tom Perry Special Collections, Harold B. Lee Library, Brigham Young University; and David O. McKay diary entry of September 13, 1963, box 54, folder 5, David O. McKay Papers, Special Collections, Marriott Library, University of Utah.

63. Udall's alienation with Mormon racial policy is ably captured in F. Ross Peterson, "'Do Not Lecture the Brethren': Stewart L. Udall's Pro-Civil Rights Stance, 1967," *Journal of Mormon History* 25 (Spring 1999): 276–277. Benson's *The Red Carpet* (Salt Lake City: Bookcraft, 1962) was his first book tracing the connection between civil rights and communism. His subsequent book on the subject, *An Enemy Hath Done This* (Salt Lake City: Parliament, 1969), offered a more detailed version than his earlier book tying civil rights to communism. Both works distill ideas from Cleon Skousen's *The Naked Communism* (Salt Lake City: Ensign, 1961), which posited a civil rights conspiracy in the postwar era. For the church's missionary efforts in Nigeria, see "Church to Open Missionary Work in Nigeria," *Deseret News*, January 11, 1963, and "Race and Religion: Churches Take More

Active Role in Negro's Fight for Equal Rights," *Wall Street Journal*, August 2, 1963. The most thorough treatment of early LDS efforts in Nigeria is James B. Allen, "Would-Be Saints: West Africa before the 1978 Priesthood Revelation," *Journal of Mormon History* 17 (1991): 207–247.

64. Prince and Wright, *David O. McKay and the Rise of Modern Mormonism*, 69.

65. See "Civil Rights Statement in Conference," in David O. McKay diary, October 6, 1963, box 55, folder 1, David O. McKay Papers, Special Collections, Marriott Library, University of Utah. The published version is in Hugh B. Brown, "The Fight between Good and Evil," *Improvement Era* 66 (December 1963): 1058; and *Conference Report* (Salt Lake: Published by the Church of Jesus Christ of Latter-day Saints, 1963), 91. McMurrin recounted these events in "A Note on the 1963 Civil Rights Statement," *Dialogue: A Journal of Mormon Thought* 12 (Summer 1979): 60–63. See also his interview with L. Jackson Newell, *in Matters of Conscience: Conversations with Sterling M. McMurrin on Philosophy, Education, and Religion* (Salt Lake City: Signature Books, 1996), 200–201.

66. Brown's squabbles with these men are well documented in D. Michael Quinn, *The Mormon Hierarchy: Extensions of Power* (Salt Lake City: Signature Books, 1997), 14, 81–82. See also Greg Prince's oral history interview with Edwin Firmage (June 6, 1995), whose discussions with his grandfather, Hugh Brown, substantiated the conflict Brown had with some of his fellow apostles. In box 22, folder 2, Gregory A. Prince Papers, Special Collections, Marriott Library, University of Utah. Firmage notes that "Grandfather was kept out of the Twelve for many, many years primarily on the basis [of the priesthood restriction]. His name was first proposed for the Twelve by President Grant, who proposed Grandfather for the Quorum of the Twelve quite a number of times. He was turned down by the Twelve each time, led by Joseph Fielding Smith." Firmage indicated that "President Grant told his grandfather about this." See Greg Prince oral history interview with Edwin Firmage, October 10, 1996, in ibid.

67. Greg Prince oral history interview with Sterling M. McMurrin, May 26, 1994, in box 22, folder 2, Gregory A. Prince Papers, Special Collections, Marriott Library, University of Utah. Despite McKay's insistence that it did not constitute an official statement, Brown believed that his civil rights statement represented "the church's stand on the subject." See his diary entry for October [n.d.], 1963, in box 52, folder 12, Richard D. Poll Papers, in ibid.

68. For Brown and First Presidency counselor N. Eldon Tanner's meeting with NAACP officials, see *Deseret News*, October 5, 1963. For Fritz's reaction to Brown's statement, see *Salt Lake Tribune*, October 6, 1963.

69. "Benson Ties Rights Issue to Reds in Mormon Rift," *Washington Post*, April 13, 1965. See also "Mormon 'Fight' over Civil Rights," *San Francisco Chronicle*, April 17, 1965.

70. Benson's life is captured in "President Ezra Taft Benson: A Sure Voice of Faith, *Ensign* (July 1994), http://tinyurl.com/kwdvmny, and Sherri Dew, *Ezra Taft Benson: A Biography* (Salt Lake City: Deseret Book, 1987). McKay would not support Benson's joining the Wallace ticket because it would "inevitably cause public relations problems for the Mormon Church," a point Dan T. Carter makes in *The Politics of Rage: George Wallace, the Origins of the New Conservatism and the Transformation of American Politics* (New York: Simon and Schuster, 1995), 356. For Benson's presidential ambitions, see Newell G. Bringhurst

and Craig L. Foster, *The Mormon Quest for the Presidency* (Independence, MO: John Whitmer Books, 2008), chapter 6.

71. See Lee Davidson, "FBI Files Shed Light on Ezra Taft Benson, Ike and the Birch Society," *Salt Lake Tribune*, November 16, 2010; Quinn, *Extensions of Power*, chapter 2. For Benson's inability to "divorce" his political views from his religious predilections, see Ernest Wilkinson diary entry of May 24, 1961, box 100, folder 4, Ernest Wilkinson Papers, L. Tom Perry Special Collections, Harold B. Lee Library, Brigham Young University.

72. "Mormons and Politics: Benson Helps Keep Church on Conservative Track," *Wall Street Journal*, August 8, 1966; and Sean Wilentz, "Confounding Fathers: The Tea Party's Cold War Roots," *The New Yorker*, October 18, 2010, http://www.newyorker.com/reporting/2010/10/18/101018fa_fact_wilentz?printable=true.

73. See Lee Davidson, "FBI Files Shed Light on Ezra Taft Benson, Ike and the Birch Society," *Salt Lake Tribune*, November 16, 2010; Quinn, *Extensions of Power*, chapter 2; and Drew Pearson, "Benson Took Birchite Tours," *Washington Post*, July 12, 1961.

74. The two men were particularly close, evident in the dozens of letters they exchanged in the 1960s (copies in Matt Harris's files). FBI Director Hoover, a prominent conservative, did not want anything to do with Benson or the Birch Society. William F. Buckley, founder of the prominent conservative publication *The National Review*, also shunned Benson and the Birch organization. See Lee Davidson, "FBI Files Shed Light on Ezra Taft Benson, Ike and the Birch Society," *Salt Lake Tribune*, November 16, 2010. See also George H. Nash, *The Conservative Intellectual Movement since 1945* (New York: Basic Books, 1976), 292–293; and William F. Buckley Jr., "The John Birch Society and the Conservative Movement," *National Review* 17 (October 19, 1965): 914–920, 925–929. The Birch Society frequently criticized Hoover because he did not support their agenda. For this point, see Curt Gentry, *J. Edgar Hoover: The Man and the Secrets* (New York: W. W. Norton, 1992), 430. Not all influential conservatives, however, shunned the Birch Society. Arizona senator Barry Goldwater praised the Birch Society in general and Benson in particular. See Rick Perlstein, *Before the Storm: Barry Goldwater and the Unmaking of the American Consensus* (New York: Hill and Wang, 2009), 118. For a broader view of the Birch Society, see D. J. Mulloy, *The World of the John Birch Society: Conspiracy, Conservatism, and the Cold War* (Nashville, TN: Vanderbilt University Press, 2014).

75. On this point, see D. Michael Quinn, "Ezra Taft Benson and Mormon Political Conflicts," *Dialogue: A Journal of Mormon Thought* 26 (Summer 1993): 1–87.

76. Brown wrote that "we have had quite a number of letters referring to the matters mentioned in your letter . . . and it is really surprising to note how much interest there is in the question of extremism." Brown referred to Benson's anticommunist agenda. See Brown to John Peterson, April 16, 1962 (Matt Harris's files). "Hugh B. Brown's File on the John Birch Society" has several letters in it about members who complained about Benson. See box 48, folder 21, Edwin B. Firmage Papers, Special Collections, Marriott Library, University of Utah. BYU religion professor Gustive Larson also complained to Brown. See his letter of November 1, 1962, box 10, folder 12, Gustive O. Larson Papers, L. Tom Perry Archives, Harold B. Lee Library, Brigham Young University. Brown's file on Benson's "John Birch activities" highlights the seriousness of the issue and how the First Presidency viewed Benson's crusading tendencies.

77. Brown to Gustive Larson, November 11, 1962, box 10, folder 12, Gustive O. Larson Papers, L. Tom Perry Special Collections, Harold B. Lee Library, Brigham Young University.

78. D. Michael Quinn, *Extensions of Power*, 68, writes: "Although Benson was never a member of record, his wife Flora and sons Reed and Mark all allegedly joined the John Birch Society." In one public Birch meeting, Benson decided not to introduce Welch at a fundraiser in Salt Lake after the "Birch issue was raised by other leaders in the church." See Wallace Turner, "Birch Dinner in Salt Lake City Vexes Mormons: Church Leaders Embarrassed by Appearance of Welch," *New York Times*, May 8, 1966. For Benson's son Reed's role in the Birch society, see Willard Clopton, "Cookies, Talk of Treason Served at Opening of Birch Headquarters," *Washington Post*, September 18, 1965; "Benson-Birch Tie Disturbs Utahans," *New York Times*, November 4, 1962; "Ezra Benson's Son Takes Birch Society Post," *Sacramento Bee*, October 27, 1962; "Reed A. Benson's Son Takes Post in Birch Society," *Deseret News*, October 27, 1962.

79. See the First Presidency's (David O. McKay, Henry D. Moyle, Hugh B. Brown) "Statement . . . on the John Birch Society," February 15, 1963 (Matt Harris's files).

80. Benson made these comments in three high-profile speeches in late 1963: "A Race against Time" (December 10, 1963) at Provo, Utah; "An Address by Ezra Taft Benson at a Patriot's Meeting" (December 13, 1963) at Logan, Utah; "'An Internal Threat Today': An Address by Ezra Taft Benson at a Public Meeting Sponsored by the Treasure Valley Freedom Forum" (December 19, 1963), at Boise, Idaho. All are in Matt Harris's files.

81. Ernest Wilkinson diary entry describing Harding's harangue against apostle Benson, September 27, 1963, box 101, folder 3, Ernest Wilkinson Papers, L. Tom Perry Special Collections, Harold B. Lee Library, Brigham Young University. Wilkinson wrote that Harding contacted Hugh Brown prior to the speech to secure his support (see ibid.).

82. "Speech of Hon. Ralph Harding of Idaho," September 25, 1963, *Congressional Record*, 3–4. The *Congressional Record* headline read, "Ezra Taft Benson's Support of John Birch Society is Criticized."

83. Though rare, Mark Petersen and Eldon Tanner, also apostles, were called to preside over missions. See Prince and Wright, *David O. McKay and the Rise of Modern Mormonism*, 298.

84. "Church Denies Mission Rumors," *Deseret News*, February 21, 1964; "Letter Denies Rebuke in Benson Call," *Salt Lake Tribune*, February 22, 1964; "Benson Says: New Duties Not 'Rebuke,'" *Salt Lake Tribune*, October 29, 1963. See also Mark Petersen's letter to the editor in response to reporter Wallace Turner's assertion that Benson was sent abroad for political reasons, in "Mormon Church," *New York Times*, February 19, 1966. Smith to Harding, December 23, 1963 (Matt Harris's files). Our thanks to John Hammond for the Smith citation. See also Drew Pearson, "Benson's Cure for Communism," *Washington Post*, January 4, 1964.

85. Ezra Taft Benson General Conference address, "Not Commanded in All Things," *Improvement Era* 68 (June 1965): 539 (describing communism "as the greatest threat to the church"). See also the unexpurgated version of the address, Scrapbook #79, David O. McKay Papers, Special Collections, Marriott Library, University of Utah (quoting that "communists were using the Civil Rights movement to promote revelation," and also the reference to "traitors in the church").

86. Gregory Prince and William Robert Wright observe that this "controversial passage was deleted from the text of the speech that was published in the official *Conference Report*." See *David O. McKay and the Rise of Modern Mormonism*, 420n48. See also Quinn, *Extensions of Power*, 81. Compare the *Improvement Era* 68 (June 1965): 539, version with the one here.

87. Benson continued his anticommunist remarks two years later in general conference, October 1967, *Conference Report*, 38. Similarly, in 1969, he published *Civil Rights: Tool of Communist Deception* (Salt Lake City: Deseret Book, 1969), and also that same year *An Enemy Hath Done This* (Salt Lake City: Parliament Publishers, 1969). Both books are recapitulations of his earlier writings and speeches.

88. A copy of McMurrin's speech can be found in box 289, folder 2, Sterling McMurrin Papers, Special Collections, Marriott Library, University of Utah. For media coverage of the speech, see "Mormon Race Practices Criticized," *Phoenix Gazette*, June 22, 1968; "Mormon Says Church to Lose 'Thousands' over Negro Stand," *Palo Alto Times*, June 22, 1968; "Bias Will Drive Out Members, Mormon Warns," *Miami Herald*, June 23, 1968; "Mormon Negro Policies Called Harmful to Church," *Middletown Journal* (Ohio), June 23, 1968; "Expert Says Racism Hurts Mormon Church," *Bridgeport Post* (Conn.), June 23, 1968. McMurrin sent a copy of the address to N. Eldon Tanner, who was then serving in the First Presidency (see McMurrin to Tanner, September 18, 1968, box 290, folder 3, McMurrin Papers, Special Collections, Marriott Library, University of Utah). For the First Presidency's response to McMurrin's speech, see David O. McKay diary entry of July 16, 1968, box 68, folder 1, David O. McKay Papers, Special Collections, Marriott Library, University of Utah.

89. Gary James Bergera, "'This Time of Crisis': The Race-Based Anti-BYU Athletic Protests of 1968–1971," *Utah Historical Quarterly* 81 (Summer 2013): 204–229, provides the most thorough analysis of the protests. Also useful is Gary James Bergera and Ronald Priddis, *Brigham Young University: A House of Faith* (Salt Lake City: Signature Books, 1985), 298–304; J. B. Haws, *The Mormon Image in the American Mind: Fifty Years of Public Perception* (New York: Oxford University Press, 2013), chapter 3; and Clifford A. Bullock, "Fired by Conscience: The 'Black 14' Incident at the University of Wyoming and Black Protest in the Western Athletic Conference, 1968–1970," *Wyoming History Journal* 68 (1996): 4–13.

90. For Stanford and BYU, see the *Salt Lake Tribune*, November 13, 1969; "Stanford Blasts Mormon Church through BYU," *Brigham Young University Alumnus*, December 1969; and "Special Report: BYU and Stanford," *The Daily Universe* (BYU student newspaper), December 15, 1969. For Tanner's remarks, see the *Salt Lake Tribune*, January 7, 1970. See also Tanner's "open letter" to BYU president Wilkinson and Stanford president Pitzer, in which he chastises both men for mishandling the situation (box 24, folder 2, JD Williams Papers, Special Collections, Marriott Library, University of Utah). Stanford did not change its policy of scheduling games against BYU until after church leaders rescinded the priesthood ban in 1978. Bergera and Priddis make this point in *Brigham Young University: A House of Faith*, 303.

91. Craig Collisson, "Manifestos, Bureaucracies, Race, and Identity: Black Student Protest at White Universities, 1967–1976" (PhD diss., University of Washington, 2008), http://depts.washington.edu/civilr/BSU_BYU.htm.

92. This account draws on the *Salt Lake Tribune*, February 6, 1970 and James Hansen II, *Democracy's College in the Centennial State: A History of Colorado State University* (Fort Collins: Colorado State University, 1977), 471–472.

93. See, in particular, the *Arizona Daily Star*, April 14, 1968; *Los Angeles Times*, August 27, 1967; *Salt Lake Tribune*, November 30, 1969; *Deseret News*, January 15, 1970; *New Yorker*, March 21, 1970; Brian Walton, "A University's Dilemma: BYU and Blacks," *Dialogue: A Journal of Mormon Thought* 6, no. 1 (Spring 1971): 31–36; Bergera and Priddis, *Brigham Young University: A House of Faith*, 297–301; and O. Kendall White Jr., "Mormonism's Anti-Black Policy and Prospects for Change," *Journal of Religious Thought* 29 (Autumn–Winter 1972): 39–60.

94. William F. Reed, "The Other Side of 'the Y,'" *Sports Illustrated*, January 26, 1970, http://sportsillustrated.cnn.com/vault/article/magazine/MAG1083285/index.htm.

95. "Wilkinson Denies LDS Negro Discrimination Claim," *Salt Lake Tribune*, March 31, 1970. See also "Wilkinson Airs Race Policy: No Policy Which Discriminates," *The Daily Universe* (BYU student newspaper), November 26, 1969. The full statement of Wilkinson's ad can be found in "Minorities, Civil Rights, and BYU," *Salt Lake Tribune*, April 3, 1970, as well as dozens of other newspapers.

96. Turner, "Mormons Weigh Stand on Negro," *New York Times*, June 7, 1963. A few years later Turner wrote a book on Mormons, critical of their race policies. See *The Mormon Establishment* (New York: Houghton, Mifflin, and Co., 1966), chapter 8 ("The Anti-Negro Doctrine").

97. Dyer was called as a "special counselor" in the First Presidency in 1967, despite protests from the apostles. Many apostles refused to sustain him, and when McKay died in 1970 they did not add him to the quorum. This was the only time in the twentieth century, Michael Quinn asserts, when an apostle "was not admitted into the Quorum of the Twelve." The apostles did not like him because of his brash temperament and because he had the ear of church president McKay. See Quinn, *Extensions of Power*, 54. Dyer's racial views are best articulated in an address he gave to missionaries in Norway. He offered a theological rationale, titled "For What Purpose," explaining why blacks could not hold the priesthood. "The reason that spirits are born into Negro bodies is because these spirits rejected the Priesthood of God in the pre-existence. This is the reason why you have Negroes upon the earth as a result of a curse placed upon them." See "For What Purpose," March 18, 1961, in LDS Church History Library. In a later work, Dyer argued that "equality of birth could not be possible because there is no equality of spirit persons." For Dyer, this applied to "cursed lineages." See Dyer's *Who Am I?* (Salt Lake City: Deseret Book, 1966), 542.

98. "LDS Leader Says Curb on Priesthood to Ease," *Salt Lake Tribune*, December 25, 1969. The most comprehensive discussion of this episode is Quinn, *Extensions of Power*, 13–14, but also useful is Edward L. Kimball, "Spencer W. Kimball and the Revelation on Priesthood," *BYU Studies* 47 (2008): 29–30. Alvin R. Dyer, a counselor in the First Presidency, indicated in the First Presidency minutes that apostle Harold B. Lee opposed Brown's efforts to rescind the priesthood ban. See "First Presidency Minutes" in David O. McKay diary, December 26, 1970, box 71, folder 2, David O. McKay Papers, Special Collection, Marriott Library, University of Utah.

99. Brown signed the statement reluctantly, trying to keep a consensus with "the Brethren"; but he opposed the statement and wept when he signed it. See Edwin B. Firmage, ed., *An Abundant Life: The Memoirs of Hugh B. Brown* (Salt Lake City: Signature Books, 1988), 142–143; Richard D. Poll, "Apostle Extraordinary—Hugh B. Brown (1883–1975)," *Dialogue: A Journal of Mormon Thought* 10 (Spring 1975–1976): 70.

100. Greg Prince oral interview with Edwin B. Firmage, June 6, 1995, box 22, folder, 2, Gregory A. Prince Papers, Special Collections, Marriott Library, University of Utah.

101. "Letter of First Presidency Clarifies Church's Position on the Negro," *Improvement Era* 73 (February 1970): 70–73; "Policy Statement of Presidency," *Church News* (January 10, 1970): 12. See also Wallace Turner, "LDS Letter Reaffirms Position on Negroes," *Salt Lake Tribune*, January 9, 1970.

102. Brown's grandson, Edwin Firmage, notes: "Grandfather managed to add language to Elder Lee's statement endorsing full civil rights for all citizens, but he still resisted signing the statement. However, he suffered from advanced age and the late stages of Parkinson's disease and was ill with the Asian flu. With Grandfather in this condition, Elder Lee brought tremendous pressure to bear upon him, arguing that with President McKay incapacitated Grandfather was obligated to join the consensus within the Quorum of the Twelve. Grandfather, deeply ill, wept as he related this story to me just before he signed the statement that bore his and President Tanner's names." In Firmage, ed., *An Abundant Life*, 142.

103. In 1968, the First Presidency decided that church leaders should refrain from answering questions about the race policy involving "the pre-existent unworthiness . . . of Negroes in receiving the curse of Cain." Such statements "only lead to confusion," they reasoned, and "the more we said about the subject, the more we shall have to explain." Any future statements on the race issue "should be clear, positive, and brief." There is no evidence, however, that the First Presidency abandoned the doctrinal framework for priesthood exclusion in 1968. What they abandoned were attempts to explain it in public because of criticisms in the press, but also because of Mormon intellectuals who did not think that such rationale for the exclusion could be defended. See First Presidency minutes in David O. McKay diary, March 1, 1968, box 67, folder 3, David O. McKay Papers, Special Collections, Marriott Library, University of Utah.

104. Henry D. Moyle to Clare Booth Luce, September 13, 1963, copy in box 509, folder 3, Ernest L. Wilkinson Papers, L. Tom Perry Special Collections, Harold B. Lee Library, Brigham Young University. See also Joseph Fielding Smith, "The [Mormon] Church can do more for the Negro than any other church on the face of the earth," quoted in Jeff Nye, "Memo from a Mormon," *Look* 27 (October 22, 1963): 75; and Harold B. Lee, "Presidency Meets the Press," *Church News* (July 15, 1972): 3: "There is no church on the face of the earth that shows greater kindness to any minority than we do."

105. Some LDS blacks accepted the ban. See, for example, Carey C. Bowles, *A Mormon Negro Views the Church* (Maplewood, NJ: Self-published, 1968); Bowles, *Experiences of a Negro Convert* (Maplewood, NJ: Self-published, 1970); and Alan Gerald Cherry, *It's You and Me, Lord!* (Provo, UT: Trilogy Arts Publication, 1970).

106. Mormon males receive the Aaronic Priesthood at age twelve, allowing them to pass the sacrament in the faith's communion services and to collect fast offerings for the

indigent. At age nineteen, they receive the Melchizedek Priesthood, which allows them to perform a two-year missionary service and to serve in various administrative positions in the church.

107. First Presidency (David O. McKay and Hugh B. Brown) to Bishop Lyman D. Perkes, July 5, 1967, and A. Hamer Reiser to David Gillispie, July 5, 1967, both in box 4, folder 16, John W. Fitzgerald Papers, Special Collections, Merrill-Cazier Library, Utah State University.

108. Joseph Fielding Smith to the First Presidency, March 30, 1955, box 64, folder 6, Spencer W. Kimball Papers, LDS Church History Library, Salt Lake City, Utah. See also Edward L. Kimball, "Spencer W. Kimball and the Revelation on Priesthood," *BYU Studies* 47 (2008): 31n66.

109. Sherri Dew, *Gordon B. Hinckley: Go Forward with Faith* (Salt Lake: Deseret Book, 1996), 296.

110. Quorum of the Twelve Minutes, [1970], box 63, folder 3, Spencer W. Kimball Papers, LDS Church History Library. Jesse L. Embry, *Black Saints in a White Church* (Salt Lake: Signature Books, 1994), 182–191, and Armand L. Mauss, *All Abraham's Children: Changing Mormon Conceptions of Race and Lineage* (Urbana: University of Illinois Press, 2003), 235–236, both provide reliable accounts of the establishment of the Genesis Group. See also "Salt Lake: Group Formed for Black Members," *Church News* (October 19, 1971): 13.

111. Wallace Turner, "Mormons Operating a Special Meeting Unit for Blacks," *New York Times*, April 6, 1972. Armand L. Mauss offers a contrasting account of the early membership, stating that "its participation levels have ranged between about twenty-five and fifty, consisting disproportionately of women, middle-aged and older people, and high school-educated skilled and semi-skilled workers." Mauss, "Fading of the Pharoahs' Curse," in Mauss and Lester E. Bush Jr., eds., *Neither White nor Black* (Midvale, UT: Signature Books, 1984), 163.

112. Dew, *Gordon B. Hinckley*, 296; Heidi S. Swinton, *To the Rescue: The Biography of Thomas S. Monson* (Salt Lake City: Deseret Book, 2010), 367–368; Lucile C. Tate, *Boyd K. Packer: A Watchman on the Tower* (Salt Lake City: Bookcraft, 1995), 227–228. For background on the Genesis Group presidency, see R. Scott Lloyd, "Revelation Rewarded Those Who Waited," *Church News* (December 18, 1999): 4–5.

113. Helen Kennedy, an early member of the group, recalled Packer's counsel to the group, in Kennedy oral history interview with Alan Cherry (April 11, 1986), MSS 7752 Series 17, African American Oral History Project, L. Tom Perry Special Collections, Harold B. Lee Library, Brigham Young University.

114. H. Michael Marquardt interview with Eugene Orr, November 7, 14, 1971, box 6, folder 3, H. Michael Marquardt Papers, Special Collections, Marriott Library, University of Utah. Orr was the second counselor in the Genesis Group presidency. Our thanks to Mike Marquardt for calling these documents to our attention. See also Helen Kennedy's account, in which she notes that the Genesis presidency approached her and said "We know we can get the priesthood." Kennedy, a black Mormon, replied, "What a minute, what are you trying to do? Look, you guys. You knew before you came in the Church how we stood on the priesthood, so you can't push this." The presidency rejoined: "Yes, we are going to have a meeting and we are going to do it." In Kennedy oral history interview with Alan Cherry.

115. Bridgeforth quoted in Peggy Olsen, "Ruffin Bridgeforth: Leader and Father to Mormon Blacks," *This People* 1 (Winter 1980): 16. Orr recalls that he formed "a special interest group" within the Genesis Group, which angered Bridgeforth. In Matt Harris phone interview with Eugene Orr, October 9, 2014 (notes in Matt Harris's files).

116. For dissention in the Genesis Group, see Bridgeforth's characterization in "Black Mormon Group Dwindling," in *Monday Magazine* (Salt Lake City), April 17, 1978. For Gray's recollection of Orr, see "Nobody Knows: The Untold Story of Black Mormons—A Script," *Dialogue: A Journal of Mormon Thought* 42 (Fall 2009): 116–117. For Bridgeforth's accounting of the apostles calling him, see Olsen, "Ruffin Bridgeforth: Leader and Father to Mormon Blacks," 17. Monson also called Monroe Fleming from the Genesis Group. See Swinton, *To the Rescue*, 395.

117. See, for example, the Genesis Group website: http://www.ldsgenesisgroup.org/. In the 1980s, other Genesis Groups were organized in the United States. For this point, see Jesse L. Embry, "Separate but Equal? Black Branches, Genesis Groups, or Integrated Wards?" *Dialogue: Journal of Mormon Thought* 23 (Spring 1990): 15–19.

Chapter 6. The 1978 Revelation and Its Implications

1. Newell G. Bringhurst, *Saints, Slaves, and Blacks: The Changing Place of Black People within Mormonism* (Westport, CT: Greenwood Press, 1981), 178–197, Armand L. Mauss, "Fading of the Pharoah's Curse: The Decline of the Fall of the Priesthood Ban against blacks in the Mormon Church," *Dialogue: A Journal of Mormon Thought* 14 (1981): 10–45, and Edward L. Kimball, "Spencer W. Kimball and the Revelation on the Priesthood," *BYU Studies* 47 (2008): 5–85, provide the most insightful treatment of the events leading up to the revelation. Also useful is O. Kendall White Jr. and Daryl White, "Abandoning an Unpopular Policy: An Analysis of the Decision Granting the Mormon Priesthood to Blacks," *Sociological Analysis* 41 (Fall 1980): 231–245; Armand L. Mauss, "Comments: White on Black among the Mormons: A Critique of White and White," *Sociological Analysis* 42 (Fall 1981): 277–282.

2. Mauss, "Mormonism and the Negro: Faith, Folklore and Civil Rights," *Dialogue: Journal of Mormon Thought* 4 (1967): 19–39. For background and context to Mauss's work in the 1960s, see his *Shifting Borders and a Tattered Passport: Intellectual Journeys of a Mormon Academic* (Salt Lake City: University of Utah Press, 2012), chapter 6.

3. For a comprehensive list of these writings, see Lester E. Bush Jr. and Armand Mauss, eds., *Neither White nor Black: Mormon Scholars Confront the Race Issue in a Universal Church* (Midvale, UT: Signature Books, 1984), 227–231.

4. Taggart, *Mormonism's Negro Policy: Social and Historical Origins* (Salt Lake City: University of Utah Press, 1970), esp. 4–33.

5. Ibid., 77–80.

6. Thomas "Memo" to BYU president Ernest Wilkinson, July 16, 1970, box 556, folder 17, Ernest L. Wilkinson Papers, L. Tom Perry Special Collections, Harold B. Lee Library, BYU.

7. Riddle "Memo" to Wilkinson, July 21, 1970, and Ludlow "Memo" to Wilkinson, July 22, 1970, both in box 556, folder 17, Ernest L. Wilkinson Papers, L. Tom Perry Special Collections, Harold B. Lee Library, BYU.

8. See "Meeting of the First Presidency," David O. McKay diary, September 17, 1969, box 70, folder 6, David O. McKay Papers, Special Collections, Marriott Library, University of Utah. For years Brown had subscribed to the view that the priesthood policy did not have "any justification in the scriptures" and, as a result, he sought a change. See Edwin B. Firmage, ed., *An Abundant Life: The Memoirs of Hugh B. Brown*, 2nd ed. (Salt Lake City: Signature Books, 1999), 129–130, 142.

9. For McKay's discussion with his sons at the Hotel Utah, see McKay diary, September 10, 1969, box 70, folder 5, David O. McKay Papers, Special Collections, Marriott Library, University of Utah. Gregory A. Prince and Wm. Robert Wright provide a contextual overview to McMurrin's conversation with McKay in 1954. See *David O. McKay and the Rise of Modern Mormonism* (Salt Lake City: University of Utah Press, 2005), 96–98. McKay read Taggart's work in manuscript form. The book was published after McKay's death.

10. See "Minutes by President Alvin R. Dyer on a meeting he had with President Hugh B. Brown," David O. McKay diary, October 8, 1969, box 70, folder 7, David O. McKay Papers, Special Collections, Marriott Library, University of Utah. These minutes are extracts from Dyer's diary. For Brown's attempt to change the racial policy, see chap. 4.

11. Porter, "'Whites, Not God, Cursed Negro,'" *Salt Lake Tribune*, May 10, 1970.

12. Wallace Turner, "Conservative and Liberal Mormons Advise Church on Negro Exclusion Policy," *New York Times*, June 21, 1970.

13. See Bush, "A Commentary on Stephen G. Taggart's Mormonism's Negro Policy: Social and Historical Origins," *Dialogue: Journal of Mormon Thought* 4 (Winter 1969): 86–103. For his interest in Mormon racial history, see Lester E. Bush Jr., "Writing 'Mormonism's Negro Doctrine: An Historical Overview' (1973): Context and Reflections, 1998," *Journal of Mormon History* 25 (Spring 1999): 233–234.

14. Fawn McKay Brodie, David O. McKay's niece, was the first person to advance the "Missouri thesis." For an exposition on this topic, see Newell G. Bringhurst, "The 'Missouri Thesis' Revisited: Early Mormonism, Slavery, and the Status of Black People," in Bringhurst and Darron T. Smith, eds., *Black and Mormon* (Urbana: University of Illinois Press, 2004), 13–33.

15. Bush, "Mormonism's Negro Doctrine: An Historical Overview," *Dialogue: Journal of Mormon Thought* 8 (Spring 1973): 11–68. The article was reprinted as a *Dialogue* monograph in 1978 and also in Bush and Mauss, eds., *Neither White nor Black*, 53–129. For the significance of Bush's article, including its importance to *Dialogue*, see Devery S. Anderson, "A History of Dialogue: Part III: Struggle toward Maturity, 1971–1982," *Dialogue: Journal of Mormon Thought* 33 (Summer 2000): 22–27 (quote at 23 n. 110). Mormon scholars also rated Bush's study as the second most influential article ever published in Mormon history, second only to Stanley Ivins' "Notes on Mormon Polygamy," *Utah Historical Quarterly* 35 (Fall 1967): 309–321. For this point, see James B. Allen, "Since 1950: Creators and Creations of Mormon History," in Davis Bitton and Maureen Ursenbach Beecher, eds., *New Views of Mormon History: A Collection of Essays in Honor of Leonard J. Arrington* (Salt Lake City: University of Utah Press, 1987), 424.

16. The LDS Church History Library has a copy of this work, as does the L. Tom Perry Special Collections at the Harold B. Lee Library, BYU.

17. Bush, "Mormonism's Negro Doctrine," esp. 18–21.

18. Ibid., 22–31, 35–39, 48.

19. Ibid., 11. See Nibley, "The Best Possible Test," *Dialogue: Journal of Mormon Thought* 8 (Spring 1973): 73–77; Thomasson, "Lester Bush's Historical Overview: Other Perspectives," *Dialogue: Journal of Mormon Thought* 8 (Spring 1973): 69–72; and England, "The Mormon Cross," *Dialogue: Journal of Mormon Thought* (Spring 1973): 78–86. None of these writers engaged Bush's central claims; all, in essence, offered personal reflections of priesthood denial.

20. As recounted by Robert Rees in Anderson, "A History of Dialogue," 26n127. See also Lester E. Bush Jr., "Writing Mormonism's Negro Doctrine: An Historical Overview" (1973): Context and Reflections, 1998," *Journal of Mormon History* 25 (Spring 1999): 260–263.

21. Bush, "Writing Mormonism's Negro Doctrine," 254–259, contains a full discussion of Bush's interactions with Packer. Bush and Packer exchanged several letters about Bush's work, which can be found in box 3, folder 36 of Lester E. Bush Papers, Special Collections, Marriott Library, University of Utah.

22. Bush, "Writing Mormonism's Negro Doctrine," 262.

23. These stories are recounted in Bush, "Writing Mormonism's Negro Doctrine," 266–267. See also Lavina Fielding Anderson, "The LDS Intellectual Community and Church Leadership: A Contemporary Chronology," *Dialogue: Journal of Mormon Thought* 26 (Spring 1993): 20–22. Tony Kimball, Spencer W. Kimball's grandson, commented that his grandfather marked up the article in *Dialogue*. However, Ed Kimball, the president's son, could not confirm that account (Ed Kimball email to Matt Harris, August 24, 2013). Our thanks to Ed Kimball for his assistance.

24. General Authority Marion D. Hanks recounted this story to Bush's friend Greg Prince. See Prince oral interview with Hanks, May 27, 1994, box 22, folder 2, Gregory A. Prince Papers, Marriott Library, University of Utah. Hanks also confided to Bush himself that Bush's work "probably had a far greater effect than was acknowledged to you or than has yet been evidence[d]. Recent conversations [with general authorities] suggest that this is so." See Hanks to Bush, July 10, 1975, box 2, folder 58, Lester E. Bush Papers, Marriott Library, University of Utah. For the general authorities' response to Bush's article, see Bush, "Writing Mormonism's Negro Doctrine," 266–267.

25. Kimball, "Spencer W. Kimball and the Revelation on the Priesthood," 44.

26. This section draws on the work of Mark L. Grover, whose seminal research on the Mormon church in Brazil constitutes a benchmark in LDS church history. See, in particular, "Religious Accommodation in the Land of Racial Democracy: Mormon Priesthood and Black Brazilians," *Dialogue: Journal of Mormon Thought* 17 (Autumn 1984): 23–34; and "The Mormon Priesthood Revelation and the São Paulo, Brazil Temple," *Dialogue: Journal of Mormon Thought* 23 (Spring 1990): 39–53. For Kimball's experiences in Brazil and South America more generally, see Francis M. Gibbons, *Spencer W. Kimball: Resolute Disciple, Prophet of God* (Salt Lake City: Deseret Book, 1995), chapter 19.

27. Haight made this statement to general authority Teddy Brewerton, May 21, 1979, Manuscript History of the "South American East Area Office of the Church of Jesus Christ of Latter-day Saints," LDS Church History Library, Salt Lake City, Utah.

28. Grover, "Mormon Priesthood Revelation," 43–44. For more on Martins' background, consult *The Autobiography of Elder Helvécio Martins*, Helvécio Martins with Mark Grover (Salt Lake: Aspen Books, 1994); Marcus H. Martins (Martins' son), *Blacks and the Mormon Priesthood* (Orem, UT: Millennial Press, 2007), 1–6; and Mark L. Grover, "Helvécio Martins: First Black General Authority," *Journal of Mormon History* 36 (Summer 2010): 27–54.

29. Martins, *Autobiography*, 66–67; Grover, "Mormon Priesthood Revelation," 48. The Brazil temple cornerstone ceremony occurred in 1977; the temple dedication was in 1978.

30. An observation Haight made to Quinn McKay, David O. McKay's nephew, 1980. McKay related this conversation in a later memoir he wrote about blacks and the Mormon church. See his "A Rural, Utah, Mormon Boy—The Blacks and the LDS Church," 2006, LDS Church History Library. Apostle LeGrand Richards made a similar statement about the importance of the Brazil temple to the reversal of the priesthood ban. See his interview with Chris Vlachos and Wesley Walters, August 16, 1978, LDS Church History Library. Paul Dunn, a popular general authority, also commented on the importance of the Brazil temple to the priesthood reversal. See his oral interview with Greg Prince, January 11, 1997, 2nd session, box 22, folder 2, Gregory A. Prince Papers, Special Collections, Marriott Library, University of Utah.

31. Bangerter oral history interview with Gordon Irving, 1981, p. 13, LDS Church History Library. Bangerter also recounts the difficulty of determining ethnicity in his autobiography. See *These Things I Know: The Autobiography of William Grant Bangerter*, compiled by Cory Wm. Bangerter (Provo, UT: BYU Print Services, 2013), 169–170. Our thanks to Cory Bangerter for sharing a copy of his father's autobiography.

32. J. Reuben Clark, a counselor in the First Presidency to David O. McKay, was the principal person opposed to opening a mission in Brazil. He believed that there was too much "mixed blood." As recounted by Daniel Shupe, oral history interview with Gordon Irving, February 22, 1973, James H. Moyle Oral History Program, p. 32, LDS Church History Library. When the mission opened, apostle Mark E. Petersen tried to close it. The church had too many problems, he said, "complicated by the ban on blacks." See Greg Prince oral history interview with Lola Gygi Timmins, March 18, 2000, box 22, folder 2, Gregory A. Prince Papers, Special Collections, Marriott Library, University of Utah. Timmins was the secretary to church president David O. McKay.

33. For an overview of Howell's "lineage lesson" program, see Campinas Branch, Brazilian Mission, Mission Circulars, 1949–1953, LDS Church History Library. The L. Tom Perry Special Collections, in the Harold B. Lee Library at BYU, also contains a collection of the Mission Circulars. The minutes from the Council of the Twelve state: "President Clark again repeated what he had previously said on a number of occasions that in South America, and particularly Brazil, we are entering into a situation in doing missionary work among these people where it is very difficult if not impossible to tell who has negro blood and who has not. He said that if we are baptizing Brazilians, we are almost certainly baptizing people of negro blood. . . ." See Council Minutes, October 9, 1947, Adam S. Bennion Papers, LDS Church History Library.

34. For the one-drop rule in American History, see Ariela J. Gross, *What Blood Won't Tell: A History of Race on Trial in America* (Cambridge: Harvard University Press, 2008),

44, 100, 106–107; and Nell Irvin Painter, *The History of White People* (New York: W.W. Norton, 2010), 386–387. The policy seems to have originated in the 1850s and then became more expansive after the Civil War. See Walter Johnson, "The Slave Trader, the White Slave, and the Politics of Racial Determination," *Journal of American History* 87 (June 2000): 13–38.

35. Grover, "Religious Accommodation," 27; Bangerter, *This I Know*, 169; and Howells oral history interview with Gordon Irving, January 18, 1973, p. 62, LDS Church History Library. There are numerous copies of the lineage lessons at the Church History Library. Missionaries were instructed to avoid teaching black Brazilians right up until the priesthood revelation in 1978. See, for example, the minutes of a Zone Conference in the Brazil São Paulo South Mission, September 22, 1975, in the "History of the South American East Area Office of the Church of Jesus Christ of Latter-day Saints," LDS Church History Library. See also "A Missionary Handbook," Brazilian Mission, 1966, p. 14, stating: "It is not permissible to confer the Priesthood of God upon one who has the lineage of Cain. For this reason, on a practical basis, it is best to avoid teaching them the discussions." Mission Handbook courtesy of Mark Grover.

36. Mark Grover email to Matt Harris, August 16, 2013. See also Grover, "Religious Accommodation," 28 ("Membership records were marked.") and Mauss, "Fading of the Pharaoh's Curse," 12–13.

37. Howells explained the church policy of tracing bloodlines out of Africa in his oral interview with Gordon Irving, January 18, 1973, p. 63, LDS Church History Library. Armand L. Mauss provides an insightful discussion of race and lineage in *All Abraham's Children: Changing Mormon Conceptions of Race and Lineage* (Urbana: University of Illinois Press, 2003). See also Bush, "Mormonism's Negro Doctrine," 68 n. 209, Kimball, "Spencer W. Kimball and the Revelation on Priesthood," 19. The policy of tracing lineage out of Africa was also applied to the South African mission. See "South African Mission Proselyting Plan," December 1951, compiled by Elder Gilbert G. Tobler, in discussion 13, p. 45–46, LDS Church History Library. The clearest exposition of church policy on lineage came from church president Harold B. Lee: "President Lee said skin color is not what keeps the Negro from the priesthood. It is strictly a matter of lineage and involves only African Negroes. In comparison, he noted, dark or black islanders, such as Fijians, Tongans, Samoans or Maoris, are all permitted full rights to the priesthood." See John Keahey, "Lee Says Complete Status for Negroes in LDS Priesthood Only Matter of Time," *Salt Lake Tribune*, September 21, 1972. The story was also reprinted in the *Ogden Standard Examiner*, September 23, 1972, and the *Daily Herald* (Provo, UT), September 26, 1972.

38. Prince and Wright, *David O. McKay and the Rise of Modern Mormonism*, 78–79; Mauss, *All Abraham's Children*, 232.

39. See Spencer W. Kimball, N. Eldon Tanner, and Marion G. Romney to "Stake and Mission Presidents, District Presidents, Bishops, and Branch Presidents," February 22, 1978, box 61, folder 3, Max Parkin Papers, Special Collections, Marriott Library, University of Utah.

40. "Brother Nunes" is a fictitious name.

41. On this point, see "Mission Presidents' Seminar," June 23, 1978, box 33, folder 4, Leonard J. Arrington Papers, Special Collections, Merrill-Cazier Library, Utah State Uni-

versity; and Edward L. Kimball, *Lengthen Your Stride: The Presidency of Spencer W. Kimball* (Salt Lake City: Deseret Book, 2005), chapter 24. See also "LDS Church Sees Growth in Black Africa," *Daily Herald*, September 6, 1979; and Newell G. Bringhurst, "The Image of Blacks within Mormonism as Presented in the Church News (1978–1988)," *American Periodicals: A Journal of History, Criticism, and Bibliography* 2 (Fall 1992): 113–123.

42. Edward Kimball, Spencer Kimball's son, makes the perceptive point that "many factors set the stage for change, although it is impossible to determine how much each contributed." See his authoritative article entitled "Spencer Kimball and the Revelation on Priesthood," *BYU Studies* 47 (2008): 43.

43. Bringhurst, *Saints, Slaves, and Blacks*, 190–191; Kimball, "Spencer Kimball and the Revelation on Priesthood," 44; Mauss, "Fading of the Pharaohs' Curse," 12–13.

44. Grover, "Religious Accommodation in the Land of Racial Democracy," 32 n. 32; Lester E. Bush, Jr., "Introduction," *Dialogue: Journal of Mormon Thought* 7 (Summer 1979): 12 n. 2. Thomas J. Fyans, a general authority, and also the executive director of the Genealogical Department, said that "he would get all these letters asking about bloodlines" and then turn them over to President Kimball. After the revelation was announced, Kimball told him that he'd no longer have to send the letters. Fyans also recounted a story when he was a general authority living in Mexico City. In 1975, a sister missionary approached him after she discovered that she had a grandfather who was black. Concerned, Fyans approached his "advisor," apostle Howard W. Hunter. Hunter asked if she was a good missionary and how much time she had left. When Fyans replied that she was a good missionary and that she only had four months remaining, Hunter told Fyans to study the issue carefully, "very carefully," and "take a minimum of four months to do it." See Greg Prince oral interview with Thomas J. Fyans, June 3, 1995, box 22, folder 2, Gregory A. Prince Papers, Special Collections, Marriott Library, University of Utah. Fryan's predecessor in the Genealogical Department, Theodore M. Burton, also a general authority, expressed similar frustration about determining lineages. See his letter to a stake president, Elden Clark Olsen, February 6, 1975, box 32, folder 4, David John Buerger Papers, Special Collections, Marriott Library, University of Utah.

45. Spencer W. Kimball, N. Eldon Tanner, and Marion G. Romney to "Stake and Mission Presidents, District Presidents, Bishops, and Branch Presidents," February 22, 1978, box 61, folder 3, Max Parkin Papers, Special Collections, Marriott Library, University of Utah. Quinn, *Extensions of Power*, 16, postulates that this policy change "was a prelude to ending the ban entirely—and soon."

46. "Mormons Pressed on Scout Policy," *New York Times*, August 3, 1974; "NAACP Files Suit in Scout Bias Case," *Pacific Stars & Stripes*, August 1, 1974. Dozens of newspapers reported on this issue. For a sampling, see *Kalamazoo*, July 19, 1974; *Bryan Times*, August 3, 1974; *Bangor Daily News*, August 2, 1974; *Tri-City Herald*, August 2, 1974; *Spokane Daily Chronicle*, August 12, 1974; *Lewiston Daily Sun*, July 24, 1974. In 1965, Daily Oliver, a black man, recalled that during his teenage years an LDS bishop instructed him that he could not attend Boy Scouts in the LDS troop because he "was a negro." See *Daily Utah Chronicle*, May 28, 1965.

47. Gibbons, *Spencer Kimball*, 277–278.

48. Ibid., 278.

49. The LDS church's lawyers, in fact, had produced a friend of the court brief in *Bob Jones* (special thanks to BYU law librarian Galen Fletcher for providing us with a copy). See "Mormons Support Bob Jones' Case, *Sumter Dailey Item*, July 31, 1981, and an unpublished report titled "Ronald Reagan and Tax Exemptions for Racist Schools," by David Whitman of Harvard's Kennedy School of Government (1984), in box 8, folder 8, Rex E. Lee Papers, L. Tom Perry Special Collections, Harold B. Lee Library, BYU.

50. For a discussion of the Bob Jones case and its impact on private schools, see Thomas Stephen Neuberger and Thomas C. Crumplar, "Tax Exempt Religious Schools Under Attack: Conflicting Goals of Religious Freedom and Racial Integration," *Fordham Law Review* 48 (1979): 241–242; Joseph H. Helm Jr., "Denying Tax Exemption to Racially Restrictive Religious Schools: An Unconstitutional Infringement Upon Religious Membership Practices," *Valparaiso Law Review* 17 (1983): 452–453; and Nicholas A. Mirkay, "Is It 'Charitable' To Discriminate?: The Necessary Transformation of Section 501(C)(3) Into the Gold Standard for Charities," *Wisconsin Law Review* 45 (2007): 61–68. For the threat of legal action at BYU, see Hollis B. Bach (Regional Civil Rights Director) to Ernest L. Wilkinson, March 27, 1969, box 35, folder 26, Richard D. Poll Papers, Special Collections, Marriott Library, University of Utah. Wilkinson's academic vice-president, Robert K. Thomas, explained that if the "racial issue" remained unresolved at BYU the university would lose government research funds and donations from private foundations. He also expressed fear that BYU would lose its general accreditation. See Thomas to Wilkinson, "President's Office Memorandum," January 1, 1969, box 556, folder 12, Ernest L. Wilkinson Papers, L. Tom Perry Special Collections, Harold B. Lee Library, Brigham Young University.

51. Arrington letter to his children, June 15, 1978, box 33, folder 4, Leonard J. Arrington Papers, Special Collections, Merrill-Cazier Library, Utah State University. Arrington repeated this assertion in his memoirs. See *Adventures of a Church Historian* (Urbana: University of Illinois Press, 1998), 183.

52. ADA to Dallin Oaks and Carl Hawkins, September 9, 1975, and Hawkins to Rex E. Lee, September 19, 1975, both in box 76, folder 2, Rex E. Lee Papers, L. Tom Perry Special Collections, Harold B. Lee Library, BYU; and Oaks' 2012 speech to the law school entitled "Unfolding in Time," in *Clark Memorandum* (Spring 2013): 15–21 (quote at 18).

53. Kimball, "Spencer Kimball and the Revelation on Priesthood," 42.

54. See "Member Ordains Black to Priesthood," *Salt Lake Tribune*, April 3, 1976; "Mormons Nullify Black's Ordination," *Denver Post*, April 3, 1976; "Ordination of Black Declared Null," *Deseret News*, April 6, 1978; "Excommunicated," *Deseret News*, April 12, 1976.

55. Kimball, *Lengthen Your Stride*, 213. On the restraining order, see Kimball, "Spencer W. Kimball and the Revelation on the Priesthood," 41; and Wallace to Spencer W. Kimball, January 20, 1977, box 3, folder 66, Lester E. Bush Papers, Special Collections, Marriott Library, University of Utah. Wallace tried unsuccessfully to sue the church.

56. Marchant's protest is recounted in *Salt Lake Tribune*, June 10, 1978. See also "Church Ousts a Mormon over Policy on Blacks," *New York Times*, October 16, 1977; "Critic of Racial Policy Says Mormons Ousted, Fired Him," *Washington Post*, Nov. 4, 1977. Marchant summoned N. Eldon Tanner for a church court, to be conducted by the presiding

bishopric. Marchant was angry because Tanner signed the First Presidency statement of 1969, making what he believed to be false statements against blacks. Hugh B. Brown, the other signatory, escaped this fate because he died in 1975. See Marchant to the Presiding Bishopric (Victor L. Brown, H. Burke Petersen, J. Richard Clark), August 18, 1977, box 3, folder 19, Lester E. Bush Papers, Special Collections, Marriott Library, University of Utah. Marchant also wrote protest letters to Kimball. See his letters of May 11, 1977, and July 29, 1974, ibid.

57. Edward Kimball interview with Sherri Dew, president of Desert Book, September 18, 1995, in Kimball, "Spencer Kimball and the Revelation on Priesthood," 44.

58. Kimball, "Spencer Kimball and the Revelation on Priesthood," 59–72, provides a solid account of church reaction to the revelation.

59. Lester Bush perceptively notes in "Mormonism's Negro Doctrine: An Historical Overview," 42–43, that an "aversion to miscegenation has been the single most consistent facet of Mormon attitudes towards the Negro. Though the attitudes towards the priesthood, slavery, or equal rights have fluctuated significantly, denunciations of interracial marriage can be identified in discourses in virtually every decade from the Restoration to the present day [1973]. Though these sentiments can never be said to have dominated Mormon thought, they did become a major theme in the years following the Second World War and are to be found in both published and private remarks, generally in connection with the civil rights discussion." See also Mauss, *All Abraham's Children*, 31.

60. See, for example, "Lesson 31: Choosing an Eternal Companion," *Aaronic Priesthood Manual* 3 (2011), on the church's website: http://lds.org/manual/aaronic-priesthood-manual-3/lesson-31-choosing-an-eternal-companion?lang=eng.

61. Quinn, *Extensions of Power*, 870. See also Kimball, "Spencer Kimball and the Revelation on Priesthood," 62 n. 185, who explains that "Petersen continued to disapprove of interracial marriage and expressed low expectations for the first mission in black Africa."

62. See "Interracial Marriage Discouraged" in the *Church News* supplement to the *Deseret News*, June 17, 1978, pp. 3–5.

63. See J. Reuben Clark, Jr. to the Young Women's Mutual Improvement Association conference, *Improvement Era* 49 (August 1946): 492. Apostle Harold B. Lee echoed similar remarks. Speaking to a youth group in 1945, he said: "Surely no one of you who is an heir to a body of more favored lineage would knowingly intermarry with a race that would condemn your posterity to penalties that have been placed upon the seed of Cain by the judgments of God." See "Youth of a Noble Birthright," May 6, 1945, typescript at LDS Church History Library.

64. First Presidency (George Albert Smith, J. Reuben Clark, David O. McKay) to Lowry Nelson, July 17, 1947, box 20, folder 1, Lowry Nelson Papers, Special Collections, Marriott Library, University of Utah; First Presidency to Virgil H. Sponberg, May 5, 1947, Adam S. Bennion Papers, LDS Church History Library.

65. First Presidency minutes in David O. McKay journal, September 26, 1961, box 48, folder 5, David O. McKay Papers, Special Collections, Marriott Library, University of Utah. See also minutes from the First Presidency meeting of January 9, 1962, in which McKay expressed great concern over Nigerians seeking baptism. He permitted baptizing

them as long as "they would stay with themselves and marry among themselves," but he feared they would migrate elsewhere and mingle with white Mormons. If that happened, McKay cautioned, "intermarriage would be an inevitable result," adding, "I don't believe in it" (box 49, folder 3, ibid.). See also a similar statement in his diary, November 10, 1965, box 61, folder 3, ibid. Mormons, of course, were not unique in opposing interracial marriage. Public opinion polls in the 1950s demonstrate that over 90 percent of whites in the United States opposed mixed marriages. On this point, see Michael J. Klarman, *From Jim Crow to Civil Rights: The Supreme Court and the Struggle for Racial Equality* (New York: Oxford University Press, 2004), 321.

66. Young made several denunciations about interracial relationships during his time as church president. See, in particular, his "Speech in the Joint Session of the Legislature," February 5, 1852, box 48, folder 3, LDS Church History Library. The Utah territorial legislature prohibited interracial sex in 1852. See Peggy Pascoe, *What Comes Naturally: Miscegenation Law and the Making of Race in America* (New York: Oxford University Press, 2009), 21.

67. The prohibition of interracial sex and marriage was a long established custom in the United States by the time Utah outlawed it in 1852 and 1888, respectively. In 1963, Utah was one of about eleven western states that had repealed anti-miscegenation laws between 1951 and 1963. See Pascoe, *What Comes Naturally*, 21, 85, 93, 118, 240–243. The Harvard legal scholar Randall Kennedy writes that "After Ohio repealed its anti-miscegenation laws in 1887, no other state followed its lead until Oregon finally did so in 1951—sixty-four years later." Kennedy, *Interracial Intimacies: Sex, Marriage, Identity, and Adoption* (New York: Pantheon Books, 2003), 258. See also Peter Wallenstein, *Tell the Court I Love My Wife: Race, Marriage, and Law—An American History* (New York: Palgrave Macmillan, 2002), 253–254; and Lawrence Freedman, *American Law in the Twentieth Century* (New Haven: Yale University Press, 2002), 111–113. A general overview of interracial marriage in Utah is Patrick Q. Mason, "The Prohibition of Interracial Marriage in Utah, 1888–1963," *Utah Historical Quarterly* 76 (Spring 2008): 108–131. In a meeting of February 7, 1963, with the Twelve Apostles, church president David O. McKay discussed the "Racial Intermarriage Statute" in Utah. McKay "said that we are facing a question of permitting the marriage of negroes with whites, and that we had better put up with a little inconvenience regarding interracial marriage to avoid greater troubles." McKay worried that Utah's anti-miscegenation laws would draw further attention to the church's checkered past with race relations. See "Council Meeting" minutes, David O. McKay diary, February 7, 1963, box 52, folder 4, David O. McKay Papers, Special Collections, Marriott Library, University of Utah.

68. For a good overview of the *Loving* case, see Wallenstein, *Tell the Court I Love My Wife*, 216–224, 231–251; Friedman, *American Law*, 294; and especially Peter Wallenstein, *Race, Sex, and the Freedom to Marry Loving v. Virginia* (Lawrence: University Press of Kansas, 2014).

69. *General Handbook of Instructions* 20 (Salt Lake City: Deseret News Press, 1968): 52. It was omitted in the 1976 handbook.

70. Kimball's speeches were reprinted in "Interracial Marriage Discouraged," *Church News* supplement to the *Deseret News*, June 17, 1978, p. 4. See also Edward L. Kimball, ed., *The Teachings of Spencer W. Kimball* (Salt Lake City: Bookcraft, 1982), 302–303.

71. Boyd Packer, "Follow the Rule," January 14, 1977, in BYU Speeches at http://speeches.byu.edu/reader/reader.php?id=6172. For the limited dating opportunities among LDS black members, see Jessie L. Embry, *Black Saints in a White Church* (Salt Lake City: Signature Books, 1984), 171.

72. Embry, *Black Saints*, 168–171; Dan LeFevre, *Salt Lake Tribune*, June 14, 1978. LeFevre said that there is "no ban on interracial marriage. If a black partner contemplating marriage is worthy of going to the Temple, nobody's going to stop him. If he's ready to go to the Temple, obviously he may go with the blessings of the church."

73. For Packer, see Embry, *Black Saints*, 170. See also Bruce R. McConkie, "Negroes," in *Mormon Doctrine*, 2nd ed. (Salt Lake City: Bookcraft, 1979), 527.

74. Edward L. Kimball, *Lengthen Your Stride: The Presidency of Spencer W. Kimball—A Working Draft* (Salt Lake City: Benchmark Books, 2009), 375.

75. In the twentieth century, Kimball and other Mormon leaders promoted a version of marital homogamy akin to other religious denominations. Marriage outside of one's faith, and marriage outside of one's race, conflicted with "time-tested strategies for marital success," noted Rebecca L. Davis. See her *More Perfect Unions: The American Search for Marital Bliss* (Cambridge, MA: Harvard University Press, 2010), 103.

76. Sterling McMurrin, the church's most persistent critic on the priesthood ban, sent the First Presidency a note congratulating them on having the "spiritual maturity" to rescind the ban. See McMurrin to Spencer W. Kimball, June 20, 1978, box 290, folder 2, Sterling M. McMurrin Papers, Special Collections, Marriott Library, University of Utah; "Carter Praises LDS Church Action," *Deseret News*, June 10, 1978; "Carter Praises Prophet's Courage," BYU *Daily Universe*, June 13, 1978.

77. Edward Kimball, *Lengthen Your Stride*, 233, comments that for "Latter-day Saints who harbored racial prejudices, the revelation came as a shock. A few people did reject the revelation and left the Church, and some lapsed into inactivity out of dissatisfaction." For the dissident ad, see "LDS Soon to Repudiate a Portion of Their Pearl of Great Price?" *Salt Lake Tribune*, July 23, 1978.

78. Quoted in Molly Ivins, "Mormon Decision on Blacks Promises Impact on Utah," *New York Times*, June 18, 1978.

79. See *Daily Herald* (Provo, UT), January 7, 1979. See also "Y Black Athletes React Favorably to Change in Priesthood Policy," BYU *Daily Universe*, June 13, 1978; "Church Officials Applaud LDS Action on Blacks," *Salt Lake Tribune*, June 10, 1978.

80. On the points, see Joseph Fielding McConkie, *The Bruce McConkie Story* (Salt Lake: Deseret Book, 2003) and Lucile C. Tate, *LeGrand Richards: Beloved Apostle* (Salt Lake: Bookcraft, 1982).

81. Richards is best known in the LDS church for his popular book, *A Marvelous Work and a Wonder* (Salt Lake City: Deseret Book, 1950), which provides an interpretive guide for missionaries to LDS scriptures and doctrine. The standard biography of Richards is Lucile C. Tate, *LeGrand Richards: Beloved Apostle* (Salt Lake City: Bookcraft, 1982).

82. The original transcript of the interview is in the LDS Church History Library. There is also a copy in the L. Tom Perry Special Collections in the Harold B. Lee Library at BYU.

83. Walters and Vlachos interview with LeGrand Richards, August 16, 1978, LDS Church History Library. A copy of the transcript is also in the L. Tom Perry Special Collections, Harold B. Lee Library, BYU.

84. David John Buerger interview with H. Michael Marquardt and Wesley Walters, August 19, 1978, box 32, folder 10, David John Buerger Papers, Special Collections, Marriott Library, University of Utah.

85. LeGrand Richards to Chris Vlachos, September 12, 1978, box 32, folder 10, David John Buerger Papers, Special Collections, Marriott Library, University of Utah. The published version of the interview can be found in Wesley P. Walters, *Interview with Mormon Apostle LeGrand Richards Concerning 1978 Negro "Revelation,"* 16 August 1978 (Phoenix, AZ: Ex-Mormons for Jesus, 1978). Box 42 of the John W. Fitzgerald Papers, Special Collections, Merrill-Cazier Library, at Utah State, contains a cassette recording of the interview. Richards did not know about the cassette recording until after the interview. Walters was a vigorous critic of the Mormon church. See, for example, *Mormonism Exposed* (Personal Freedom Outreach, 1991); Wesley P. Walters, "From Occult to Cult with Joseph Smith, Jr.," *Journal of Pastoral Practice* 1, no. 2 (Summer 1977); Wesley P. Walters, "Joseph's First Vision Story Undermined," *Quarterly Journal of Watchman Fellowship* (January–March 1988).

86. McConkie, "All Alike Unto God," address given to Seminary and Institute of Religion personnel, August 18, 1978, LDS Church History Library, Salt Lake City, Utah; McConkie, "The New Revelation on Priesthood," in (no author or editor listed) *Priesthood* (Salt Lake: Deseret Book, 1981), 126–137. All references to the talk are from the published version.

87. See E. Dale LeBaron, "Official Declaration 2: Revelation on the Priesthood," *The Heavens Are Open: The 1992 Sperry Symposium of the Doctrine and Covenants* (Salt Lake City: Deseret Book, 1993), 194–195; E. Dale LeBaron, "Revelation on the Priesthood: The Dawning of a New Day in Africa," *Doctrines for Exaltation: The 1989 Sperry Symposium on the Doctrine and Covenants* (Salt Lake City: Deseret Book, 1989), 128–129; "Official Declaration 2: 'Every, Faithful, Worthy Man,'" *Doctrine and Covenants Student Manual* (Salt Lake City: The Church of Jesus Christ of Latter-day Saints, 2002), 364–365; Mary Jane Woodger, "Revelation Attitudes: The Coming Forth of Official Declaration 2," *Religious Educator* 3, no. 2 (2002): 185–200; Richard E. Bennett, "'That Every Man Might Speak in the Name of God the Lord': A Study of Official Declaration 2," *Religious Educator* 4, no. 2 (2003): 41–56; Rachel Cope, "Teaching Official Declaration 2" (2012), *Juvenile Instructor*, http://tinyurl.com/nzvycz7.

88. McConkie, "New Revelation on Priesthood," 126.

89. Ibid., 128.

90. Ibid., 132.

91. Mauss, *Shifting Borders and a Tattered Passport*, 232n32. The 1979 edition of McConkie's *Mormon Doctrine* (Salt Lake City: Bookcraft, 1979) still contains racist teachings under headings such as "Caste System," "Cain," and "Pre-existence." Furthermore, McConkie's later writings still contained racist doctrines, particularly the hierarchy of lineages. See, for example, his *The Mortal Messiah* (Salt Lake City: Deseret Book, 1979), 1:23; *The Millennial Messiah* (Salt Lake City: Deseret Book, 1982), 182–183 and chapter 16; and *A New Witness for the Articles of Faith* (Salt Lake City: Deseret Book, 1985), 510–512 and chapter 4.

Chapter 7. Confronting the Church's Problematic Racial Past after 1978

1. Armand L. Mauss, *All Abraham's Children: Changing Mormon Conceptions of Race and Lineage* (Urbana: University of Illinois Press, 2003), and Mauss, "Casting Off the 'Curse of Cain': The Extent and Limits of Progress Since 1978," in Newell G. Bringhurst and Darron T. Smith, eds., *Black and Mormon* (Urbana: University of Illinois Press, 2004), 82–115, constitute the most aggressive effort of any Latter-day Saint to get the church to repudiate "the doctrinal residue of . . . [its] discarded racial policy" (ibid., 82).

2. See Smith, *Doctrines of Salvation: Sermons and Writings of Joseph Fielding Smith*, comp. by Bruce R. McConkie, 3 vols. (Salt Lake City: Bookcraft, 1954–56); *Answers to Gospel Questions*, 5 vols. (Salt Lake City: Deseret Book, 1957–1966); and McConkie, *Mormon Doctrine* (Salt Lake City: Bookcraft, 1958; rev. ed. 1979). *Mormon Doctrine* went out of print in 2010; as of 2015, *Doctrines of Salvation* and *Answers to Gospel Questions* are still in print.

3. Ronald W. Walker, David J. Whittaker, and James B. Allen, *Mormon History* (Urbana: University of Illinois Press, 2001), 241.

4. See the preface in Ludlow et al., eds., *Encyclopedia of Mormonism*, 1:lxii.

5. Notable exceptions include Jan Shipps, a Methodist scholar of Mormonism, and James Charlesworth, a biblical scholar at the Princeton Theological Seminary. Two high-profile Mormon scholars were excluded from the project: former BYU history professor D. Michael Quinn, a prolific scholar of Mormonism, and University of Utah philosophy professor Sterling M. McMurrin. Quinn and McMurrin were omitted because of their controversial writings and their unorthodox beliefs and practices.

6. See "Acknowledgements" in Ludlow et al., eds., *Encyclopedia of Mormonism*, 1:lxiv.

7. From a conversation in 1994 that Matt Harris had with Ronald W. Walker, a professor of history at BYU and one of the contributors to the *Encyclopedia of Mormonism*.

8. Embry and Cherry collaborated on an earlier project on blacks and the LDS church. Since 1985, they had been conducting oral interviews with LDS African Americans. Their work resulted in a book titled *Black Saints in a White Church: Contemporary African American Mormons* (Salt Lake City: Signature Books, 1994). Cherry is a convert to the LDS church.

9. Scholars acknowledged black priesthood ordination long before Embry and Cherry recognized it in the *Encyclopedia of Mormonism*. See, for example, Lester E. Bush Jr., "Mormonism's Negro Doctrine: An Historical Overview," *Dialogue—A Journal of Mormon Thought* 8 (Spring 1973): 11–68; Newell G. Bringhurst, *Saints, Slaves, and Blacks: The Changing Place of Black People within Mormonism* (Westport, CT: Greenwood Press, 1981); and Lester E. Bush Jr. and Armand Mauss, *Neither White nor Black: Mormon Scholars Confront the Race Issue* (Salt Lake City: Signature Books, 1984). In 1920, Assistant Church Historian Andrew Jensen acknowledged Elijah Abel's priesthood ordination, but years later apostle Joseph Fielding Smith denied that Abel was ordained (see Smith's letter to Floren S. Preece, January 18, 1955, S. George Ellsworth Papers, Special Collections, Merrill-Cazier Library, Utah State University). See Jenson, *Latter-day Saint Biographical Encyclopedia*, 4 vols. (Salt Lake City: Andrew Jenson History Co., 1901–1936), 3:577. On another occasion,

Joseph Fielding Smith claimed that there were two Elijah Abels—one white and one black. For this point, see Newell G. Bringhurst, "Elijah Abel and the Changing Status of Blacks within Mormonism," *Dialogue: A Journal of Mormon Thought* 12 (Summer 1979): 22–36.

10. For a brief account of this story, see Richard N. Ostling and Joan K. Ostling, *Mormon America: The Power and the Promise* (San Francisco: Harper Collins, 1999), 103; and Armand L. Mauss, *Shifting Borders and a Tattered Passport: Intellectual Journeys of a Mormon Academic* (Salt Lake City: University of Utah Press, 2012), chapter 6.

11. Jackson to Gordon Hinckley, October 9, 1995 (in Matt Harris's files).

12. F. Michael Watson, the secretary to the First Presidency, responded to Jackson's letter, directing him to the bishop, who would "be pleased to read the answering letter to you." Watson to Jackson, October 25, 1995 (in Matt Harris's files). Richard and Joan Ostling, *Mormon America*, 103, speculate that the First Presidency did not want to give a copy of the letter to Jackson "because that would have put headquarters on record."

13. Jackson email to Harris, December 5, 2011.

14. Gladwell titled his survey "Implications of the 1978 Revelation" (in Matt Harris's file). It draws heavily from Lester Bush's authoritative article, "Mormonism's Negro Doctrine: An Historical Legacy," *Dialogue: A Journal of Mormon Thought* 8 (Spring 1973): 11–68. See also Gladwell to Jensen, October 15, 1996 (in Matt Harris's files).

15. Armand Mauss email to Matt Harris, December 1, 2011. Mauss confirmed that David Jackson's wife, Betty, also attended the luncheon. See also Mauss, *Shifting Borders*, 108–109.

16. Mauss, "Racial Ideas as a Continuing Problem in the Church," July 1998 report presented to Marlin K. Jensen of the First Quorum of Seventy (in Matt Harris's files). See also Mauss, "Casting Off the 'Curse of Cain,'" in Bringhurst and Smith, eds., *Black and Mormon*, 90–91; and Mauss, *All Abraham's Children*, 248–250. Mauss's credentials on Mormons and race are impeccable. For a sampling of his voluminous writings, see *All Abraham's Children*, 314–315.

17. Mauss writes that "the black member of the ad hoc committee, who had initiated the process in the first place, became impatient" ("Casting Off the 'Curse of Cain,'" in Bringhurst and Smith, eds., *Black and Mormon*, 91–92); Stammer, "Mormons May Disavow Old View on Blacks," *Los Angeles Times*, May 18, 1998. Jackson vigorously disputes that he leaked the story, claiming that the story had already been out by the time Larry Stammer contacted him (Jackson email to Matt Harris, January 6, 2013).

18. A church spokesman conveyed to KSL TV Channel 5, the church's television station, that the story was "totally erroneous," May 18, 1998 (http://www.ksl.com/TV/newsslocb.htm). See also the "*Los Angeles Times* story on Blacks and the Priesthood: First Presidency Statement" (press release from the LDS Public Affairs Department, May 18, 1998). See also Peggy Fletcher Stack, "Church Leaders Haven't Discussed Racial Issues, LDS President Says," *Salt Lake Tribune*, May 19, 1998.

19. Mauss commented that the committee "was chagrined and irritated that one of its own members had leaked the story to the media," noting that Jensen "presumably suffered some embarrassment at the raised eyebrows of some of his superiors" ("Casting Off the 'Curse of Cain,'" in Bringhurst and Smith, eds., *Black and Mormon*, 92). See also Stammer, "Mormon Leader Defends Race Relations," *Los Angeles Times*, September 12,

1998, in which he regretted that "all efforts to bring about the change have stopped." The "project is on hold indefinitely," he lamented.

20. Larry B. Stammer, "Mormon Plan to Disavow Racist Teachings Jeopardized by Publicity," *Los Angeles Times*, May 24, 1998.

21. Along with Mauss, Lester E. Bush and Newell G. Bringhurst also called for church leaders to renounce its racial heritage. See Stammer, "Mormon Plan to Disavow Racist Teachings Jeopardized by Publicity," *Los Angeles Times*, May 24, 1998. See also Eugene England, "Becoming a World Religion: Blacks, the Poor—All of Us," *Sunstone* 21, no. 2 (June–July 1998): 49–60; Keith E. Norman, "The Mark of the Curse: Lingering Racism in Mormon Doctrine," *Dialogue: A Journal of Mormon Thought* 31 (1999): 119–136, who writes a heartfelt plea for the church to move beyond its "hypocrisy" and "forsake the darkness of the past" (quotes at 136); Darron Smith, "The Persistence of Racialized Discourse in Mormonism," *Sunstone* 126 (March 2003): 31–33, who implores the church to repudiate the notion that "blacks are descendants of Cain, that they merited lesser earthy privilege because they were 'fence sitters' in the War in Heaven, and that, science and climatic factors aside, there is a link between skin color and righteousness" (quote at 31); and Robert A. Rees, "Black African Jews, the Mormon Denial of Priesthood to Blacks, and Truth and Reconciliation," *Sunstone* 127 (October 2004): 62–67, commenting that "Until the Church makes a clear, clean break from its racist teachings and practices instead of ambiguously distancing itself from them, racism will continue its ugly and corrosive effect on the social and spiritual fabric of the Church" (quote at 66). Some black Mormons do not think a repudiation is necessary, while others want "a correction by church leaders." See Lee Davidson, "Controversy Is Over, Say LDS Blacks," *Deseret News*, May 24, 1998; Bill Broadway, "Black Mormons Resist Apology Talk," *Washington Post*, May 30, 1998; and Margaret Ramirez, "Mormon Past Steeped in Racism: Some Black Members Want Church to Denounce Racist Doctrines," *Chicago Tribune*, July 26, 2005.

22. Larry B. Stammer, "Mormon Leader Defends Race Relations," *Los Angeles Times*, September 12, 1998.

23. Kimball, *Lengthen Your Stride*, 244; Alexander B. Morrison, "No More Strangers," *Ensign* 30 (September 2000): 16.

24. The church does not keep membership data based on race or ethnicity; however, at the end of the twenty-first century, most estimates place the number of blacks in the church at about 500,000. See *Deseret News 1999–2000 Church Almanac* (Salt Lake City: Deseret News, 2000), 119.

25. One study suggests that black growth in the church has been exaggerated. See Newell G. Bringhurst, "The Image of Blacks within Mormonism as Presented in the *Church News*, 1978–1988," *American Periodicals* 2 (Fall 1992): 113–123. For growth rates in Africa, see Carrie A. Moore, "Flood of Converts Alters the Face of the LDS Church," *Deseret News*, October 7, 2002; E. Dale Lebaron, "The Church in Africa," in *Out of Obscurity: The LDS Church in the Twentieth Century* (Salt Lake City: Deseret Book, 2000), 177–189.

26. Scholars at the "Pew Forum on Religion and Public Life" estimate that nearly 90 percent of Mormons in the United States are white; just 3 percent of Mormons in the United States are African American. See "A Portrait of Mormons in the U.S." at http://

pewforum.org/Christian/Mormon/A-Portrait-of-Mormons-in-the-US.aspx. For the difficulty of black assimilation in the church, see Jesse L. Embry, *Black Saints in a White Church: Contemporary African-American Mormons* (Salt Lake City: Signature Books, 1994).

27. As of 2008, 158 of the 30,426 students at BYU were black. See Amy K. Stewart, "Being a Black Student at BYU Can Be Difficult," *Deseret News*, February 27, 2008.

28. Helvécio Martins (with Mark Grover), *The Autobiography of Elder Helvécio Martins* (Salt Lake City: Aspen Books, 1994). See also Mark L. Grover, "Helvécio Martins: First Black General Authority," *Journal of Mormon History* 36 (Summer 2010): 27–54.

29. Claudia Bushman, *Contemporary Mormonism*, 94–95; Mauss, *All Abraham's Children*, 244–245. A month after the priesthood revelation was announced, some "concerned Latter-day Saints" paid for a full-page advertisement in the *Salt Lake Tribune* (July 23, 1978) in which they denounced the decision to allow blacks to hold the priesthood.

30. Mauss, *All Abraham's Children*, 219–228; see also Mauss's article "Mormonism and Secular Attitudes toward the Negroes," *Pacific Sociological Review* 9 (Fall 1966): 91–99. Cardell Jacobson, a sociologist at BYU, reaffirms Mauss's work. He notes that "despite the relative isolation of the church and the low number of African American members, the attitudes of white LDS members historically have not been and are not today much different than those of whites nationally." See his "African American Latter-day Saints: A Sociological Perspective," in Bringhurst and Smith, eds., *Black and Mormon*, 118.

31. Carrie A. Moore, "Racism Still Runs through LDS Culture, Y Researcher Says," *Deseret News*, March 5, 2005.

32. See Darron T. Smith, "These House-Negroes Still Think We're Cursed: Struggling against Racism in the Classroom," *Journal of Culture Studies* 19 (July 2005): 439–454. See also Smith's "Unpacking Whiteness in Zion: Some Personal Reflections and General Observations," in Bringhurst and Smith, eds., *Black and Mormon*, 148–166.

33. Eugene England, "Becoming a World Religion: Blacks, the Poor—All of Us," *Sunstone* 21 (June–July 1998): 58. See also Keith E. Norman, "The Mark of the Curse: Lingering Racism in Mormon Doctrine?" *Dialogue: A Journal of Mormon Thought* 32, no. 1 (Spring 1999): 119–136.

34. Story recounted in the documentary *Nobody Knows: The Untold Story of Black Mormons* (2008), produced by Margaret Young and Darius Gray. See also Eugene England, "All Are Alike unto God?: Prejudice against Blacks and Women in Popular Theology," *Sunstone* 15 (April 1990): 18.

35. Mauss, *All Abraham's Children*, 244.

36. See William A. Wilson and Richard C. Poulsen, "The Curse of Cain and Other Stories: Blacks in Mormon Folklore," *Sunstone* 5 (November/December 1980): 9–13.

37. An overview of Hinckley's life can be found in Sherri L. Dew, *Go Forward with Faith: The Biography of Gordon B. Hinckley* (Salt Lake City: Deseret Book, 1996).

38. See Margaret Young, "All God's Critters: Some Thoughts on the Priesthood Restriction and Differing Opinions—Part III," at http://bycommonconsent.com/2011/07/24/all-gods-critters-some-thoughts-on-the-priesthood-restriction-and-differing-opinions-part-iii/. Young is a BYU professor of English and a close friend and collaborator with Darius

Gray. Both have worked together on numerous projects discussing Mormon racial issues, including a trilogy of historical novels and a film. See also the transcript of a telephone interview Armand Mauss conducted with Gray, May 25, 1999, in which Gray notes that he "receives many phone calls during the year from all over the country," as many as "100" a year. "Many of these deal with the distress which black Saints feel at having encountered the various racial myths in LDS meetings or from white LDS friends." In box 42, folder 3, Armand Mauss Papers, Utah State Historical Society, Salt Lake City.

39. Gordon B. Hinckley, "The Need for Greater Kindness," *Ensign* 36 (May 2006): 58–61.

40. Richard N. Osling, "Mormonism Enters a New Era," *Time* (August 7, 1978): 55. Interview also recounted in Kimball, *Lengthen Your Stride*, 238.

41. LeGrand Richards interview with Wesley P. Walters and Chris Vlachos, August 16, 1978, transcript at LDS Church History Library and L. Tom Perry Special Collections, Harold B. Lee Library, Brigham Young University.

42. Dallin H. Oaks interview with the Associated Press, *Daily Herald* (Provo, Utah), June 5, 1988.

43. Hinckley interview in Australia, November 9, 1997, quoted in "On the Record: 'We Stand for Something,'" *Sunstone* 21, no. 4 (December 1998): 71.

44. Morrison, interview with Salt Lake City local news station KTVX, channel 4, June 8, 1998.

45. See, among others, Joseph Fielding McConkie, *Answers: Straightforward Answers to Tough Gospel Questions* (Salt Lake City: Deseret Book, 1998), 30.

46. See Juan Henderson's paper "A Time for Healing: Official Declaration 2," as part of the 29th Annual Sidney B. Sperry Symposium, published in *Out of Obscurity: The LDS Church in the Twentieth Century* (Salt Lake City: Deseret Book, 2000), 151–160. For Ballard's remarks, see Lynn Arave, "Monument in S.L. erected in honor of black pioneer," *Deseret News*, September 30, 2002. The *Encyclopedia of Mormonism*, which had strong church support, contained a passage stating that "the reasons for these restrictions have not been revealed." See Jesse Embry and Alan Cherry's entry on "Blacks," in ibid., 1:125.

47. The documentary aired on April 30 and May 1, 2007. Such meetings are rare, as high-ranking Mormon officials do not generally give interviews to the media. One exception, however, is church president Gordon B. Hinckley, whose background in journalism made him comfortable in front of the camera. In the 1990s Hinckley interviewed with CBS reporter Mike Wallace, CNN's Larry King, and a host of other high-profile journalists. Hinckley's predecessor, Howard W. Hunter, and his successor, Thomas S. Monson, generally avoided interviews with the media. See Dew, *Go Forward with Faith*, 537–547.

48. Church president Gordon Hinckley, apostles Dallin Oaks and Boyd Packer, and general authority and church historian Marlin Jensen also interviewed with Whitney.

49. For a biographical sketch of Holland, see the church's website at http://newsroom.lds.org/topic/quorum-of-the-twelve-apostles.

50. Holland interview with Whitney, March 4, 2006 (http://www.pbs.org/mormons/interviews/holland.html). LDS sociologist Armand Mauss has been urging leaders for years to distance the church from earlier racial views. Mauss was particularly concerned that books with racial folklore were still being sold in LDS bookstores, a point Holland

alludes to in his interview with Whitney. See Mauss's *All Abraham's Children*, 248; "Casting Off the 'Curse of Cain': The Extent and Limits of Progress since 1978," in Newell G. Bringhurst and Darron T. Smith, eds., *Black and Mormon* (Urbana: University of Illinois Press, 2004), 82–115; and "Dispelling the Curse of Cain: Or, How to Explain the Old Priesthood Ban without Looking Ridiculous," *Sunstone* 134 (October, 2004): 54–59. See also Keith E. Norman, "The Mark of the Curse: Lingering Racism in Mormon Doctrine?" *Dialogue: A Journal of Mormon Thought* 31, no. 2 (Spring 1999): 119.

51. In 2008, on the thirtieth anniversary commemorating the extension of the priesthood to African descent, church public-relations spokesperson Mark Tuttle noted: The "folklore is not part of and never was taught as doctrine by the Church" (Peggy Fletcher Black, "Mormon and Black," *Salt Lake Tribune*, June 6, 2008). Similarly, general authority Sheldon Child taught: "When you think about it, that's just what it is—folklore. It's never really been official doctrine" (Carrie A. Moore, "LDS Marking 30-Year Milestone," *Deseret News*, June 7, 2008). See also the church press release of February 29, 2012, "The Church and Race: All Are Alike unto God": "The origins of priesthood availability are not entirely clear. Some explanations with respect to this matter were made in the absence of direct revelation and references to these explanations are sometimes cited in publications. These pervious personal statements do not represent Church doctrine" (http://www.mormon newsroom.org/article/race-church).

52. Jason Horowitz, "The Genesis of a Church's Stand on Race," *Washington Post*, February 28, 2012. In addition, Mormon leaders have taught that God is discriminatory. See the First Presidency statement of 1969, in "Letter of First Presidency Clarifies Church's Position on the Negro," *Improvement Era* 73 (February 1970): 70–71.

53. Peterson blog, February 28, 2012, http://www.patheos.com/blogs/danpeterson/ 2012/02/an-unfortunate-attempt-to-explain-the-pre-1978-priesthood-ban.html; see also "LDS Church condemns past racism 'inside and outside the church,'" *Deseret News*, February 29, 2012.

54. Ball, quoted in Kate Bennion, "Washington Post article on black priesthood ban spurs concern, outrage," *The Universe* (BYU student newspaper), February 29, 2012.

55. Armand L. Mauss, "Casting Off the 'Curse of Cain,'" in Bringhurst and Smith, eds., *Black and Mormon*, 82–115, and Mauss, *All Abraham's Children*, 231–266. See also Norman, "The Mark of the Curse," 119–136. BYU religion professor J. B. Haws, *The Mormon Image in the American Mind: Fifty Years of Public Perception* (New York: Oxford University Press, 2013), 272, writes that "church leaders had disavowed the very types of rationales quoted in the [*Washington*] *Post*" story, conveying the impression that Bott was acting out of line when he rehashed Mormonism's erstwhile racial teachings. Church leaders, however, did not officially repudiate these teachings until 2013, when they issued the "Race and the Priesthood" document. See chapter 7 for a broader discussion of this historic document.

56. The 1979 edition of Bruce McConkie's *Mormon Doctrine*, 2nd ed. (Salt Lake City: Bookcraft, 1979), contains racist teachings under headings such as "Cain," "Caste System," and "Pre-existence." Even though the priesthood ban was lifted the previous year, McConkie's book still taught that "Cain, Ham, and the whole negro race have been cursed with a black skin, the mark of Cain" (ibid., 114). Though *Mormon Doctrine* went out of print in

2010 (Peggy Fletcher Stack, "Landmark 'Mormon Doctrine' goes out of print," *Salt Lake Tribune*, May 21, 2010), McConkie's other books are still in print and affirm this racist rhetoric. See, for example, his *The Mortal Messiah* (Salt Lake City: Deseret Book, 1979), 23; *The Millennial Messiah* (Salt Lake City: Deseret Book, 1982), 182–183 and chapter 16; and *A New Witness for the Articles of Faith* (Salt Lake City: Deseret Book, 1985), 510–512 and chapter 4. As of 2014, two other books are still in print that advance the divine curse: see Joseph Fielding Smith, *Doctrines of Salvation: Sermons and Writings of Joseph Fielding Smith*, ed. Bruce R. McConkie (Salt Lake City: Bookcraft, 1954; repr. 1998), 61, 65–66, 279; and Smith's *Answers to Gospel Questions*, 5 vols. (Salt Lake: Deseret Book, 1957–66), 2:175–178, 184–188.

57. A good recounting of the church's community outreach to people of color can be found in Mauss, *All Abraham's Children*, 245–252; and William Lobdell, "New Mormon Aim: Reach Out to Blacks," *Los Angeles Times*, September 21, 2003. Don Harwell, the president of the Genesis Group, a support group for black Latter-day Saints, called Bott's thinking "vile" (Jason Horowitz, "The Genesis of a Church's Stand on Race," *Washington Post*, February 28, 2012). For other reactions in the LDS black community, go to Darron T. Smith, "How Does It Feel to Be a Curse," March 9, 2012, http://www.darronsmith.com/2012/03/how-does-it-feel-to-be-a-curse-mitt-romney-and-the-continuing-problems-of-race-in-lds-church/; Max Mueller, "Is Mormonism Still Racist? Comments from a BYU Professor Stir Up a Troubling Past," March 2, 2012, http://www.slate.com/articles/life/faithbased/2012/03/mormon_church_and_racism_a_new_controversy_about_old_teachings_.single.html; Joseph Walker, "Genesis Members, Others Respond to LDS Racism Statement," *Deseret News*, March 6, 2012.

58. Nathan B. Oman, "Race, Folklore and Mormon Doctrine," *Deseret News*, February 29, 2012; Daniel Burke, "Will Mormons' Racial History Be a Problem for Mitt Romney," *Washington Post*, January 31, 2012; John G. Turner, "Why Race Is Still a Problem for Mormons," *New York Times*, August 18, 2012; "Mormon History with Race Could Haunt Romney," *Salt Lake Tribune*, April 10, 2012; Philip Rucker, "Romney Confronted over Mormon Doctrines," *Washington Post*, April 2, 2012, and Joanna Brooks, "Romney Faces Sticky Questions about LDS 'Doctrines' on Race," April 4, 2012, *Religious Dispatches*, http://www.religiondispatches.org/dispatches/joannabrooks/5853/romney_faces_sticky_questions_about_lds_%E2%80%9Cdoctrines%E2%80%9D_on_race. For an insightful analysis of Mitt Romney's presidential run, see Newell G. Bringhurst, "Mormonism, Mitt Romney, and Race in the 2012 Presidential Campaign," *John Whitmer Historical Society Journal* (Fall 2013): 1–14.

59. John H. Bunzel, "Is America Ready for a Mormon President," *Boston Globe*, February 19, 2006; Max Perry Mueller, "Has the Mormon Church Truly Left Its Race Problem Behind?" *New Republic*, November 15, 2011. Mitt Romney interview with Tim Russert on NBC News's *Meet the Press*, December 16, 2007, http://www.presidency.ucsb.edu/ws/index.php?pid=77749.

60. "Church Statement Regarding 'Washington Post Article on Race and the Church," February 29, 2012, http://www.mormonnewsroom.org/article/racial-remarks-in-washington-post-article.

61. "Race and the Church: All Are Alike unto God," February 29, 2012, http://www.mormon newsroom.org/article/race-church.

62. A private conversation Matt Harris had with one of Bott's colleagues, September 22, 2012. As of 2008, KBYU TV, a church-owned television station, was still airing podcasts of BYU religion faculty teaching the "curse of Cain," drawing support from the *Pearl of Great Price*, one of the four books of scripture in the Mormon canon.

63. For Bott's webpage, see http://religion.byu.edu/randy_bott. Bott was ranked "professor of the year" by a student website called "Rate My Professor." See Tad Walch, "BYU Professor Sits Atop National Rankings," *Deseret News*, December 11, 2008.

64. Tad Walch, "LDS Church enhances web pages on its history, doctrine," *Deseret News,* December 10, 2013.

65. Peggy Fletcher Stack, "Mormon Church Traces Black Priesthood Ban to Brigham Young," *Salt Lake Tribune*, December 16, 2013.

66. Mormon leaders have long asserted that Joseph Smith instituted the ban, most prominently in a First Presidency statement of 1969 (see chapter 5). More recently, church officials acknowledged that church records were not clear on why and precisely when the ban began—a position they retracted with the "Race and Priesthood" document. See "Updated edition of the English Scriptures," March 1, 2013, on LDS church website: https://www.lds.org/scriptures/dc-testament/od/2.

67. Two of the more prominent Internet sites critical of Mormon history and theology include "Mormon Think" (http://mormonthink.com/) and "Mormon—Reddit" (http://www.reddit.com/r/mormon/). For news coverage of Latter-day Saints leaving the church, consult Carrie Sheffield, "A Mormon Church in Need of Reform," *Washington Post*, January 29, 2012; Peggy Fletcher Stack, "Mormons Tackling Tough Questions in Their History," *Salt Lake Tribune*, February 3, 2012; Peter Henderson and Kristina Cooke, "Special Report: Mormonism Besieged by the Modern Age," *Reuters* (January 31, 2012): http://tinyurl.com/6s7l239. These news stories were influenced by general authority Marlin K. Jensen's candid admission in 2012 that the church was experiencing its greatest "apostasy" since Kirkland—a reference characterizing Mormons' disaffection during Joseph Smith's day. For this admission, see his discussion with Utah State University students, hosted by the John A. Widsoe Association for Mormon Studies, November 11, 2011, audiotape at http://www.fileswap.com/dl/5iKOuShH9D/ElderJensenQandAInterlacedEdited.mp3.

68. Snow and Pieper both quoted in Tad Walch, "LDS Church Enhances Web Pages on Its History, Doctrine," *Deseret News*, December 9, 2014. For other essays devoted to difficult Mormon teachings, see Peggy Fletcher Stack, "Abraham to Blacks to Brigham—Mormon Essays Confront Tough Questions," *Salt Lake Tribune*, July 14, 2014; and the "gospel topics" page on the LDS church's website, https://www.lds.org/topics.

69. Tad Walch, "LDS blacks, scholars cheer church's essay on priesthood," *Deseret News*, June 8, 2014.

70. Peggy Fletcher Stack, "Mormon Church Traces Black Priesthood Ban to Brigham Young," *Salt Lake Tribune*, December 16, 2013.

71. Walch, "LDS Blacks, Scholars Cheer Church's Essay on Priesthood."

72. Ibid.

73. Darron Smith, "The Mormon Church Quietly Disavows Its Racist Past: What Next," December 2013. Copy of essay provided by Darron Smith to Newell G. Bringhurst and Matt Harris.

74. Armand Mauss email to Tad Walch, December 13, 2013, copy provided by Mauss in an email to Newell G. Bringhurst. Portions of Mauss's statements were contained in Tad Walch. "LDS Blacks, Scholars Cheer Church's Essay on Priesthood."

75. As quoted in Tad Walch, "LDS Blacks, Scholars Cheer Church's Essay on Priesthood."

76. As quoted in Peggy Fletcher Stack, "Mormon Church Traces Black Priesthood Ban to Brigham Young."

Bibliography

Allen, James B. "Would-Be Saints: West Africa before the 1978 Priesthood Revelation." *Journal of Mormon History* 17 (1991): 207–247.
"Are Negroes Children of Adam?" *Millennial Star* 65 (December 3, 1903): 776–778.
Authority of the Legislative Assembly. *Acts, Resolutions, and Memorials, passed by the First Annual, and Special Sessions, of the Legislative Assembly, of the Territory of Utah, Begun and Held at Great Salt Lake City, on the 22nd Day of September, A.D., 1851 . . . 1852.*
Arrington, Leonard J. *Brigham Young: American Moses*. New York: Alfred Knopf, 1985.
Beller, Jack. "Negro Slaves in Utah." *Utah Historical Quarterly* 2 (October 1929): 123–126.
Bennett, Wallace R. "The Negro in Utah." *Utah Law Review* 3 (Spring 1953): 340–348.
Benson, Ezra Taft. *Civil Rights: Tool of Communist Deception*. Salt Lake City: Deseret Book, 1968.
Bergera, Gary James. "'This Time of Crisis': The Race-Based Anti-BYU Athletic Protests of 1968–1971." *Utah Historical Quarterly* 81 (Summer 2013): 204–229.
Bergera, Gary James, and Ronald Priddis. *Brigham Young University: A House of Faith*. Salt Lake City: Signature Books, 1985.
Berrett, William E. "The Church and the Negroid People." In John J. Stewart. *Mormonism and the Negro*. Orem, UT: Bookmark, 1960.
Book of Mormon. Salt Lake City: The Church of Jesus Christ of Latter-day Saints, 1981.
Botham, Fay. *Almighty God Created the Races: Christianity, Interracial Marriage, and American Law*. Chapel Hill: University of North Carolina Press, 2009.
Bowman, Matthew. *The Mormon People: The Making of an American Faith*. New York: Random House, 2012.
Bradford, Mary Lythgoe. *Lowell L. Bennion: Teacher, Counselor, Humanitarian*. Salt Lake City: Dialogue Foundation, 1995.
Brewer, David L. "Religious Resistance to Changing Beliefs about Race." *Pacific Sociological Review* 13 (Summer 1970): 163–170.

Bringhurst, Newell G. "An Ambiguous Decision: The Implementation of Mormon Priesthood Denial for the Black Man—A Re-examination." *Utah Historical Quarterly* 46 (Winter 1978): 45–64.

———. "Charles B. Thompson and the Issues of Slavery and Race." *Journal of Mormon History* 8 (1981): 37–47.

———. "'The Descendants of Ham' in Zion: Discrimination against Blacks along the Shifting Mormon Frontier, 1830–1920." *Nevada Historical Quarterly* 24 (Winter 1981): 298–318.

———. "Elijah Abel and the Changing Status of Blacks within Mormonism." *Dialogue: A Journal of Mormon Thought* 12 (Summer 1979): 22–36.

———. "Forgotten Mormon Perspectives: Slavery, Race, and the Black Man as Issues among Non-Utah Latter-day Saints, 1844–1873." *Michigan History* 61 (Winter 1977): 353–370.

———. "The Mormons and Black Slavery—A Closer Look." *Pacific Historical Review* 50 (November 1981): 329–338.

———. *Saints, Slaves, and Blacks: The Changing Place of Black People within Mormonism.* Westport, CT: Greenwood Press, 1981.

Bringhurst, Newell G., and Darron T. Smith, eds. *Black and Mormon.* Urbana: University of Illinois Press, 2006.

Burke, Daniel. "Will Mormons' Racial History Be a Problem for Mitt Romney?" *Washington Post*, January 31, 2012.

Bush, Lester E., Jr. "A Commentary on Stephen G. Taggart's *Mormonism's Negro Policy: Social and Historical Origins, Dialogue: A Journal of Mormon Thought* 4 (Winter 1969): 86–103.

———. "Introduction [to issue on the priesthood revelation of 1978]." *Dialogue: A Journal of Mormon Thought* 12 (Summer 1979): 9–12.

———. "Mormonism's Negro Doctrine: An Historical Overview." *Dialogue: A Journal of Mormon Thought* 8 (Spring 1973): 11–68.

———. "Writing 'Mormonism's Negro Doctrine: An Historical Overview' (1973): Context and Reflections, 1998." *Journal of Mormon History* 25 (Spring 1999): 229–271.

Bush, Lester E., Jr., and Armand L. Mauss. *Neither White nor Black: Mormon Scholars Confront the Race Issue.* Midvale, UT: Signature Books, 1984.

Bushman, Claudia L. *Contemporary Mormonism: Latter-day Saints in Modern America.* Westport, CT: Praeger, 2006.

Bushman, Richard Lyman. *Joseph Smith and the Beginnings of Mormonism.* Urbana: University of Illinois Press, 1984.

———. *Joseph Smith: Rough Stone Rolling.* New York: Alfred Knopf, 2005.

Chappell, David L. *A Stone of Hope: Prophetic Religion and the Death of Jim Crow.* Chapel Hill: University of North Carolina Press, 2004.

"Church Statement Regarding 'Washington Post Article on Race and the Church.'" February 29, 2012, http://www.mormonnewsroom.org/article/racial-remarks-in-washington-post-article.

Coleman, Ronald G. "'Is There No Blessing for Me?' Jane Elizabeth James, a Mormon African American Woman." In *African American Women Confront the West, 1600–2000.*

Edited by Quintard Taylor and Shirley Ann Wilson Moore. Norman: University of Oklahoma Press, 2003.

Crapo, Richley H. "Grassroots Deviance from the Official Doctrine: A Study of Latter-day Saint (Mormon) Folk Beliefs." *Journal for the Scientific Study of Religion* 26 (December 1987): 465–486.

Davidson, Karen Lynn, et al., eds. *The Joseph Smith Papers: Histories, Vol. 2: Assigned Histories, 1831–1847*. Salt Lake City: Church Historian's Press, 2012.

Davis, David Brion. *Inhuman Bondage: The Rise and Fall of Slavery in the New World*. New York: Oxford University Press, 2006.

Deseret News. Salt Lake City, UT.

Doctrine and Covenants. Salt Lake City: The Church of Jesus Christ of Latter-day Saints, 1981.

Douglas, Norman. "The Sons of Lehi and the Seed of Cain: Racial Myths in the Mormon Scriptures and Their Relevance to the Pacific Islands." *Journal of Religious History* 8 (June 1974): 90–104.

Dyer, Alvin R. "For What Purpose?" Address to missionary conference, Oslo, Norway, March 18, 1961. LDS Church History Library.

Embry, Jessie L. *Black Saints in a White Church: Contemporary African American Mormons*. Salt Lake City: Signature Books, 1994.

———. "Separate But Equal?: Black Branches, Genesis Groups, or Integrated Wards." *Dialogue: A Journal of Mormon Thought* 23 (Spring 1990): 11–36.

England, Eugene. "Becoming a World Religion: Blacks, the Poor—All of Us." *Sunstone* 21, no. 2 (June–July 1998): 49–60.

———. "The Mormon Cross." *Dialogue* 8 (Spring 1973): 78–86.

Ensign. Salt Lake City: The Church of Jesus Christ of Latter-day Saints.

Esplin, Ronald K. "Brigham Young and Priesthood Denial to the Blacks: An Alternative View." *BYU Studies* 19 (Spring 1979): 394–402.

Finkelman, Paul, ed. *Defending Slavery: Proslavery Thought in the Old South*. Boston: Bedford/St. Martin's, 2003.

Firmage, Edwin B., ed. *An Abundant Life: The Memoirs of Hugh B. Brown*. Second edition. Salt Lake City: Signature Books, 1999.

First Presidency of the Church of Jesus Christ of Latter-day Saints. "First Presidency Statement [on blacks], August 17, 1949." LDS Church History Library.

First Presidency of the Church of Jesus Christ of Latter-day Saints. "First Presidency Statement [on blacks], December 15, 1969." LDS Church History Library.

First Presidency of the Church of Jesus Christ of Latter-day Saints. "First Presidency Statement [on blacks], February 22, 1978." LDS Church History Library.

First Presidency of the Church of Jesus Christ of Latter-day Saints. "First Presidency Statement [on priesthood], June 8, 1978." LDS Church History Library.

First Presidency of Church of Jesus Christ of Latter-day Saints (on *Los Angeles Times* story). Press release from LDS Public Affairs Department, May 24, 1998. LDS Church History Library.

Frederickson, George. *Racism: A Short History*. Princeton, NJ: Princeton University Press, 2003.

Givens, Terryl L. *By the Hand of Mormon: The American Scripture that Launched a New World Religion*. New York: Oxford University Press, 2002.

Goldenberg, David M. *The Curse of Ham: Race and Slavery in Early Judaism, Christianity, and Islam*. Princeton, NJ: Princeton University Press, 2003.

Gordon, Sarah Barringer. *The Mormon Question: Polygamy and Constitutional Conflict in Nineteenth Century America*. Chapel Hill: University of North Carolina Press, 2002.

Gross, Ariela J. *What Blood Won't Tell: A History of Race on Trial in America*. Cambridge, MA: Harvard University Press, 2008.

Grover, Mark L. "Helvécio Martins: First Black General Authority." *Journal of Mormon History* 36 (Summer 2010): 27–54.

——. "The Mormon Priesthood Revelation and the São Paulo, Brazil Temple." *Dialogue: A Journal of Mormon Thought* 23 (Spring 1990): 39–53.

Gutjahr, Paul C. *The Book of Mormon: A Biography*. Princeton, NJ: Princeton University Press, 2012.

Hamilton, Keith N. *Last Laborer: Thoughts and Reflections of a Black Mormon*. Salt Lake City: Ammon Works, 2011.

Hansen, Klaus. *Mormonism and the American Experience*. Chicago: University of Chicago Press, 1980.

Harris, Matthew L. "Mormonism's Problematic Racial Past and the Evolution of the Divine-Curse Doctrine." *John Whitmer Historical Association Journal* 33 (Spring/Summer 2013): 90–114.

Haws, J. B. *The Mormon Image in the American Mind: Fifty Years of Public Perception*. New York: Oxford University Press, 2013.

Haynes, Stephen R. *Noah's Curse: The Biblical Justification of American Slavery*. New York: Oxford University Press, 2007.

Hill, Donna. *Joseph Smith: First Mormon*. New York: Doubleday, 1977.

Hinckley, Gordon B. "The Need for Greater Kindness." *Ensign* 36 (May 2006): 58–61.

Horowitz, Jason. "The Genesis of a Church's Stand on Race." *Washington Post*, February 28, 2012.

Improvement Era. Salt Lake City: The Church of Jesus Christ of Latter-day Saints.

Jackson, W. Kesler. *Elijah Abel: The Life and Times of a Black Priesthood Holder*. Springville, UT: Cedar Fort, 2013.

Jensen, Robin Scott, et al., eds. *The Joseph Smith Papers, Revelations and Translations: Manuscript Revelation Books*. Salt Lake City: Church Historian's Press, 2009.

——. *Joseph Smith Papers: Revelations and Translations, Vol. 2: Published Revelations*. Salt Lake City: Church Historian's Press, 2011.

Jordan, Winthrop. *White over Black: American Attitudes toward the Negro, 1550–1812*. Chapel Hill: University of North Carolina Press, 1968.

Journal of Discourses. 26 volumes. London: Latter-day Saints' Book Depot, 1855–1886.

Juvenile Instructor. Salt Lake City: The Church of Jesus Christ of Latter-day Saints, September–November 1868.

Kidd, Colin. *The Forging of Races: Race and Scripture in the Protestant Atlantic World, 1600–2000*. Cambridge: Cambridge University Press, 2006.

Kimball, Edward L. *Lengthen Your Stride: The Presidency of Spencer W. Kimball*. Salt Lake City: Deseret Book, 2005.

———. "Spencer W. Kimball and the Revelation on Priesthood." *BYU Studies* 47 (2008): 5–85.

———, ed. *The Teachings of Spencer W. Kimball*. Salt Lake City: Bookcraft, 1982.

Kenney, Scott G., ed. *Wilford Woodruff's Journal, 1833–1898*. 9 vols. Salt Lake City: Signature Books, 1983–1985.

Klarman, Michael J. *From Jim Crow to Civil Rights: The Supreme Court and the Struggle for Racial Equality*. New York: Oxford University Press, 2004.

LeBaron, E. Dale. "Official Declaration 2: Revelation on the Priesthood." In *The Heavens Are Open: The 1992 Sperry Symposium on the Doctrine and Covenants and Church History*. Salt Lake City: Deseret Book, 1993.

LeBaron, E. Dale, ed. *"All Are Alike unto God."* Salt Lake City: Deseret Book, 1990.

"Letter of First Presidency Clarifies Church's Position on the Negro." *Improvement Era* 73 (February 1970): 70–71.

Ludlow, Daniel H., et al., eds. *Encyclopedia of Mormonism*, 4 volumes. New York: Macmillan Publishing Company, 1992.

Lund, John Lewis. *The Church and the Negro: A Discussion of Mormons, Negroes and the Priesthood*. Salt Lake City: Paramount Publishers, 1967.

Lythgoe, Dennis L. "Negro Slavery and Mormon Doctrine." *Western Humanities Review* 21 (1957): 327–338.

———. "Negro Slavery in Utah." *Utah Historical Quarterly* 39 (Winter 1971): 40–54.

Martins, Marcus H. *Blacks and the Mormon Priesthood: Setting the Record Straight*. Orem, UT: Millennial Press, 2007.

Mason, Patrick Q. "The Prohibition of Interracial Marriage in Utah, 1888–1963." *Utah Historical Quarterly* 76 (Spring 2008): 108–131.

Mauss, Armand L. *All Abraham's Children: Changing Mormon Conceptions of Race and Lineage*. Urbana: University of Illinois Press, 2003.

———. "Comments: White on Black among the Mormons: A Critique of White & White." *Sociological Analysis* 42 (Fall 1981): 277–283.

———. "The Fading of the Pharaoh's Curse: The Decline and Fall of the Priesthood Ban against Blacks in the Mormon Church." *Dialogue: A Journal of Mormon Thought* 14 (Fall 1981): 10–45.

———. "Moderation in All Things: Political and Social Outlooks of Modern Urban Mormons." *Dialogue: A Journal of Mormon Thought* 7 (Spring 1972): 57–69.

———. "Mormonism and the Negro: Faith, Folklore and Civil Rights." *Dialogue: A Journal of Mormon Thought* 4 (Winter 1967): 19–39.

———. "Mormonism and Secular Attitudes toward Negroes." *Pacific Sociological Review* 9 (Fall 1966): 91–99.

———. *Shifting Borders and a Tattered Passport*. Salt Lake City: University of Utah Press, 2012.

McConkie, Bruce R. "All Are Alike unto God." Address to Seminary and Institute of Religion personnel. Brigham Young University, August 18, 1978. LDS Church History Library.

———. *Mormon Doctrine*. Salt Lake City: Bookcraft, 1958, 1966, 1979 editions.

———. "The New Revelation on Priesthood." In *Priesthood*. Salt Lake City: Deseret Book, 1981.

McConkie, Joseph Fielding. *Answers: Straightforward Answers to Tough Gospel Questions*. Salt Lake City: Deseret Book, 1998.

McMurrin, Sterling M. "A Note on the 1963 Civil Rights Statement." *Dialogue: A Journal of Mormon Thought* 12 (Summer 1979): 60–63.

McMurrin, Sterling M., and L. Jackson Newell, eds. *Matters of Conscience: Conversations with Sterling M. McMurrin on Philosophy, Education, and Religion*. Salt Lake City: Signature Books, 1996.

Moore, Carrie A. "Racism Still Runs through LDS Culture, Y Researcher Says." *Deseret News*, March 5, 2005.

Moyle, Henry D. "What of the Negro?" Address to French East Mission, Geneva, Switzerland, October 30, 1961. LDS Church History Library.

Mueller, Max Perry. "Has the Mormon Church Truly Left Its Race Problem Behind?" *New Republic*, November 15, 2011.

———. "Playing Jane: Re-presenting Black Mormon Memory through Reenacting the Black Mormon Past." *Journal of Africana Religions* 1:4 (2013): 513–561.

Nelson, Lowry. *In the Direction of His Dreams: Memoirs*. New York: Philosophical Library, 1985.

———. "Mormons and Blacks." *Christian Century* 91 (October 1974): 949–950.

———. "Mormons and the Negro." *Nation* 174 (May 24, 1952): 488.

Newell, Quincy D. "The Autobiography and Interview of Jane Elizabeth Manning James." *Journal of Africana Religions* 1:2 (2013): 251–291.

Nibley, Hugh W. "The Best Possible Test." *Dialogue: A Journal of Mormon Thought* 8 (Spring 1973): 73–77.

Norman, Keith E. "The Mark of the Curse: Lingering Racism in Mormon Doctrine." *Dialogue: A Journal of Mormon Thought* 31 (1999): 119–136.

O'Donovan, Connell. "Brigham Young, African Americans, and Plural Marriage: Schism and the Beginnings of Black Priesthood Denial." In *The Persistence of Polygamy: From Joseph Smith's Martyrdom to the First Manifesto, 1844 to 1890*. Edited by Newell G. Bringhurst and Craig L. Foster. Independence, MO: John Whitmer Books, 2013.

———. "The Mormon Priesthood Ban and Elder Q. Walker Lewis: An Example for His More Whiter Brethren to Follow." *John Whitmer Historical Association Journal* 26 (2006): 47–99.

Oliver, David H. *A Negro on Mormonism*. Salt Lake City: D. H. Oliver, 1963.

Oman, Nathan B. "Race, Folklore and Mormon Doctrine." *Deseret News*, February 29, 2012.

Pascoe, Peggy. *What Comes Naturally: Miscegenation Law and the Making of Race in America*. New York: Oxford University Press, 2009.

Pearl of Great Price. Salt Lake City: The Church of Jesus Christ of Latter-day Saints, 1981.

Petersen, Boyd Jay. "'One Soul Shall Not Be Lost': The War in Heaven in Mormon Thought." *Journal of Mormon History* 38 (Winter 2012): 1–50.

Petersen, Mark E. "Race Problems—As They Affect the Church." Address at Brigham Young University, August 27, 1954. LDS Church History Library.

Peterson, H. Ross. "'Blindside': Utah on the Eve of *Brown v. Board of Education*." *Utah Historical Quarterly* 73 (2005): 4–20.

———. "'Do Not Lecture the Brethren': Stewart L. Udall's Pro-Civil Rights Stance, 1967." *Journal of Mormon History* 25 (Spring 1999): 272–287.

Phelps, William W. "Free People of Color," *Evening and Morning Star*. Independence, MO: The Church of Jesus Christ of Latter-day Saints, July, 1833.

Prince, Gregory A. "David O. McKay and Blacks." *Dialogue: A Journal of Mormon Thought* (Spring 2002): 145–153.

Prince, Gregory A., and William Robert Wright. *David O. McKay and the Rise of Modern Mormonism*. Salt Lake City: University of Utah Press, 2005.

Quinn, D. Michael. *Elder Statesman: A Biography of J. Reuben Clark*. Salt Lake City: Signature Books, 2002.

———. "Ezra Taft Benson and Mormon Political Conflicts." *Dialogue: A Journal of Mormon Thought* 26 (Summer 1993): 1–87.

———. *The Mormon Hierarchy: Extensions of Power*. Salt Lake City: Signature Books, 1997.

———. *The Mormon Hierarchy: Origins of Power*. Salt Lake City: Signature Books, 1994.

"Race and the Church: All Are Alike unto God." February 29, 2012, http://www.mormon newsroom.org/article/race-church.

"Race and the Priesthood" (2013): https://www.lds.org/topics/race-and-the-priesthood.

Reeve, W. Paul. *Religion of a Different Color: Race and the Mormon Struggle for Whiteness*. New York: Oxford University Press, 2015.

Rich, Christopher B., Jr. "The True Policy for Utah: Servitude, Slavery, and 'An Act in Relation to Service.'" *Utah Historical Quarterly* 80 (2012): 54–74.

Roberts, B. H. *New Witness for God*, vol. 3. Salt Lake City: Deseret News, 1909.

———. *The Contributor*, vol. 6, 1885. *Salt Lake Tribune*. Salt Lake City, UT.

Shipps, Jan B. "Second-Class Saints." *Colorado Quarterly* 11 (1962–1963): 183–190.

Smart, M. Neff. "The Challenge of Africa." *Dialogue: A Journal of Mormon Thought* 12 (Summer 1979): 54–57.

Smith, Elmer R. *The Status of the Negro in Utah*. Salt Lake City: NAACP Salt Lake Branch, 1956.

Smith, George D., Jr. "The Negro Doctrine—An Afterview." *Dialogue: A Journal of Mormon Thought* 12 (Summer 1979): 64–67.

Smith, George D., Jr., ed. *An Intimate Chronicle: The Journals of William Clayton*. Salt Lake City: Signature Books, 1995.

Smith, Joseph Fielding, Jr. *Answers to Gospel Questions*. 4 volumes. Salt Lake City: Deseret Book, 1957–1963.

———. *Doctrines of Salvation: Sermons and Writings of Joseph Fielding Smith*, 3 vols. Compiled by Bruce R. McConkie. Salt Lake City: Bookcraft, 1954–1956.

———. "The Negro and the Priesthood." *Improvement Era* 27 (April 1924): 564–565.

———. *The Way to Perfection*. Salt Lake City: Deseret Book, 1931.

Smith, Joseph, Jr. *History of the Church*. 2nd ed., 7 vols. Salt Lake City: Deseret Book, 1976.

Stack, Peggy Fletcher. "Mormon Church Traces Black Priesthood Ban to Brigham Young." *Salt Lake Tribune*, December 16, 2013.

———. "Mormons Tackling Tough Questions in Their History." *Salt Lake Tribune*, February 3, 2012.

Stammer, Larry B. "Mormon Leader Defends Race Relations." *Los Angeles Times*, September 12, 1998.
———. "Mormon Plan to Disavow Racist Teachings Jeopardized by Publicity." *Los Angeles Times*, May 24, 1998.
———. "Mormons May Disavow Old View on Blacks." *Los Angeles Times*, May 18, 1998.
Stevenson, Russell W. "'A Negro Preacher': The Worlds of Elijah Abels." *Journal of Mormon History* 39 (Spring 2013): 165–254.
———, ed. *For the Cause of Righteousness: A Global History of Blacks and Mormonism, 1830–2013*. Salt Lake City: Greg Kofford Books, 2014.
Stewart, John J. *Mormonism and the Negro*. Orem, UT: Community Press, 1960.
Taggart, Stephen G. *Mormonism's Negro Policy: Social and Historical Origins*. Salt Lake City: University of Utah Press, 1970.
"The Negro and the Priesthood." *The Elders' Journal* 5 (1908): 1164–1167.
Thomasson, Gordon C. "Lester Bush's Historical Overview: Other Perspectives." *Dialogue: A Journal of Mormon Thought* 8 (Spring 1973): 69–72.
Times and Seasons. 6 volumes. Nauvoo, Illinois, 1839–1846.
Trank, Douglas M. "The Negro and the Mormons: A Church in Conflict." *Western Speech* 35 (Fall 1971): 220–230.
Turner, John G. *Brigham Young: Pioneer Prophet*. Cambridge, MA: Harvard University Press, 2012.
———. "Why Race Is Still a Problem for Mormons." *New York Times*, August 18, 2012.
Underwood, Grant. *The Millenarian World of Early Mormonism*. Urbana: University of Illinois Press, 1994.
Walch, Tad. "LDS Blacks, Scholars Cheer Church's Essay on Priesthood." *Deseret News*, June 8, 2014.
———. "LDS Church Enhances Web Pages on Its History, Doctrine." *Deseret News*, December 9, 2014.
Walton, Brian. "A University's Dilemma: BYU and Blacks." *Dialogue: A Journal of Mormon Thought* 6 (Spring 1971): 31–36.
White, O. Kendall, Jr., and Daryl White. "Abandoning an Unpopular Policy: An Analysis of the Decision Granting the Mormon Priesthood to Blacks." *Sociological Analysis* 41 (Fall 1980): 231–245.
———. "Reply to Mauss' Critique of Our Analysis of Admitting Blacks into the Mormon Priesthood." *Sociological Analysis* 42 (Fall 1981): 283–288.
Wilson, William A., and Richard C. Poulsen. "The Curse of Cain and Other Stories: Blacks in Mormon Folklore." *Sunstone* 5 (November–December 1980): 9–13.
Wolfinger, Henry J. "A Test of Faith: Jane Elizabeth James and the Origins of the Utah Black Community." In *Social Accommodation in Utah*. Edited by Clark Knowlton. American West Center, Occasional Papers, University of Utah, Salt Lake City, 1975.

Index

Abel, 2, 11, 36–38, 52, 54, 56–57, 73, 99–100, 104, 136
Abel, Elijah, 19, 26, 46, 51, 90–91, 98; biography, 25–26; missionary work, 26; patriarchal blessing, 26–27, 158n11, 195n9
abolitionist movement, 15, 17–18, 21–22
abolition of slavery, 27
Abraham, 12–14, 57–58, 91, 104, 113; seed of, 31
Adam, 11–13, 37–39, 50, 56, 60, 73, 104
African Americans, 11, 18–19, 28, 30–32, 39–40, 42, 49, 55, 66, 68, 72, 74, 79, 80–82, 94, 96–101, 105–6, 112–14, 117, 121–22, 128–30, 171n24, 171n29, 172n31, 176n62
"All Are Alike unto God," 113, 138–39
Alvord, James W., 21–22
American Bar Association, 106–7
"An Act in Relation to Service," 33–35
antimiscegenation laws, 3, 44, 110
Appleby, William L, 31, 35
Arrington, Leonard J., 95, 107

Bailey, Thurl, 4
Ball, Joseph T., 19, 30, 32
Ball, Terry, 136
Ballard, M. Russell, 134
Bangerter, William Grant, 102
baptism, 17, 62, 70, 102, 104, 164n1
baptismal certificates, 102
Bennion, Lowell, 69
Benson, Ezra Taft, 68, 75–78
Benson, Reed, 77
Black Pete, 19, 97

blacks, 65, 67–68, 84–85, 89–90, 105, 115, 120–21, 128–29, 149n24
Blacks and the Scriptures, 142
blood atonement, 42, 162n34
Bob Jones University, 106
Book of Abraham, 11–14, 31, 35, 44, 58, 60, 91, 99, 104, 113, 116, 138, 153n32
Book of Covenants, 2, 25
Book of Mormon, 2, 5–10, 44, 115, 118, 138
Book of Moses, 11–12, 44, 60, 122
Bott, Randy, 118, 136–39
Brazil, 92, 101–2, 106, 112, 114, 116, 131
Bridgeforth, Ruffin, 84–85, 91
Brigham Young University, 69, 77, 90, 93, 106–7, 111, 117, 119, 121, 132, 198n27; 134; boycotts of, 64, 79
Brown, Hugh B., 64, 74–78, 80–81, 83, 93–94, 176n59, 177n66, 182n102
Brown v. the Board of Education, 67
Bush, Lester E., Jr., 26, 93–95, 97, 105, 154–55n38, 185n15, 186n24
Bushman, Richard L., 142

Cain, 2–3, 7, 11–12, 31, 33, 36–39, 43, 45, 49, 52, 54–58, 60, 73–74, 99–100, 113, 115, 118, 122, 126–27, 136–37; descent from/lineage of, 66, 70, 73, 98–99, 103–5, 117–18, 122, 124–25, 128, 130, 133, 138, 143, 167n43, 182n103, 197n21; as Perdition, 72, 125
California, 32
Canaan, 24, 33, 39, 45, 55–58, 100, 113, 117
Canaanites, 13, 31, 57, 73, 115

Cannon, Angus M., 52
Cannon, George Q., 114, 117
caste system, 72–73
Chaldeans, 12
Cherry, Alan, 119
children of Israel, 31
civil rights, 3, 63–64, 66–69, 74–81, 110
Civil Rights Act of 1964, 75, 106
Civil War, 43–44, 81, 90
Clark, J. Reuben, 64–65, 68, 110, 122
colonization of freed blacks, 27–28
Coltrin, Zebedee, 45–46
Communism, 76–78
communists, 79
compensated emancipation, 27–28
Compromise of 1850, 32
Congo, 131
Contributor, 48, 99
Costa Rica, 107
Cowdery, Oliver, 22
Cuba, 64
curse/cursed, 2–3, 7, 9, 11, 14, 24, 37–38, 40, 57–58, 60, 65, 68, 70, 72–73, 91, 94, 97–98, 109, 112–13, 115, 117–18, 128, 130, 133, 136–38, 143, 181n97

dark skin, 6–8, 10, 29, 70, 73, 92, 106, 143
Deseret Book, 113, 118, 128–29, 134
Dialogue, A Journal of Mormon Thought, 94–95
Doctrine and Covenants, 2, 5–6, 15–16, 44, 48, 108, 122, 126. See also *Book of Covenants*
Dominican Republic, 131
Dube, Edward, 150n25
Dyer, Alvin R., 80, 93–94, 181n97

Egyptians, 12, 58
Egypt, 12, 49, 57
Egyptus, 13, 49–50, 58, 73–74, 113, 117, 138
Eisenhower, Dwight D., 76–77
Embry, Jesse, 119
Encyclopedia of Mormonism, 119
England, Eugene, 95
Enoch, 12, 45, 70, 104
Ephraim, 2, 31, 45
eunuchs, 42
European Christians, 2–3
Evans, William S. "Bill," 123, 131
Evening and Morning Star, 11, 15, 18–20

fair and delightsome, 10
folklore, 133–35, 142, 200n51
"For What Purpose," 181n97
"Free People of Color," 20

Fritz, Albert, 75–76
Fugitive Slave Law, 40
fundamentalist Mormons, 112

General Handbook of Instructions, 110
Genesis Group, 84–86, 89–90, 132, 141, 183n114, 201n57
Ghana, 131
Gibbons, Francis, 106
Gillespie, David, 83–84, 86, 89
Gladwell, Dennis A., 122–23, 126–27, 130–31
Gray, Darius, 84–85, 132–33, 141
Greeley, Horace, 40–41
Greene, John P., 46
Grover, Mark, 101

Haight, David B., 101
Haiti, 131
Ham, 2–3, 13; 33, 40, 49, 55–58, 60, 73, 90–91, 95, 100, 113, 117, 127; descendants of, 7, 12, 31, 35, 40, 57, 98, 128, 164n1
Harding, Ralph, 78
Harwell, Don, 141
Hebrews, Epistle to, 58
Heson, Alexis, 141
Hiltbrand, Jeff, 126
Hinckley, Gordon B., 4, 85, 90, 122, 124, 130–34, 140
Holland, Jeffrey, 133–36
Hooper, William H, 33
Horowitz, Jason, 136
Howard, F. Burton, 107
Howells, Rulon S., 102
Hyde, Orson, 14

idolatry, 13
Illinois, 18, 34
Indians, 7–8, 39, 115. See also Native Americans
intelligences, 13
Internal Revenue Service, 106
interracial marriage, 37, 41, 64, 68, 70, 101, 106, 108–11
Ivory Coast, 131

Jackson, A. David, 122–24, 127, 130–31, 137
Jackson, Betty, 123
Jackson, W. Kesler, 26
Jamaica, 131
James, Isaac, 40, 51–52, 54
James, Jane Elizabeth Manning, 40, 50–52, 54–55
Japheth, 58, 62
Jaredites, 7

Jensen, Marlin K., 122–23, 127, 130–31
Jews, 2, 39–40
Jim Crow laws, 3, 44
John Birch Society, 77–78
Johnson, Lyndon, 75
Jones, Earl, 91
Joseph (sold into Egypt), 2, 45, 58

Kennedy, John F., 75
Kimball, Edward, 96, 107
Kimball, Spencer W., 3, 64, 77, 80, 85, 95–96, 101, 103, 105–9, 111–17, 134, 141
Kirtland, Ohio, 21–22, 25, 46, 116
Knight, Gladys, 4
Ku Klux Klan, 44, 69

Lamanites, 6–10, 70, 138
Lamech, 12
Latter Day Saints' Messenger and Advocate, 21, 23
LDS Afro-American Oral History Project, 121
Lee, Harold B., 68, 71, 75, 77, 80, 176n59
LeFevre, Don, 111
Lewis, Enoch Lovejoy, 19, 42
Lewis, Quock Walker, 19, 31, 36, 51–52
Liahona: The Elder's Journal, 55
Liberty Stake, 84, 90
Lincoln, Abraham, 42
lineage, 2, 31, 35, 73, 91, 95, 98–100, 102–4, 109, 118, 122, 124–25, 143
lineage lesson, 102–3, 187n33
Ludlow, Daniel H., 93

Madsen, Truman G., 95
Manifest Destiny, 28
Manning, Isaac, 52
Marchant, Byron, 107–8
Marquardt, Michael, 86, 89–90
Marsh, Thomas B., 46
Martins, Helvécio, 101, 132, 149n25
Mason, Patrick, 142
Mauss, Armand L., 92, 114, 123, 126–27, 131, 142
McCary, William (Werner), 30–32, 35–36
McConkie, Bruce R., 4, 68, 71–72, 95, 111–14, 116, 118, 122
McKay, David O., 63, 65, 67–68, 71–72, 74–78, 80, 83–84, 86, 90, 93–94, 105, 110, 122
McMurrin, Sterling, 75, 79, 94
Meeks, Heber, 64–65
Mexico, 28, 32
Millennial Star, 45
Missouri, 15–16, 18–20, 43, 93, 96–97; Missouri Mormon War, 20

Mitchell, Devan, 141
Monson, Thomas S., 85, 90
Mormon Doctrine, 71–72, 111, 114, 122
"Mormon ethnicity," 31
"Mormonism's Negro Doctrine: An Historical Overview," 94, 97
"Mormonism's Negro Policy: Social and Historical Origins," 93
Mormons, The, 134–35
"Mormons May Disavow Old View on Blacks," 129
Morrison, Alexander B., 134
Moses, 58
Moyle, Henry D., 68, 176n62
Mozambique, 131
mulattoes, 19–21, 42

National Association for Colored People/NAACP, 44, 75–76, 79, 106
Native Americans, 7
Nauvoo, Illinois, 19, 26, 50
"Need for Greater Kindness, A," 132–33
"Negro," 72
"The Negro and the Priesthood," 55–56
negro blood, 3, 112–14
negroes. *See* African Americans
Nelson, Lowry, 64–65
Nephites, 6–8
New Mexico, 32
"New Revelation on the Priesthood, The," 113–14
New Testament, 2, 5, 9, 11, 22, 24, 48
Nibley, Hugh W., 95
Nigeria, 75, 90, 131
1978 black priesthood revelation, 1, 3, 72, 92, 105, 108–9, 112, 114, 121, 123, 125, 128, 130
Noah, 13, 31, 49–50, 55–58

Oaks, Dallin H., 107, 134
Ohio, 17, 21, 46
Old Testament, 2, 5, 11, 22, 31, 48
Orr, Eugene, 84–86, 89, 90–91
Ostling, Richard, 134

Packer, Boyd K., 85, 90, 95, 111
Parrish, Warren, 22, 46
Patten, David W., 46
Pearl of Great Price, 2, 5–6, 11–12, 44–45, 48–49, 55–58, 60, 62, 99–100, 112, 118, 136
Perkins, Frank, 51
Perkins, Marvin, 142
Petersen, Mark E., 67–69, 72, 77, 95, 110
Peterson, Daniel, 136

Pharaoh, 12–13, 49, 58, 90–91, 104, 113, 117
Phelps, William W., 19–20, 97
Philanthropist, The, 22
Pieper, Paul B., 141
plural marriage/polygamy, 30–32, 41–42, 45, 59
Porter, Roger, 94
Pratt, Parley P., 7, 19, 31, 35
preexistence, 12–14, 48, 74, 100, 115, 124, 138, 143, 154–55n38
priesthood, 1–2, 12–13, 19, 26, 30–31, 35, 38, 49–50, 58–60, 66, 81, 83–85, 91, 94–95, 101–6, 110, 119, 136; would be a curse, 59, 139
priesthood ban, 1, 3–5, 12, 30, 35–37, 44, 46, 48–50, 52, 55, 59–60, 64–67, 72, 74, 78, 80–81, 83–85, 91–96, 101, 103, 105, 110, 112–14, 118, 128–29, 134–37, 140–43, 160n2, 162n30
Puerto Rico, 131

"Race and the Priesthood," 4, 137, 140–41, 143
"Race Problems—As They Affect the Church," 67, 69
racial environmentalism, 7
"Racial Ideas as a Continuing Problem in the Church," 123
Rees, Robert, 95
Reeve, Paul, 142
Reiser, A. Hamer, 84
Rich, Charles C., 33
Richards, Franklin D., 45
Richards, LeGrand, 112–14, 134
Riddle, Chauncey C., 93
Roberts, Brigham H., 48–49, 55, 99–100
Romney, George, 75
Romney, Marion G., 72, 109
Romney, Mitt, 4–5, 118, 137
Russert, Tim, 137

Santo Domingo, 131
São Paulo, Brazil, 101
Satan, 3, 11–12, 56–57, 60, 125; followers, 14
segregated/segregation, 12, 63–64, 67–74, 84, 110, 175n58
Shem, 58, 62
Sitati, Joseph, 149n25
slaveholders, 10
slavery, 1–2, 6, 10, 15–17, 18–21, 23–24, 28, 32, 37, 39, 93, 97–99; in Utah Territory, 1, 30, 32–33, 40–41, 98–99
slaves, 10, 32–33
Smith, Darron, 142
Smith, David, 90
Smith, Eldred G., 91

Smith, Emma, 51
Smith, George Albert, 65, 110, 122
Smith, Joseph, Jr., 1, 5–7, 11–13, 15–19, 21, 25–27, 44, 46, 51–52, 59–60, 62, 81, 97–98, 104, 119, 140–41; and antislavery views, 27, 139; and black priesthood, 82, 93–94, 100, 119, 138, 140; campaign for President, 1, 27–29; and slavery, 99, 159n33
Smith, Joseph, Sr., 26
Smith, Joseph F., 45–46, 52, 54–55, 59
Smith, Joseph Fielding, 3–4, 59–60, 68, 71–72, 75, 77–78, 80, 84, 118, 196n9
Smith, William, 30–31
Smoot, Abraham O., 33, 45–46
Snow, Lorenzo, 36
Snow, Steven E., 141
South Africa, 63, 131
Stack, Peggy Fletcher, 140
Stammer, Larry B., 123–24, 129
Stokes, Catherine, 141

Taggart, Stephen, 93–95, 105
Tanner, N. Eldon, 75, 77, 80, 83, 109
Taylor, John, 44–45, 51, 91, 99
temple ordinances, 30, 44, 50–52, 89, 101, 105, 164n1
Thomas, Robert K., 93, 95
Thomasson, Gordon C., 95
Times and Seasons, 12, 18
"To the Youth of Israel," 48, 55
Turner, Wallace, 69, 80, 94
"twin relics of barbarism," 42

Udall, Stewart L., 75
Utah Territorial Legislature, 32–37, 40, 99, 110
Utah Territory, 30, 40

"Views of the Powers and Policy of the Government," 28
Vlachos, Chris, 112–14
Voting Rights Act of 1965, 75

Walch, Tad, 140
Wallace, Douglas, 107
Wallace, George C., 76
Walters, Wesley, 112–14
war in heaven, 3, 14, 48, 100
"The Way to Perfection: Short Discourses on Gospel Themes," 59–60
West Indies, 131
Welch, Robert, 77
White, Kendall, 68

"white and delightsome," 115, 152n13
whiteness, 31, 152n13, 161n8
Whitney, Helen, 134–35
Wilkinson, Ernest, 77, 79
Williams, LaMar, 90
Winter Quarters, 31, 36
Woodruff, Wilford, 52, 54, 66

Young, Brigham, 1, 3–4, 30–31, 38–41, 43, 46, 51, 56, 58, 60, 62, 94–95, 99–100, 110, 114, 117, 122, 140–41, 143; as Governor, 32–33, 35–37, 40, 42; began priesthood ban, 66, 98, 122, 138, 140; on "seed of Cain," 133; time will come when seed of Cain will receive all privileges, 66, 120
Young, Brigham, Jr., 46
Young, Zina D. Huntington, 54

Zimbabwe, 131
Zion, 15, 18, 96

MATTHEW L. HARRIS is a professor of history at Colorado State University-Pueblo. He is the coauthor of *The Founding Fathers and the Debate over Religion in Revolutionary America*.

NEWELL G. BRINGHURST is a professor emeritus of history and political science at College of the Sequoias. He is the author of *Saints, Slaves, and Blacks: The Changing Place of Blacks within Mormonism*.

The University of Illinois Press
is a founding member of the
Association of American University Presses.

———————————————————

University of Illinois Press
1325 South Oak Street
Champaign, IL 61820-6903
www.press.uillinois.edu